Archaeology and Geoinformatics

CARIBBEAN ARCHAEOLOGY AND ETHNOHISTORY

Series Editor Antonio L. Curet

Archaeology and Geoinformatics
Case Studies from the Caribbean

Edited by Basil A. Reid

THE UNIVERSITY OF ALABAMA PRESS
Tuscaloosa

Copyright © 2008
The University of Alabama Press
Tuscaloosa, Alabama 35487-0380
All rights reserved
Manufactured in the United States of America

Typeface: ACaslon

∞
The paper on which this book is printed meets the minimum requirements of American National Standard for Information Sciences-Permanence of Paper for Printed Library Materials, ANSI Z39.48-1984.

Library of Congress Cataloging-in-Publication Data

Archaeology and geoinformatics : case studies from the Caribbean / [edited by] Basil A. Reid.
    p. cm. — (Caribbean archaeology and ethnohistory)
  Includes bibliographical references and index.
  ISBN 978-0-8173-1601-3 (cloth : alk. paper) — ISBN 978-0-8173-5470-1 (pbk. : alk. paper) — ISBN 978-0-8173-8053-3 (electronic) 1. Indians of the West Indies—Antiquities. 2. Archaeological geology—Caribbean Area. 3. Excavations (Archaeology)—Geographic information systems—Caribbean Area. 4. Caribbean Area—Antiquities. I. Reid, Basil A., 1961–
  F1619.A73 2008
  972.900285—dc22

2007036716

Contents

List of Illustrations   vii

Acknowledgments   xiii

Introduction
Archaeology and Geoinformatics: Case Studies from the Caribbean
Basil A. Reid   1

PART I: ARCHAEOLOGY, GIS, AND VISIBILITY MODELS
1. The Caribbean: A Continent Divided by Water
Joshua M. Torres and Reniel Rodríguez Ramos   13

PART II: ARCHAEOLOGY, GIS, AND CULTURAL RESOURCE MANAGEMENT
2. Developing Weights-of-Evidence Predictive Models for the Cultural Resource Management of Pre-Columbian Sites in Trinidad
Basil A. Reid   33

3. Forward Planning: The Utilization of GIS in the Management of Archaeological Resources in Barbados
Kevin Farmer   74

4. Developing an Archaeological Information System for Trinidad and Tobago
Bheshem Ramlal and Basil A. Reid   86

PART III: ARCHAEOLOGY, GIS, CARTOGRAPHY, GPS, SATELLITE IMAGERY, AERIAL PHOTOGRAPHY, AND PHOTOGRAMMETRY
5. Maps, *Matricals,* and Material Remains: An Archaeological GIS of Late-Eighteenth-Century Historic Sites on St. John, Danish West Indies
Douglas V. Armstrong, Mark W. Hauser, David W. Knight, and Stephan Lenik   99

6. Understanding Nevis: GPS and Archaeological Field Survey in a Postcolonial Landscape
   Roger H. Leech   127

7. The Use of Imagery to Locate Taino Sites in Jamaica in a GIS Environment
   Parris Lyew-Ayee and Ivor Conolley   137

   PART IV: ARCHAEOLOGY AND GEOPHYSICS

8. Geophysics and the Search for Raleigh's Outpost on Trinidad
   Eric Klingelhofer   155

9. Geophysics and Volcanic Islands: Resistivity and Gradiometry on St. Eustatius
   R. Grant Gilmore III   170

Conclusion
Postscript: Archaeology and Geoinformatics from a Caribbeanist Perspective
Basil A. Reid   184

Glossary of Terms   195

References Cited   205

Contributors   225

Index   229

Illustrations

Figures

1.1. Map of the Caribbean Basin with GTOPO30 digital elevation model (DEM) and political boundaries 14

1.2. Recalculated DEM using Bowditch's standard distance to the visible horizon formula 18

1.3. Recalculated DEM using Bowditch's standard distance to the visible horizon formula showing sample points from/to which visibility is possible 20

1.4. Visibility ranges based on point sample 21

1.5. Map showing variability in distances between coasts and landmass visibility ranges 23

1.6. Overlapping visibility areas in the Greater Antilles 24

1.7. Overlapping visibility areas in the Lesser Antilles 27

2.1. Map of Trinidad showing the location of the three watersheds selected for this study 34

2.2. Map of Trinidad showing the location of the watersheds in relation to the island's physiography 35

2.3. Map of Trinidad and Tobago showing a sample of pre-Columbian sites on the island 38

2.4. Flow chart of weights-of-evidence procedure used in this study 39

2.5. Output weights of Landform evidential theme (Cipero watershed) 49

2.6. Output weights of Soil Texture evidential theme (Cipero watershed) 49

2.7. Output weights of Land Capability evidential theme (Cipero watershed) 50

2.8. Output weights of Relief evidential theme (Cipero watershed) 50
2.9. Output weights of Landform evidential theme (South Oropouche watershed) 51
2.10. Output weights of Land Capability evidential theme (South Oropouche watershed) 51
2.11. Output weights of Relief evidential theme (South Oropouche watershed) 51
2.12. Output weights of Landform evidential theme (Rest North watershed) 52
2.13. Output weights of Soil Texture evidential theme (Rest North watershed) 52
2.14. Output weights of Land Capability evidential theme (Rest North watershed) 52
2.15. Output weights of Relief evidential theme (Rest North watershed) 53
2.16. Posterior probability of Cipero watershed 62
2.17. Posterior probability of South Oropouche watershed 63
2.18. Posterior probability of Rest North watershed 64
2.19. Archaeological site favorability for Cipero watershed 65
2.20. Archaeological site favorability for South Oropouche watershed 66
2.21. Archaeological site favorability for Rest North watershed 67
3.1. Map of Barbados showing prehistoric site locations 77
4.1. Entity-relationship diagram of conceptual model 92
4.2. Attribute data entry form 93
4.3. Map of Trinidad created using the archaeological sites data set 93
4.4. Map of Trinidad created using the land-use data set 94
4.5. Selected sites that are within 500 m of a river and/or the coastline 95
4.6. Sites intersected with digital elevation model 95
5.1. Oxholm's map of St. John, 1780 101
5.2. Oxholm's map of St. John, 1800 102
5.3. Beck's map of St. Croix, 1754 107
5.4. Map of Coral Harbor, 1720 108
5.5. Oxholm's 1777 draft map of St. John 111
5.6. Fortification of Cruz Bay (Oxholm drawing) 112
5.7. Fort at Coral Bay (Oxholm drawing) 113

5.8. Color aerial survey/base map, 1994   117
5.9. Field survey: Mark Hauser using GPS to locate sites   118
5.10. Identification of historic sites (Cinnamon Bay Plantation)   119
5.11. GIS plot of sites dating to 1780 and 1800 (quarter boundaries also shown)   120
5.12. Plantation production by estate and quarter (sugar, cotton, provision), 1780 versus 1800   122
5.13. Change in distribution of unfree (enslaved) population from 1780 to 1800   123
6.1. Map of Nevis showing the "divisions"   131
6.2. Mountravers: the plantation landscape   132
6.3. Upper Woodland plantation, plans from archaeological survey   133
6.4. Parris's Garden, an eighteenth-century villa   134
7.1. Map of the parish of Trelawny located in north-central Jamaica   139
7.2. An example of how the X-parallax is observed   143
7.3. An infrared image of the study area   145
7.4. Land-cover classifications of the study area   147
7.5. Map showing potential areas for future Taino site exploration   149
8.1. Locational map of Los Gallos Point, Trinidad   157
8.2. Site map of Los Gallos Point, also depicting the possibly contemporary aboriginal Quemada Point site   158
8.3. Mercer team employing magnetometer at Los Gallos Point in 1998   159
8.4. Plan of the 1998 magnetometer surveys   160
8.5. Mercer team using Mark 1 prototype resistivity meter in 2002   162
8.6. Magnetometer survey (1998) of the Main Survey Area, with the smaller 2002 resistivity survey area imposed   163
8.7. Detail of the 1998 magnetometer survey with the same area of the 2002 resistivity survey   164
8.8. Mercer team taking soil temperature readings in 2002   165
8.9. Test Unit 9, 2004   166
8.10. Test Unit 10, 2004; east–west soil stain of possible slot   167
9.1. Geographical location of St. Eustatius   173
9.2. Location of Pleasures Estate Plantation and English Quarter Plantation on St. Eustatius   175

9.3. Several distinct foundation areas evident in the resistivity meter results for English Quarter Plantation   178
9.4. English Quarter Plantation as depicted on the 1781 P. F. Martin map; the Pleasures Estate Plantation as depicted on the same map   179
9.5. Geophysics identified additional structural remains at the Pleasures Estate Plantation   180

TABLES

2.1. Sites in Cipero watershed   42
2.2. Sites in South Oropouche watershed   42
2.3. Sites in Rest North watershed   43
2.4. Details of the analysis parameters of selected watersheds   43
2.5. Attributes of output weights of Landform evidential theme (Cipero)   44
2.6. Attributes of output weights of Soil Texture evidential theme (Cipero)   44
2.7. Attributes of output weights of Land Capability evidential theme (Cipero)   45
2.8. Attributes of output weights of Relief evidential theme (Cipero)   45
2.9. Attributes of output weights of Landform evidential theme (South Oropouche)   45
2.10. Attributes of output weights of Soil Texture evidential theme (South Oropouche)   46
2.11. Attributes of output weights of Land Capability evidential theme (South Oropouche)   46
2.12. Attributes of output weights of Relief evidential theme (South Oropouche)   47
2.13. Attributes of output weights of Landform evidential theme (Rest North)   47
2.14. Attributes of output weights of Soil Texture evidential theme (Rest North)   47
2.15. Attributes of output weights of Land Capability evidential theme (Rest North)   48
2.16. Attributes of output weights of Relief evidential theme (Rest North)   49
2.17. Attributes of weights-of-evidence (Cipero)   54
2.18. Attributes of response theme (Cipero)   54

Illustrations / xi

2.19. Attributes of posterior probability (Cipero)   55
2.20. Attributes of conditional independence (Cipero)   56
2.21. Attributes of weights-of-evidence (South Oropouche)   56
2.22. Attributes of response theme (South Oropouche)   56
2.23. Attributes of posterior probability (South Oropouche)   57
2.24. Attributes of conditional independence (South Oropouche)   58
2.25. Attributes of weights-of-evidence (Rest North)   58
2.26. Attributes of response theme (Rest North)   59
2.27. Attributes of posterior probability (Rest North)   60
2.28. Attributes of conditional independence (Rest North)   61
2.29. Archaeological site predictive model for Cipero watershed   68
2.30. Archaeological site predictive model for South Oropouche watershed   68
2.31. Archaeological site predictive model for Rest North watershed   69
4.1. Major applications of the AIS   88
4.2. Data required for the AIS   89
4.3. Major attributes stored for archaeological sites   90
7.1. Land-cover characteristics of the study region   148
9.1. Relative shipping activity in colonial ports   172

Acknowledgments

I wish to thank all the authors of the various chapters for their stellar contributions. It was indeed a pleasure working with them. Their essays, which reflect tremendous insight and an excellent grasp of the subject matter, are well appreciated and will, no doubt, serve to develop a better appreciation of geoinformatics within the context of Caribbean archaeology. I wish to express my profound gratitude to Narissa Seegulam, Daren Dhoray, Tariq Khan, John De Sormeaux, Kerry Bullock, Chris Riley, Naseema Hosein, Maria Peter-Joseph, Lystra Baksh-Moti, Marcela Boatswain, Serene Joseph, Kimika Lai Tan, Luke Mahase, and Dale Flemming for assisting with various aspects of the project such as typing, collating, and enhancing maps, figures, and tables coupled with compiling both the glossary and references in the volume. Heather Cateau provided useful information on references relating to West Indian plantation societies. Her contribution is gratefully acknowledged. I am particularly grateful to my wife, Joan, and our son, Gavin, for their moral support and incomparable patience as I sat up long hours in the nights vetting and editing the various chapters. Finally, thanks to the staff of the University of Alabama Press for their encouragement at every stage of this publication.

Basil A. Reid

Archaeology and Geoinformatics

Introduction

Archaeology and Geoinformatics: Case Studies from the Caribbean

Basil A. Reid

This volume, *Archaeology and Geoinformatics: Case Studies from the Caribbean*, presents a miscellany of both interesting and informative essays on the use of geoinformatics in Caribbean archaeology. The contributions are based on case studies drawn from specific island territories, namely, Barbados, St. John, Jamaica, Nevis, St. Eustatius, Puerto Rico and Trinidad and Tobago, with Chapter 1, which focuses on interisland interaction and landscape conceptualization in the Caribbean region, being the exception. Geoinformatics is one of the relatively new emphases in archaeology and can be defined as an interdisciplinary field that develops and uses information science and science infrastructure to address the problems of geosciences. In order to achieve its objectives, geoinformatics employs a battery of integrative and innovative approaches in analyzing, modeling, and developing extensive and diverse data sets. Several disciplines fall within the general purview of geoinformatics, namely, geographic information systems (GIS), global positioning systems (GPS), satellite imagery, aerial photography, photogrammetry, cartography, and geophysical surveys. However, while these techniques are increasingly being utilized in archaeology (e.g., Allen et al. 1990; Brophy and Cowley 2005; Carr 1982; Clarke 1990; Knowles 2002; Lock and Stancic 1995), most publications largely revolve around North American and European case studies, with scant attention being paid to the Caribbean. By demonstrating that this region—like anywhere else in the world—is fertile ground for the application of geoinformatics in archaeology, this volume places a well-needed scholarly spotlight on the Caribbean.

THE USEFULNESS OF GEOINFORMATICS IN CARIBBEAN ARCHAEOLOGY

The Caribbean is fertile ground for the following reasons. To begin with, the hive of archaeological activity in the region since the 1980s has led to an increasing demand for state-of-the-art technologies. Fourteen years ago,

William Keegan (1994:255) exclaimed that "Caribbean archaeology is riding the wave of an exponential curve," as myriad Caribbeanists had begun to "address questions of adaptation, evolution, social and political organization, mythology, cosmology, and ideology" (Ayubi and Haviser 1991; Robinson 1991; Siegel 1989). No longer is research in the Caribbean based almost exclusively on conventional survey and reconnaissance methods such as trial trenching, shovel test pitting, field walking, and ground surveys. Indeed, the various papers presented at the Twenty-First Congress of the International Association for Caribbean Archaeology (IACA), held in Trinidad and Tobago in July 2005, underscored the extent to which research agendas are being increasingly informed by a holistic mix of archaeological data, field methods, and scientific techniques, including geoinformatics.

The following examples favorably reflect the growing popularity of geoinformatics within the context of Caribbean archaeology. In 1998, geophysical surveys of a Jewish cemetery in Nevis resulted in the identification of at least 44 possible burials within the cemetery in addition to the 19 marked burials (Terrell 1998). Recent studies of St. Kitts's prehistoric settlement patterns incorporated not only reconnaissance site visits and field surveys but also the use of GIS-generated maps, including the production of 500-m buffer zones depicting possible site catchment zones (Farag and Ramlal 2005). Another example pertains to the innovative creation of a system by Landon and Seales (2005) for building three-dimensional models for Caribbean petroglyphs based on reconstructions of Taino petroglyphs at Caquana, Puerto Rico. According to Landon and Seales (2005) these digital models were aimed at allowing digital access to and preservation of petroglyphs in remote areas that often remain unprotected from the elements. By coupling aerial photographs with highly accurate survey techniques, large-scale area excavation, and a fully automated barcode-based computer system, Kappers, Fitzpatrick, and Kaye (2007) successfully created a three-dimensional model of the fast-disappearing site of Grand Bay in Carriacou. Essentially, the resulting GIS data set provided the means to construct three-dimensional modeling of the site, a necessary component for developing future strategies dedicated to investigating and protecting archaeological sites on the island (Kappers et al. 2007). Given these important developments, this volume is both timely and relevant, as it epitomizes a significant trend in Caribbean archaeology that is proving to be increasingly useful to scholarly pursuits in the region.

Another important reason for this volume relates to the negative impacts on archaeological sites of sprawling urban growth, agriculture, mining, and land erosion in various Caribbean territories. These impacts have been particularly damaging to pre-Columbian sites, as these sites tend to be generally less visible on the landscape than their historic period counterparts. For instance, since the first systematic archaeology was conducted on the island in 1985, Anguilla has experienced a dramatic loss of its Amerindian archaeological heritage as a result of two decades of hotel development along the coastline where the sites are situated (Crock 2005). Michiel Kappers (2004) indicated that in March/April 2003, 11 site locations in Carriacou were surveyed and mapped. Most sites in Carriacou were found to be endangered by erosion through wave, storm, and tidal action and sand dredging by the local population, with the site of Grand Bay being the primary example.

The realization that archaeological resources are finite and diminishing (Drewett 2001:7) has prompted greater cultural resource management efforts in some Caribbean territories, as evidenced by the creation of heritage and planning organizations such as the Jamaica National Heritage Trust, the Institute of Jamaica, and the Town and Country Planning Authority in Jamaica; the National Trust, the Town and Planning Division, and the Tobago Trust in Trinidad and Tobago; the Barbados Museum and Historical Society and the Archaeological Museum of Aruba. There is also growing recognition among archaeologists, heritage managers, and policy makers in the Caribbean that geoinformatics is the preferred technique in heritage management, as it generally allows for more efficient data collection, analysis, and retrieval than conventional paper-based methods. Aerial photography is particularly useful for "preventive prospecting," which means detecting and documenting sites before their destruction. These may be especially relevant in the face of the growing destruction of archaeological sites as a result of flooding, land erosion, mining, and road and building construction, which often result in the complete destruction of archaeological sites, despite the presence of heritage management organizations throughout the region.

Caribbean geography is also well suited to the application of geoinformatics. The island chain is divided into three parts. The Lesser Antilles form an arc extending northward from Trinidad and Tobago to the Virgin Islands; the Greater Antilles stretch westward from there to the Yucatan Peninsula; and the islands of the Bahamian Archipelago form a triangle in the Atlantic Ocean between the Greater Antilles and Florida (Rouse 1992:3). Although the islands in the Caribbean are generally small, their myriad microenvironments such as river valleys, forested areas, grasslands, coastlines, plains, hills, and mountains often pose significant challenges with respect to both site visibility and accessibility. Visibility refers to "the extent to which a site has been buried or covered by soil aggradation and vegetation since its occupation" (MacManamon 1984:224). James Zeidler (1995:11) discusses how low to nonexistent visibility because of dense vegetation cover is a common problem throughout the neotropics, which includes much of the Caribbean. This can be caused by old-growth forest vegetation with dense understory, more recent secondary-growth forest, or the dense ground cover of tall grasses used for pasturage. Trinidad and Tobago, which was connected to the South American mainland as recently as 10,000 years ago and remains in close proximity to the South American mainland, can be cited as a case in point. Comprising approximately 90 percent of the land area (Davis et al. 1986), the forests of the twin island republic not only share the same flora with South America but also, more significantly, these forests conceal many archaeological sites on the ground. Often, even cultivated plots exhibit completely obscured ground surfaces (Zeidler 1995:11). For instance, extensive sugar and rice cultivation on the plains of St. Catherine in south-central Jamaica has significantly reduced the visibility of archaeological sites within this particular area.

Accessibility, on the other hand, can be defined as the ability to physically inspect a given area of terrain (Zeidler 1995:12). Cases of low accessibility can be caused by difficult terrain or dense vegetational growth, which may impede or reduce mobility. Recent landscape modifications in the Caribbean may have completely destroyed evidence of archaeological occupations or covered them entirely with large expanses of soil, water, or modern construction. Because of ongoing land erosion, much of Canoe Bay, a large Amerindian site on the southwest coast of Tobago, has now been inundated by the sea, thereby making much of the site inaccessible to serious investigators.

Clearly, these land surface conditions can have drastic consequences for discovery probability and logistical efficiency in archaeological surveys within the Caribbean. This is primarily because conventional surveys require the use of labor-intensive subsurface testing programs and/or pedestrian surface inspections that may be both costly and time consuming (see Siegel 1995). Geoinformatics—which includes noninvasive techniques such as satellite remote sensing, cartography, aerial photography, photogrammetry, GIS, GPS, and geophysical surveys—can facilitate rapid reconnaissance of relatively large areas of archaeological interest that have been adversely affected by both low or nonexistent site visibility and accessibility. As shall be demonstrated in this volume, geoinformatics can lead to better site detection and more efficient data collection and management both in the field and in the laboratory. The results generated by geoinformatics can also facilitate more "targeted" excavations of selected sites in the Caribbean, thus significantly reducing time and monetary costs.

CHAPTER DESCRIPTIONS

Part I: Archaeology, GIS, and Visibility Models

The chapters in this volume have been organized under various themes, called Parts I, II, III, and IV. Part I focuses on the versatility of GIS applications in creating visibility models. Generically defined as any computer-based capability for the manipulation of geographical data (Bernhardsen 1999:4), GIS has been utilized in a variety of scenarios, including creating representations of social landscapes and associated landscapes (Harris and Lock 1995:355). These representations enable archaeologists to address questions of cognition among the cultures they study (Wheatley 1993).

Joshua Torres and Reniel Rodríguez Ramos's essay in Chapter 1 is a quintessential example of this approach. Both Torres and Rodríguez Ramos seriously challenge notions of insularity and isolationism associated with the Caribbean archipelago by using visual sight analysis to show connectivity between islands as well as neighboring continental landmasses. They also critically examine the implications of their models in relation to pre-Columbian migratory patterns and cultural interactions throughout the region. Although it has been argued that visibility models should be treated with great care, since it is not at all clear how we might compute modern cognition in the landscape with GIS (Baldwin et al. 1996), the reality is that the visible area around a site presents a measure of the cognitive environment of the site. According to Gaffney and van Leusen (1995), this is related to the fact that the visible area is indeed a measure of the area seen and the locations visible and, as such, a possible measure of the value of the site location and other locations visible to it. In applying their visibility models to the Caribbean, Torres and Rodríguez Ramos's incisive chapter reflects the breadth of perspective that can be achieved through the astute use of GIS.

Part II: Archaeology, GIS, and Cultural Resource Management

An underlying theme running through a significant number of the chapters in this volume is cultural resource management (CRM), which can be succinctly defined as the management and preservation of cultural resources, such as cultural landscapes, archaeological sites, historical records, historic buildings, and industrial heritage and artifacts. The twinning of GIS and CRM in the contributions of Basil Reid, Kevin Farmer, and Bheshem Ramlal and Basil Reid in Chapters 2, 3, and 4, respectively, is clearly premised on the growing recognition throughout the Caribbean that GIS is a powerful tool for the management of heritage sites.

Certainly, one of the central tenets of CRM is predictive modeling, which is predicated on the simple assumption that patterns exist in the places where people locate their activities, camps, or settlements in the landscape. On the basis of GIS weights-of-evidence analysis of prehistoric sites and their areal association with evidential themes, Reid in Chapter 2 produces archaeological predictive models for three watersheds in Trinidad. This study is designed to enhance CRM of Trinidad's pre-Columbian sites, an important but seriously threatened heritage resource on the island. Although weights-of-evidence is invariably used for geological prospecting (Bonham-Carter et al. 1988), Reid's chapter clearly demonstrates the utility of this technique in archaeological predictive modeling.

Farmer's and Ramlal and Reid's contributions (in Chapters 3 and 4, respectively) both bring into sharp perspective the significant role that GIS has been playing in some Caribbean territories, like Barbados and Trinidad and Tobago, in collecting, archiving, managing, retrieving, analyzing, and outputting geographic and other related kinds of attribute data. Farmer's discussion revolves around a project to develop a "Sites and Monuments Inventory System" at the Barbados Museum and Historical Society through a grant from UNESCO—a project driven by the need to properly document sites that are being threatened by rapid urbanization in the small Caribbean nation. Ramlal and Reid place the spotlight on the design and development of an Archaeological Information System (AIS) for the Archaeology Centre at the University of the West Indies, St. Augustine, using ArcView GIS (ESRI) and Microsoft Access software. Considered as far superior to conventional paper-based methods, the AIS would not only provide a means for accessing information but also a digital database that may be maintained and updated with new information as it becomes available.

What is clear from Farmer's and Ramlal and Reid's essays is that—like all GIS operations—converting source material into spatial and attribute data for the sake of CRM can be very time consuming. Although GIS can be used quickly to make maps and tables, archaeologists, historians, and cultural resource managers should be prepared to invest considerable time in designing their systems, acquiring data, and converting material from manuscript and print sources (including paper maps) into digital forms (see Knowles 2002: xvii). Despite this, the rewards of such investment are considerable, as GIS enables us to generate permanent records of sites, combine and jointly analyze diverse sources, understand how cultural heritage relates spatially to its surrounding natural and human environment, communicate knowledge and network databases, test proposed development models and conservation strategies, facilitate monitoring and management of sites, and map one's material in the course of research.

Part III: Archaeology, GIS, Cartography, GPS, Satellite Imagery, Aerial Photography, and Photogrammetry

Part III presents an eclectic mix of case studies based on other important geoinformatics techniques such as cartography, GPS, GIS, satellite imagery, aerial photography, and photogrammetry. In Chapter 5, Douglas Armstrong, Mark

Hauser, David Knight, and Stephan Lenik reconstruct the social context of ownership and control in eighteenth-century St. John in the Danish West Indies by utilizing an impressive collage of Peter L. Oxholm's historical maps, satellite imagery, archaeological data, documentary evidence, and tax records (*matricals*) within a GIS environment. Their research reveals the consolidation of sugar estates under a few key planters and the emergence of a free colored group who became owners of both land (cotton and provisioning estates) and slaves. In Chapter 6, working with an assortment of mid-twentieth-century maps coupled with field surveys of abandoned landscapes with the help of handheld GPS equipment, Roger Leech provides insights into the process of estate consolidation of colonial Nevis.

What is perhaps most instructive about these two research papers is the critical reading of maps as a key data source. This approach is symptomatic of emerging trends in what Knowles (2002) refers to as "Historical GIS" and is premised on the belief that maps hold information retained by no other written source, such as place names, boundaries, and physical features that have been modified or erased by modern development (Rumsey and Williams 2002). Despite the fact that the historical maps themselves challenge GIS users to understand the geographic principles of cartography, particularly scale and projection, they also reflect the prevailing attitudes and worldviews of those who created them.

Increasingly being used for archaeological research worldwide, GPS determines (by triangulation) the location of features, using data from orbiting satellites. In archaeological fieldwork, GPS may well be used for mapping find-spots, earthworks, and other archaeological features without the need of conventional techniques (i.e., triangulation and offset grids). The correct choice of GPS for specific projects depends upon the level of accuracy required in the field. Many archaeologists are happy with the level of accuracy obtained by handheld GPS (navigation grade) for archaeological fieldwork (Souterrain Archaeological Services, Ltd. 2004). While this is an increasingly indispensable (and inexpensive) item of equipment for field reconnaissance and walk-over surveys—especially in the more remote regions—it is clearly inappropriate for positioning evaluation trenches or conducting field-walking surveys, where tighter controls are required over each transect to be walked (Souterrain Archaeological Services, Ltd. 2004). Like Roger Leech (Chapter 6) and Kevin Farmer (Chapter 3), Parris Lyew-Ayee and Ivor Conolley (in Chapter 7) highlight GPS as an integral method in collecting site location data in the field. The two authors utilize aerial photographs, photogrammetry, multispectral satellite imagery, and three-dimensional images within a GIS environment to create a physical profile of Taino locations in Trelawny, Jamaica. This is designed to produce predictive models of where Taino sites are likely to be found in the parish. However, the use of remotely sensed data, though useful, poses significant limitations because of Trelawny's thick forest canopy covers. GPS, given its high mobility survey capacity, is therefore used by Lyew-Ayee and Conolley to locate Taino sites in the field.

GPS aside, Lyew-Ayee and Conolley should be commended for incorporating a panoply of remote sensing techniques in their study, such as aerial photography, photogrammetry, and infrared satellite imagery. Although infrared satellite images and aerial photographs, as well as the stereoscopic images generated by photogrammetry, capture contemporary environmental conditions in Trelawny, the two authors were able to use these tools to digitally create environmental profiles of Taino sites in order to determine possible site locations. Overall, the contributions of Armstrong and colleagues, Leech, and Lyew-Ayee and Conolley clearly indicate that multiple data sources, if subjected to careful analysis, can be of considerable interpretive value in better understanding past societies of the Caribbean.

Part IV: Archaeology and Geophysics

The final two chapters, by Eric Klingelhofer (Chapter 8) and R. Grant Gilmore III (Chapter 9), both present informative discourses on the use of geophysics in archaeological research. Defined as the study of the various physical properties of the earth and the composition and movement of its component layers of rock, geophysics is increasingly being applied to detect archaeologically significant areas of interest. As is characteristic of this volume, both Klingelhofer's and Gilmore's chapters reflect a multidisciplinary approach. While geophysics is the primary technique in Klingelhofer's attempt to locate Sir Walter Raleigh's outpost in Trinidad, archaeological, documentary, and cartographic sources are also part and parcel of his research methodology. The Elizabethan outpost is yet to be found, hence the project, in Klingelhofer's words, is "a work in progress." The ongoing work of Klingelhofer and his Mercer University team is indeed justified, as historical records and maps point to locations in Trinidad as possible bases for early English exploration and colonization.

In Chapter 9, Gilmore discusses the significant role of geophysics in guiding future research designs and in confirming cartographic evidence on the English Quarter sugar plantation in St. Eustatius. While dry soil and vegetation were the primary deterrents to using the resistivity meter at Pleasures Estate, also in St. Eustatius, this equipment helped to identify the location of a slave village at English Quarter Plantation, including slave quarters and sugar/rum-processing buildings. Clearly, therefore, although certain soil conditions can militate against the effectiveness of geophysical surveys, these surveys can produce optimal results if used in the "right" conditions. The results of geophysical surveys can help the archaeologist to subsequently focus his or her limited resources on specific areas of each site, thereby significantly reducing costs relating to capital outlay, equipment, and labor.

CONCLUSION

This book's approach is both interpretive and multidisciplinary, drawing not only on archaeological data and geoinformatics but also on a rich array of documentary and cartographic sources. The essays in this volume represent exciting new directions in Caribbean archaeology and will be a useful store of information as well as a critical frame of reference for archaeologists, historians, heritage managers, museologists, geographers, environmentalists, geoinformatics specialists, and interested members of the public.

I
Archaeology, GIS, and Visibility Models

1
The Caribbean
A Continent Divided by Water

Joshua M. Torres and Reniel Rodríguez Ramos

Current conceptualizations of the relatedness of islands within the Caribbean Basin are typically characterized by notions of insularity and isolationism based on the archipelagic configuration of the region. In this chapter, we utilize theoretical concepts associated with phenomenology and landscape approaches to show levels of connectivity between islands (as well as neighboring continental landmasses) that have previously been ignored. In particular, we focus on aspects of visual sight analysis, through the use of geographic information systems (GIS) to promote a view of interisland interaction and landscape conceptualization characterized by continentality rather than insularism. Critically, we explore the implications of this perspective in terms of pre-Columbian migrations and movements through the Caribbean and the potential interaction spheres associated with native populations of the region.

Current conceptualizations of the Caribbean landscape depict it as a group of islands lineally arranged with "its tail stretching from Trinidad and Tobago, at the mouth of the Orinoco River in South America, and its arms reaching to the peninsulas of Yucatan in Middle America and Florida in North America" (Rouse 1992:1) (Figure 1.1). This lineal configuration has led to consideration of this landscape as an ideal laboratory for addressing questions about human migration and cultural evolution. Traditionally, migration into the Antilles has been characterized by a stepping-stone model of movement northward through the islands from South America (Rouse 1953, 1992). However, the origins and pace of that movement are still points of contention (Callaghan 1995, 2001, 2003; Curet 2005; Wilson et al. 1998). The most common perspective of cultural migrations and evolution in the Caribbean is that, once peoples reached these islands, they developed in situ in monocultural landscapes (i.e., at the series level), until social or environmental pressures necessitated their expansion to the next suitable island (see Curet 2005:28–30 for a detailed discussion). In this sense, the islands have become the major spatial units of analysis

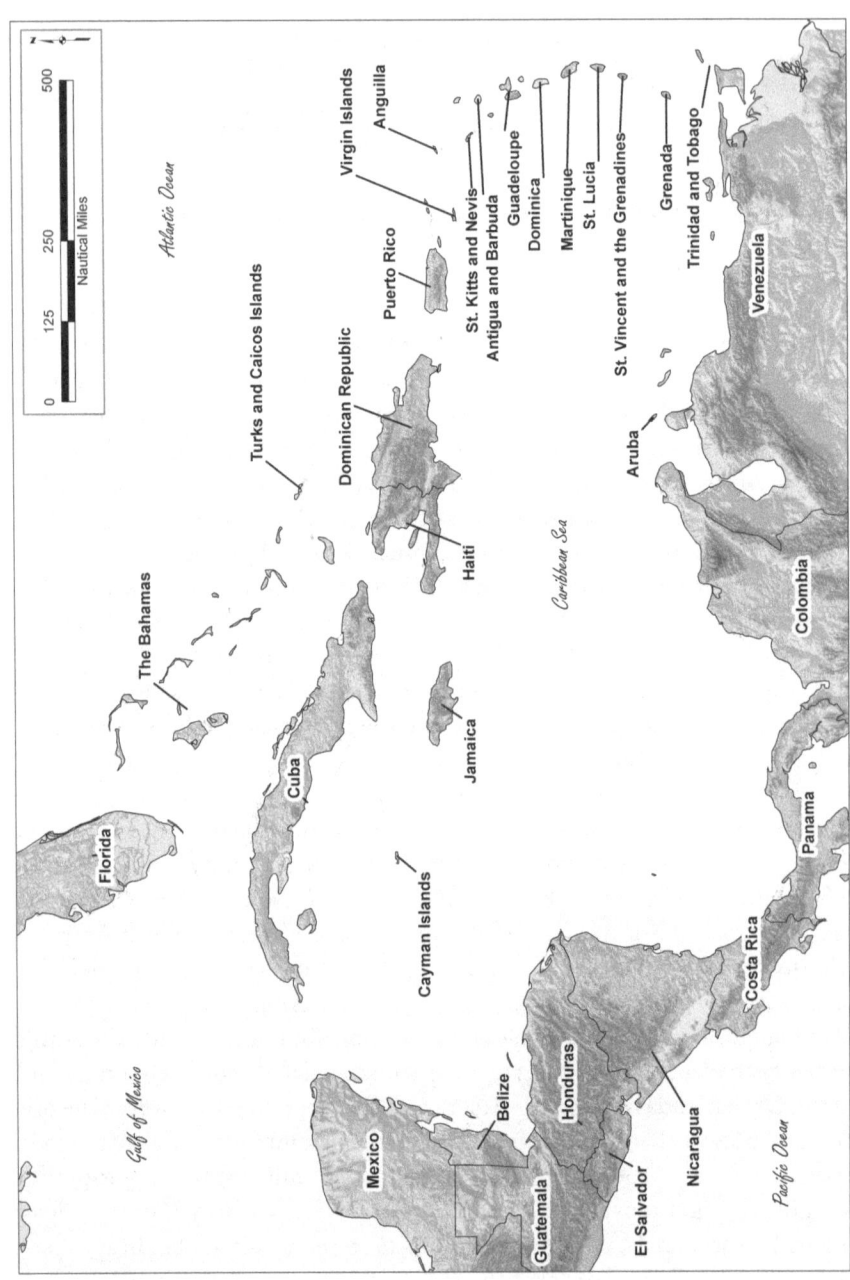

Figure 1.1. Map of the Caribbean Basin with GTOPO30 digital elevation model (DEM) and political boundaries.

at the macrolevel, with a general neglect for the sociocultural processes occurring at varying scales within them and between them.

In geographic terms, the islands have been defined as terrestrial bodies surrounded by water. In this sense, the boundary of each island is delimited at the point where land touches water. This has led to the idea that processes within those islands occur in "insularity," as if "oceanic islands are somehow unto themselves bounded environments because they are surrounded by water and separated from other places physically as well as mentally" (Fitzpatrick 2004:3). This idea of the "primitive isolate" (Lape 2004) has influenced archaeological conceptualizations of the pre-Columbian social landscape of the Antilles, which in turn has influenced the frameworks developed for modeling the colonization of the region and the degrees of intraregional and interregional interaction among precolonial populations. However, as was stated by Rouse (1992) and has been recently documented in several works dealing with the articulation of political (Crock 2000) and economic (e.g., Haviser 1991; Knippenberg 1999a, 1999b; Rodríguez 2002; Watters 1997) interaction spheres, the processes that occur in the spaces between landmasses are an extension of the ones that occur within them. Within this context the sea can be conceived of as a continuum of terrestrial social landscapes, as they too are places of experience and action. As such, we promote the notion that the Antillean social landscapes are spatially fluid in that they can be defined by the spaces not only where land touches water but also where land becomes water (Cooney 2003). Current theoretical conceptualizations of social landscapes have focused on phenomenological approaches in which action and movement in the physical world are part of the process of its construction (Bradley 2003; Certeau 1984; Gray 1999; Ingold 1993; Knapp and Ashmore 1999). Importantly, the key component to any phenomenological approach to landscapes is the way they are perceived and experienced by social actors and the relational nature of the physical world (Heidegger 1977; Ingold 1993; Tilley 1994). Within the context of a relational and conceptual landscape, visibility becomes an intrinsic element in the definition of what it means to experience and perceive and is key to the process of orienting oneself within the world (Ingold 1993; Merleau-Ponty 1962). Critical to this perspective, and an important part of this essay, is the process by which social actors relate to their physical world through action and experience.

Caribbean archaeologists have usually considered interisland visibility an important variable in people's decision to migrate from one island to the other. From this perspective, visibility has been construed as what people could see from land. However, as previously noted, if the sea was an extension of land vis-à-vis human action and experience, then part of that perceived landscape includes what you can see from water and thus the boundaries of landmasses extended much farther than the limits of their shores (Cooney 2003). Sometimes though, when at sea, before one loses visual contact with the place of origin, one is able to detect the presence of another landmass (e.g., when traveling from the Orinoco to Trinidad). These critical spaces of intersecting visibility provide a continuum between islands that perhaps played similar roles, although on a larger scale, as those of river drainages within the islands. For instance, on the island of Puerto Rico it has been suggested that sociopolitical units, while connected in webs of relational social networks, were organized on the basis of the boundaries of river drainages during late Saladoid and Early Ostionoid times (cf. Curet et al. 2004). From this perspective, islands were related in networks of social action and interaction, which were connected by water rather than separated by it. Therefore water, traditionally conceived of as separating these places, actually serves as a relational space connecting the islands and their continental neighbors through human action and experience.

The negotiation and development of landscapes are based on the actions of human agents (Bourdieu 1977; Ingold 1993). Within the contexts of the prehistoric settlement of the Caribbean, successful migrations would have relied upon being able to navigate and orient oneself on the seas in ways similar to a terrestrial landscape. By this we mean that the orientation and travel within either space requires movement through it and the utilization of referents in the physical world through the concomitant process of moving and orienting or "wayfinding" (Ingold 2000). However, as one on land is oriented based on landscape features, orientation within a seascape would have necessitated different frames of reference or waypoints such as islands in relation to one another or celestial bodies (see Irwin 1992 for discussion in relation to Pacific Islanders).

Critically, this process of orienting oneself and traveling through space is divorced from traditional European notions of maps and two-dimensional reference systems. Rather, wayfinding (Ingold 2000), or landscape as an event (Hirsch 1995), is part of a process of "being in the world" (Heidegger 1977) and represents a body of knowledge that would have been necessary for the successful colonization of and subsequent travel through the Caribbean (Curet 2005). Therefore, in order to understand the landscapes of the past, we must contextualize those referents from an experiential and relational perspective. Only then can one begin to discuss the relationships between people and place in the development of past societies.

In order to illustrate this alternative perspective of the Caribbean landscape, we present an exploratory analysis of the interconnectivity of the islands of the Caribbean Basin and their continental neighbors through the use of line-of-sight analysis with the aid of geographic information systems (GIS) technology.[1] Through this exploratory analysis, we suggest that the region is much more interconnected than previously conceived, representing more of a "continental" landscape than an archipelagic one. Critically, we suggest that the bodies of water served to connect places and that these spaces are as much a part of the social landscape as settings on land. We then present the potential implications of landscape visibility for prehistoric interaction and travel throughout the region as well as suggestions for further research.

METHODS

The primary data set used in this analysis was the GTOPO30 digital elevation model (DEM) of the Caribbean Basin developed by the U.S. Geological Survey (see Figure 1.1).[2] The GTOPO30 data set is a 30-arc second grid, where each cell represents a 1-km^2 area with elevation values recorded for each cell. Landmasses under 1 km^2 are not represented within the DEM. Unfortunately, smaller-scale (i.e., higher resolution) DEMs do not exist for the entire region. However, even though the GTOPO30 data set represents a relatively coarse scale, we do not feel that this precludes its use in our analysis, as the data are primarily used for generating approximate distances from which landmasses are visible from sea and from one another.

Visual sight analysis has become an increasingly useful tool in modern archaeological research contexts (e.g., Madry and Rakos 1996; Swanson 2003) and has been an important component of phenomenological perspectives of landscapes of the past (e.g., Scarre 2002). Line-of-sight analysis typically entails a calculation of the maximum distance of visibility from a given point on the landscape based on the height, or elevation, of the observer as well as the height of the object being observed and any obstructions that would inhibit visibility between the observer and the target area (cf. Wheatley and Gillings 2002:201–216).

For the present study, the first step in the analysis was to address how to create a model representing maximum visibility ranges from land. This was done to model not only how far from land one could see but also how far land could be seen from the water. To do this with some level of control, it was necessary to create a model showing visibility distances for each cell in the DEM. Utilization of the built-in ArcView visibility applications was deemed impractical, as this would have required running the application for every cell in the DEM for multiple target locations. Instead, the DEM elevations were recalculated and substituted with values representing the maximum distance range visible from the cell to the horizon, or how far away any given point could be seen (Figure 1.2). In this regard, we used Bowditch's (1995:340) standard distance to the visible horizon formula, which is *DHNM = (1.17) × (vH)*, where *DHNM* is the distance to the horizon in nautical miles, 1.17 is the factor for the

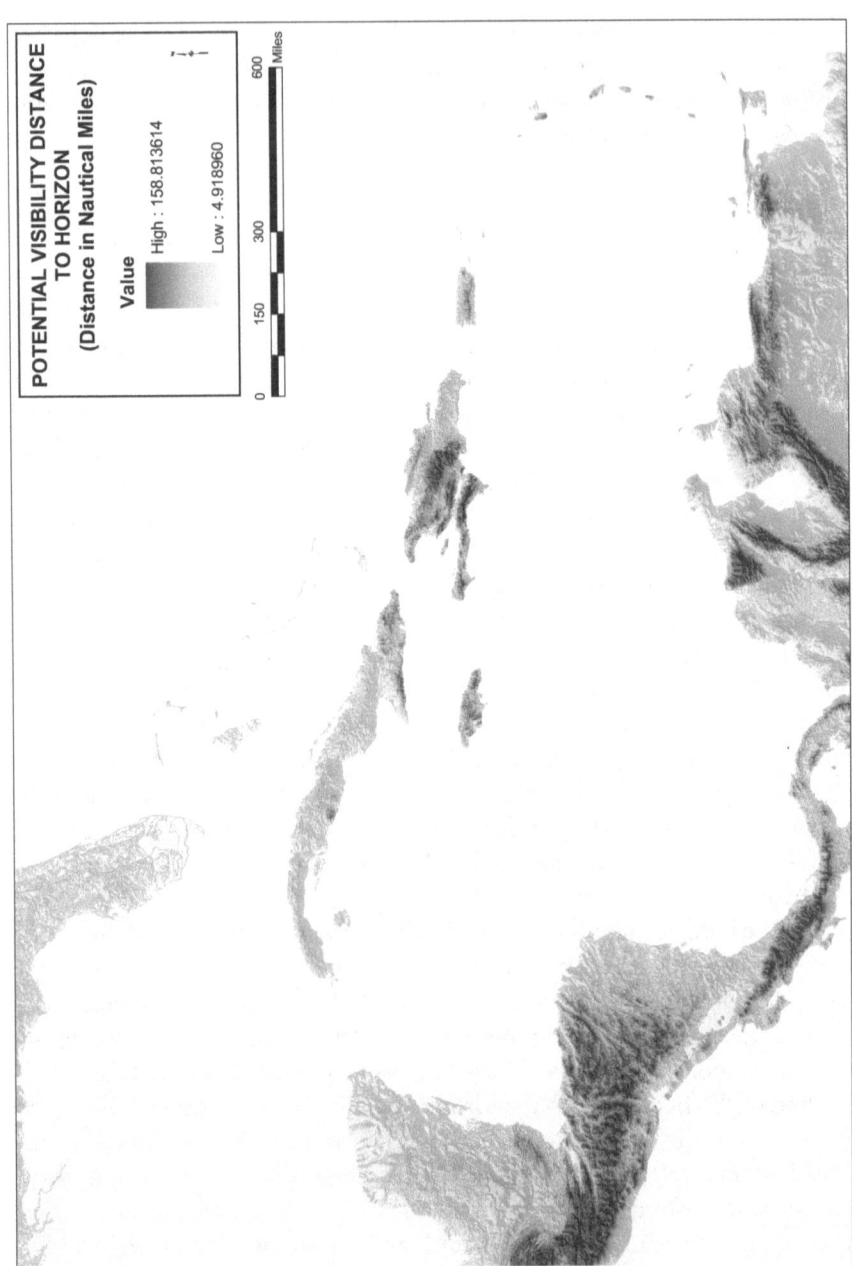

Figure 1.2. Recalculated DEM using Bowditch's (1995:340) standard distance to the visible horizon formula.

distance to the visible horizon, and vH is the square root of the height of the eye of the observer in feet. This model assumes conditions of perfect visibility with no looming effects and similar environmental conditions to those currently registered. It also assumes a height of the observer of 1.75 m above water and does not take into consideration the additions in elevations due to the height of vegetation on landmasses.

Observation points (n = 104) for visibility were based on two factors in order to maximize visibility ranges: (1) proximity to the coast and (2) the height of the observation point, which tended to be the highest point of elevation on an island or continental upland adjacent to the coast. Points were placed on these locations and attributed with the underlying cell value representing visible distance to the horizon. Subsequently these points were buffered to the underlying distance value of the point (Figure 1.3). No observation points were put in either the Bahamas or Florida as preliminary testing showed that the elevations on those areas were too low to have any substantial visual effect. Moreover, we would like to note that all areas within the buffered zone are not completely visible from the selected points (and vice versa), although the high points of landmasses and their visual sight distances from water are generally unobstructed at their maximal range.

DISCUSSION

Based on a cursory examination of the visibility ranges, it is clear that the projection of Caribbean landmasses and Circum-Caribbean continental landscapes extends far beyond their shores. This projection range based on visibility has several important implications. To begin with, visual continuity between the areas where land is visible can be inferred where line-of-sight buffers overlap (Figure 1.4). This visual range would have provided sea travelers with an important tool for orienting themselves, as they could see land from any point within that range. It is very likely that these areas would have served as important visual and navigational landmarks for seafarers and that they would have been utilized continually once established.

As humans interacted with their visual surroundings at sea, they most likely developed connections of spatial relationality that were used to orient themselves within the world. This becomes important both in consideration of the development of a conceptual "map" in the minds of pre-Columbian peoples of the Caribbean and in consideration of the importance of the knowledge of this "map" in terms of orientation and sea travel (Ingold 2000; Irwin 1992). Both archaeological and anthropological researchers have recently presented the significance of this transmitted knowledge in the contexts of cultural tradition, experience, and navigation (Curet 2005). From this perspective, throughout

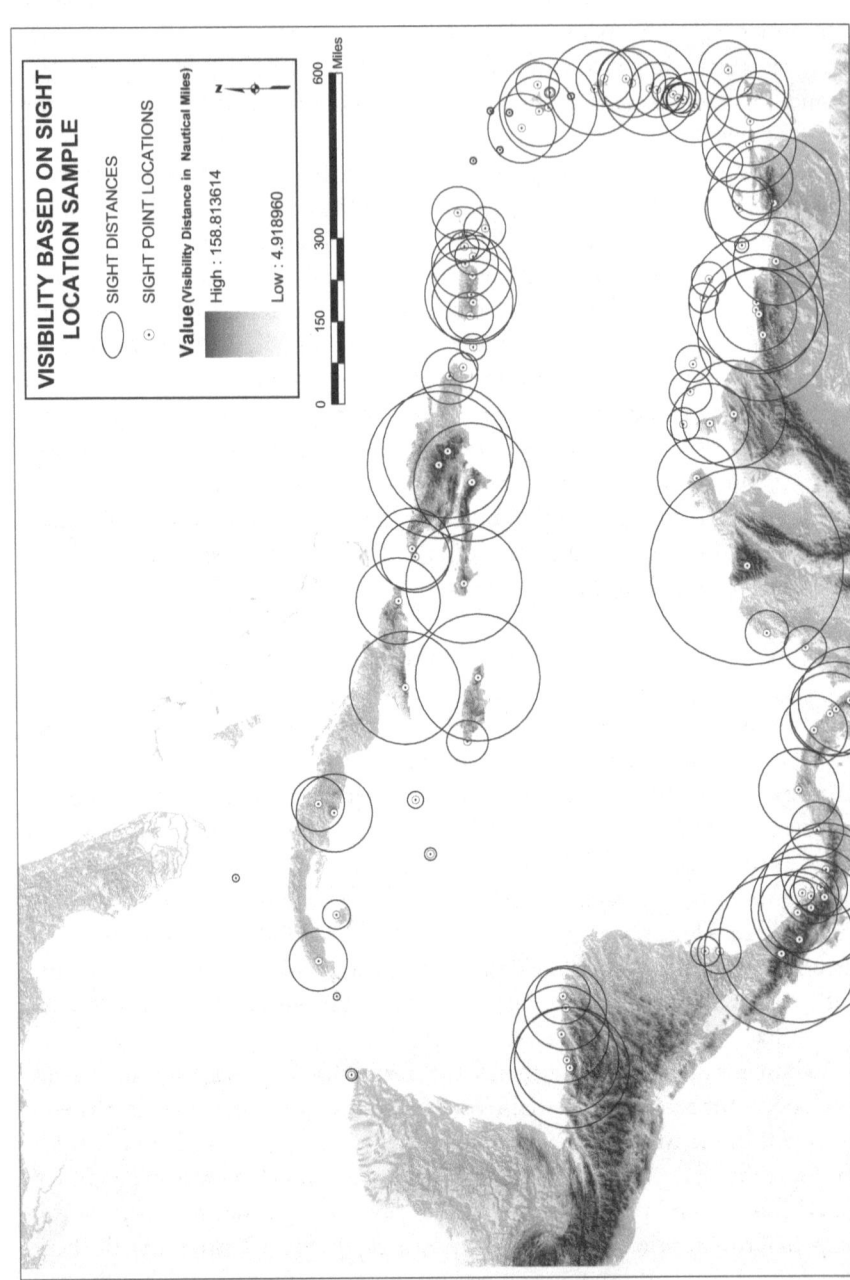

Figure 1.3. Recalculated DEM using Bowditch's (1995:340) standard distance to the visible horizon formula. Map also shows sample points from/to which visibility is possible.

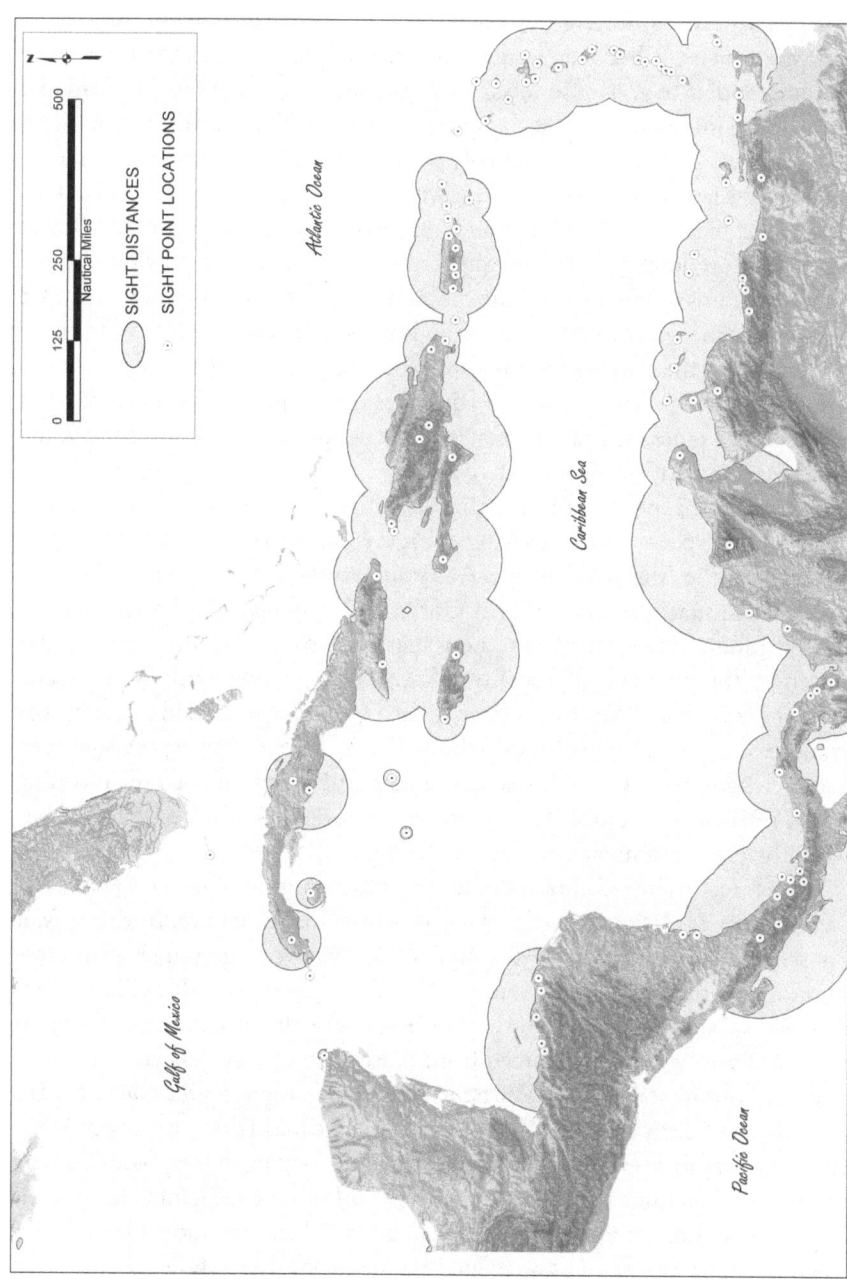

Figure 1.4. Visibility ranges based on point sample. The base map is the GTOPO30 DEM.

most of the Greater and Lesser Antilles, the landmasses are visually contiguous, providing a sense of continuity, a sense of continentality. This continuum contrasts with the notions of the "big jumps" that were registered in areas where land was not visible between islands, assumed in previously suggested island-hopping models (e.g., Rouse 1992). For instance, areas between Trinidad and Grenada are joined by intersecting visibility ranges, thus posing a scenario in which the two landmasses are actually within sight of each other (Figure 1.5).

Perceived landscape continuity between two landmasses can also be seen with respect to southeastern Cuba and northeastern Jamaica (Figure 1.6). These two islands are joined by the heightened range of visibility provided by the Blue Mountains of Jamaica and the Sierra Maestra of Cuba, both of which are actually within sight of each other from both the sea and the land. This connection makes the reasons for the supposed late peopling date for Jamaica (a date of ca. A.D. 650 from the Little River site in St. Ann on the north coast of Jamaica) even more intriguing when in Cuba people were occupying the island as early as 7000 B.P. (Wilson et al. 1998).

Obviously, this does not imply that seafarers of the Antilles did not travel through blind spaces. When looking at Figure 1.4, one is able to detect a major blind spot in the Anegada Passage. According to the projections in our model, this negative space between Virgin Gorda and Anguilla is approximately 80 nautical miles. However, we do know that this space was crossed, as is evidenced by the presence of flint from Antigua and radiolarian limestone and porphyry from Saint Martin to Puerto Rico (Knippenberg 1999a, 1999b; Rodríguez 2001, 2002). This obviously shows that interaction spheres existed even in areas where there was no visual continuity, and therefore open sea traveling was an intrinsic element in the maritime networks that were established between the pre-Columbian societies of the region.

Therefore, this interconnectivity forces us to reconsider the landscape of the Caribbean as a relational space, which is continental in nature. In this way, it is possible to alleviate some of the myopic perspectives regarding social interaction and cultural development in the Caribbean. Ever since Rouse's (1953) article testing Steward's Circum-Caribbean Theory, the processes occurring in the Caribbean have been divorced from those that were evidenced in the surrounding continental regions. With the exception of the accepted contacts with northeastern South America during precolonial times (Boomert 2000; Watters 1997), very little emphasis has been placed on looking at the possibilities of sustained interactions between the Antilles and other continental areas, with some notable exceptions (e.g., Callaghan 2003; Chanlatte 2003; Garcia 1984; McGinnis 1997; Rodríguez 2002; Sued Badillo 1979). Even though some areas such as Belize (Wilson et al. 1998), northwestern Venezuela (Zucchi 1984), and Florida (Febles and Baena 1995) have been considered as sources of migration

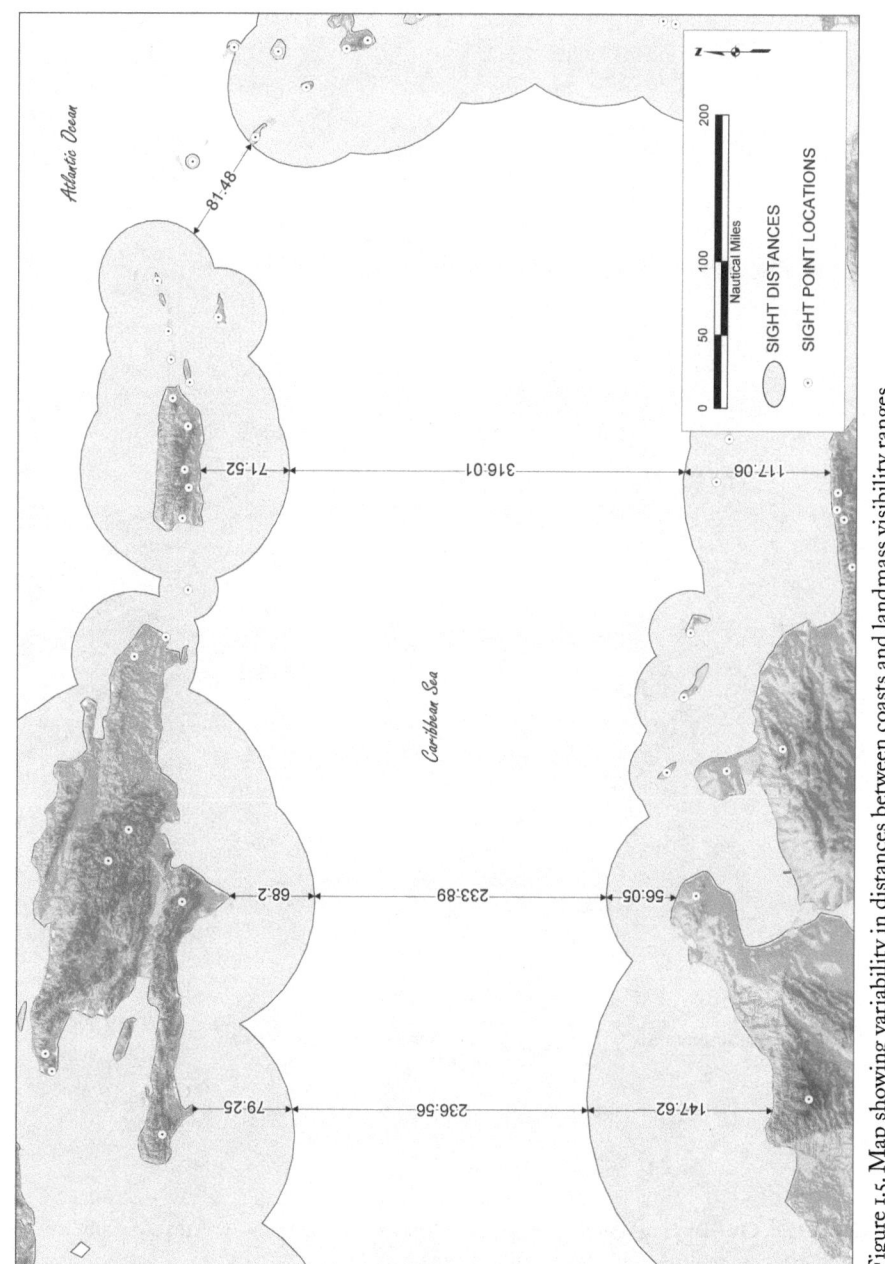

Figure 1.5. Map showing variability in distances between coasts and landmass visibility ranges.

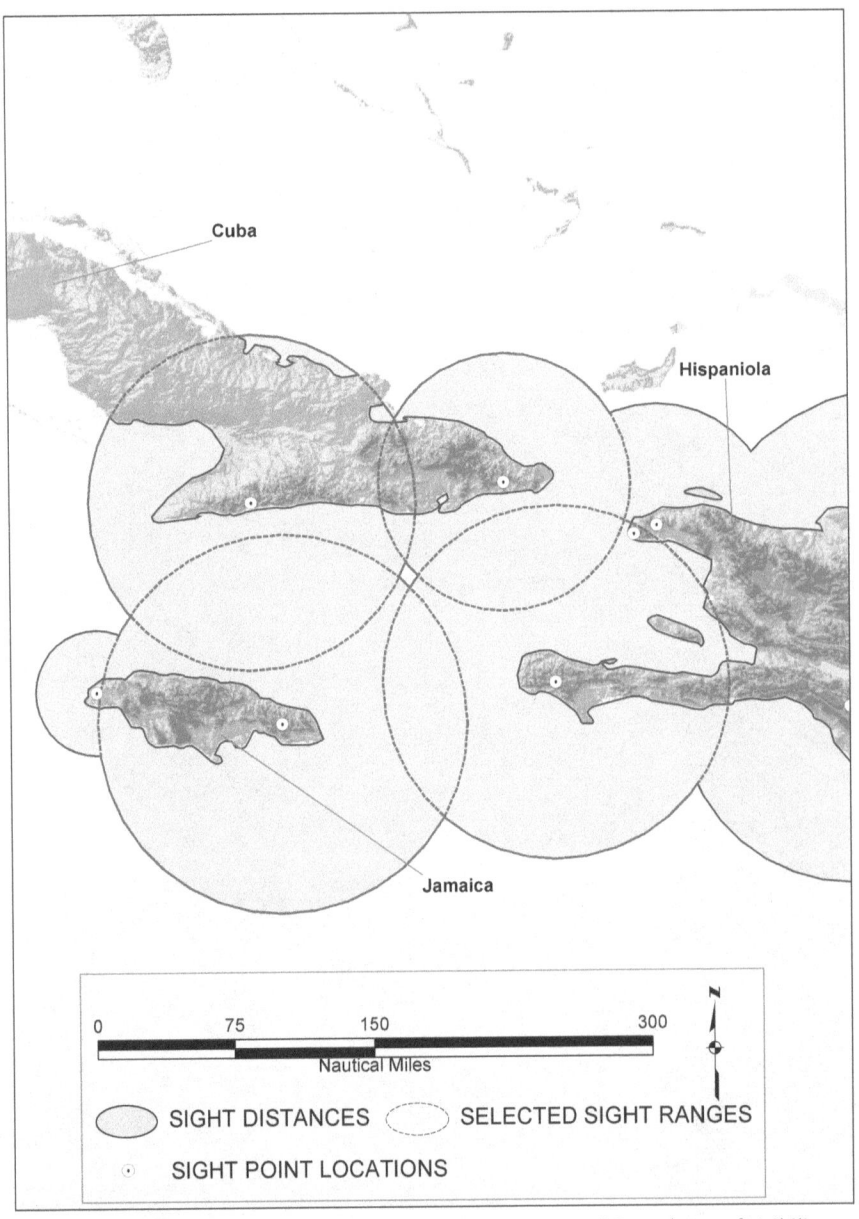

Figure 1.6. Overlapping visibility areas in the Greater Antilles. (Note: Areas of visibility overlap where multiple islands are visible from water.)

to the islands, the possibility of continuous contact with people from such regions after the initial population movement had been considered unlikely. Factors such as sea currents and distance between areas, among others, have been used as arguments for isolating the Caribbean from the Circum-Caribbean region.

For instance, interaction with Florida is often negated. However, if we consider that the distance of the negative space of the Anegada Passage (121 nautical miles coast to coast) is considerably larger than that between southern Florida and northern Cuba (86 nautical miles coast to coast), then the reasons for such a lack of interaction become untenable. The currents have been used as an argument to establish the unlikelihood of contact between those two areas (e.g., Bullen 1974; Rouse 1992). Yet as Polynesians were able to travel across distances that covered around a fourth of the circumference of the globe even in very difficult seafaring conditions (Kirch 1984:1), it might have been possible for the pre-Columbian navigators of the Caribbean to travel across large stretches in the open sea. Obviously the currents and other environmental contingencies were important elements to consider in delineating the navigational routes that needed to be followed to reach target destinations; but as with the Polynesians, it is almost certain that the peoples of the islands were able to circumvent these constraints by their extensive knowledge of spatial referents in the physical world that formed a network of related places between seascapes, landscapes, and human action.

The extension of the visual landscape to the sea also results in a perceptual decrease in the distance to be traveled to detect a landmass. Specifically, our analysis shows that when we extend the range of visibility between two landmasses to the sea, the chance discovery of a landmass or the occurrence of a conceptual "landfall" is augmented dramatically as the space between landmasses is decreased. For instance, people usually consider travel distances from coast to coast or land to land. In our model, the visual range of landmasses supplements coastal distances because we suggest that once visual contact has been made with a landmass, physical contact is more or less imminent. Importantly, once visual contact is made with a landmass it becomes part of the relational network between places and part of the cognitive representation of human experience within the world.

This observation is particularly important when considering the possibilities of contact between northwestern South America and the Greater Antilles. The large distance between these two areas has been used as an argument against the possibilities of direct contacts between them. However, if one takes into consideration the extended visual ranges observed in northeastern Colombia and southern Hispaniola, then the distance for making a virtual landfall decreases from 463 to 236 nautical miles, which is just 115 nautical miles longer than the negative space of the Anegada Passage (Figure 1.7). This dramatically increases the chances of accidentally detecting the Greater Antilles and provides further support for the modeling of navigational routes to the Caribbean from South America proposed by Callaghan (2003). If we add to this the effects of clouds and bird movements that were definitely additional referents used by seafarers in the process of wayfinding to reckon the presence of "nearby" land, then it should not be so surprising that people could have moved directly and intentionally from northwestern and/or north-central South America to the Greater Antilles.

In terms of interconnectivity, there are several areas that show where multiple landmasses would have been visible from the sea. These areas of intersecting visibility between islands might have been used as navigational routes or areas of interaction, as groups would have been able to maintain visual connection to their given terrestrial points of origin. This visibility might have provided more options in the directionality of movement between landmasses, thus promoting the articulation of multidimensional interactions rather than exclusively bi-dimensional (i.e., east–west) ones based on modern Western conceptualizations of space and maps (Ingold 2000; Tilley 1994).

This intersecting visibility of two landmasses from different points at sea could have also encouraged greater levels of cultural interactions between two landmasses connected by water than between two extremes within the same island, as indicated in Rouse's (1992) "passage area" concept. For instance, Rouse has suggested that stronger cultural relationships existed between an island and its adjacent island neighbor rather than among the populations within an island. An example of this can be seen on the island of Puerto Rico and the suggested interaction areas characterized by the Mona Passage and Vieques Sound areas,[3] respectively (Rouse 1992). Perhaps in such cases, it was less costly to travel to and therefore be connected to adjacent island neighbors than to travel to opposite ends of the same island.

CONCLUSION

The visual analysis shows that most of the Caribbean landmasses are visible at considerable distances from the water. This distance would have provided a safe range from land within which sea travelers could skirt visible landmasses as navigational landmarks. Furthermore, these visual extensions of the terrestrial landmasses decreased the distance between areas in which people would travel blindly between considerable spaces. These aspects of the West Indian landscape would have been realized by seafaring peoples and very likely influenced their conceptualization of the Caribbean as a whole, which, as we suggest here, consisted not only of landmasses but also of the water that connected

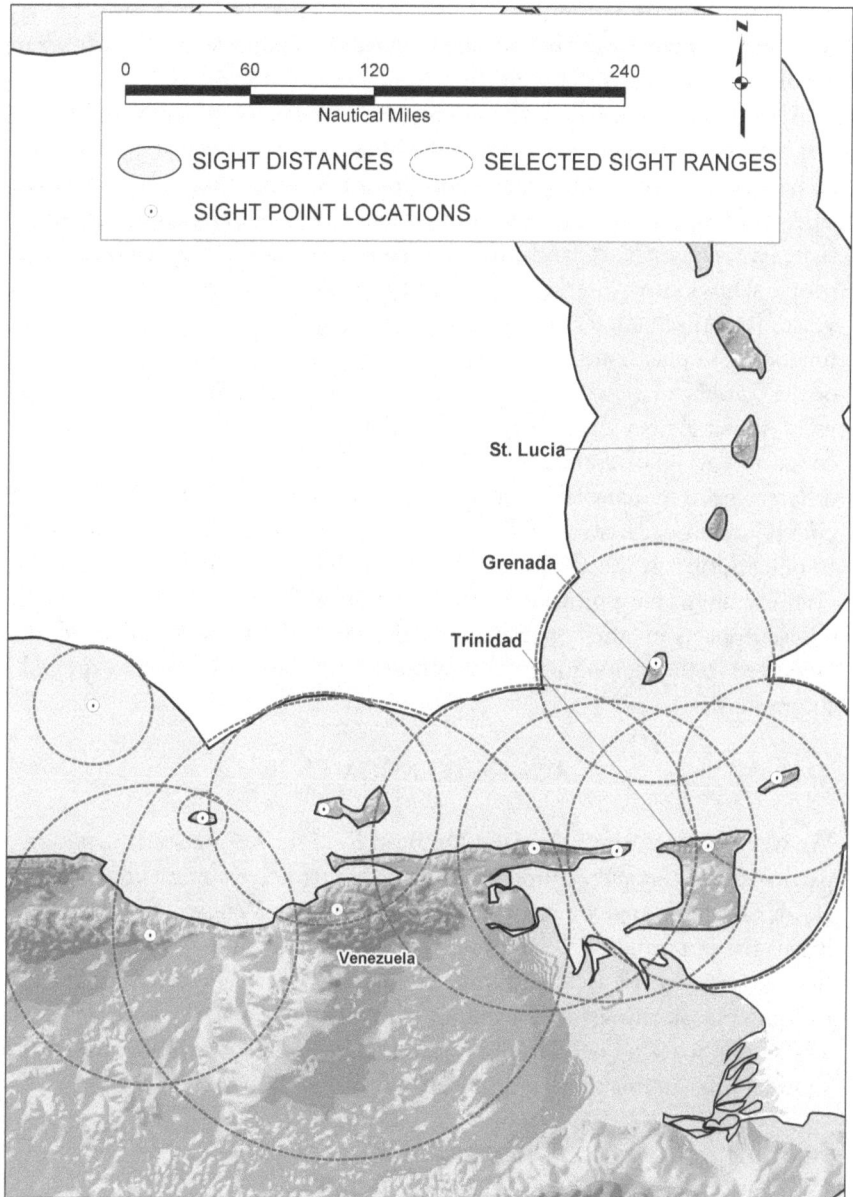

Figure 1.7. Overlapping visibility areas in the Lesser Antilles. (Note: Areas of visibility overlap where multiple islands are visible from one another.)

them by virtue of visibility. Importantly, these visual landscapes undoubtedly influenced the way in which peoples experienced, conceived of, and interacted in their world. Examining the material correlates between areas based on high visual connectivity would help to shed more light on the usefulness of applying visual sight analysis at this scale.

Although we do not deny the uniqueness of the environmental and physiographic island settings and some of the idiosyncrasies of social processes that occurred on certain islands of the Antilles, we feel that these landscapes form part of a larger relational network of human action and experience. In this sense, we suggest that landscapes are conceived and conceptualized by the people who occupy, interact, create, and negotiate their social realities within spaces (cf. Anschuetz et al. 2001:160; Gray 1999; Ingold 1993). Therefore, the functional implications of landscape conceptualizations, within the contexts of the Caribbean, need not stop at the shores of its constituent islands. In this work, we single out the particularity of the Caribbean landscape as an interconnected group of landmasses surrounded by continents, which is markedly different from more isolated archipelagic environments such as the South Pacific (Curet 2004; Keegan and Diamond 1987). The proximity of the islands to one another in the Caribbean Basin and their interconnectivity based on visibility might have provided a sense of continuity, a sense of continentality, whose impacts on the regional interaction and social development of those who lived in the region in pre-Columbian times should be further explored in future studies.

ACKNOWLEDGMENTS

We wish to thank the following: Dr. Basil Reid for his gracious invitation to participate in this publication and for his constructive comments on our essay during the course of its development; Professor William Keegan for giving us the opportunity to work on this essay as part of a class assignment at the University of Florida; and three anonymous reviewers for taking the time to comment on this essay. This material is based upon work supported under a National Science Foundation Graduate Research Fellowship. Any errors or shortcomings in this chapter are solely our responsibility.

NOTES

1. The analysis was conducted using ESRI's ArcView 3.2 software.
2. For more information regarding the development of the GTOPO30 data set please refer to http://edcdaac.usgs.gov/gtopo30/gtopo30.asp (accessed 11/30/04),

or write to U.S. Geological Survey, EROS Data Center, 47914 252nd Street, Sioux Falls, SD 57198-0001.

3. The Mona Passage separates the Dominican Republic from Puerto Rico and has a reputation for unpredictable currents and choppy seas. Vieques is an island-municipality of Puerto Rico. It is located to the east of the Puerto Rican mainland.

II
Archaeology, GIS, and Cultural Resource Management

2
Developing Weights-of-Evidence Predictive Models for the Cultural Resource Management of Pre-Columbian Sites in Trinidad

Basil A. Reid

Aimed at enhancing cultural resource management of Trinidad's pre-Columbian sites, this chapter discusses weights-of-evidence models for three watersheds in the south and southwest of Trinidad. Pre-Columbian sites and their areal association with evidential themes (such as landform, relief, soils, and land capability) formed the basis of these predictive models. The study suggests that the pre-Columbian sites in south and southwestern Trinidad are likely to be found in areas of hilly relief, land capability characterized by either fairly good land or land unsuitable for agriculture because of slope and/or water limitations, upland landforms, and areas with "free internal drainage" along the south coast of the island. Most weights-of-evidence models revolve around North American case studies. This chapter is therefore significant as it provides a useful example of how weights-of-evidence models can be created and interpreted on the basis of environmental data sets specific to a Caribbean island. I argue that the models generated in this chapter can significantly improve the cultural resource management of Trinidad's pre-Columbian sites by (a) reducing the monetary and time costs of fieldwork on the island, (b) facilitating more effective land-use management, and (c) helping archaeologists and cultural resource managers create, update, and protect Trinidad's archaeological database.

Developed in this chapter are three weights-of-evidence models relating to the South Oropouche, Rest North, and Cipero watersheds of Trinidad (see Figures 2.1 and 2.2). Given that these predictive models are yet to be subjected to field verification, they should be considered as a working hypothesis for future archaeological surveys on the island and elsewhere in the Caribbean. Of more immediate significance, these models provide a modus operandi for those entrusted with the enormous responsibility of identifying, assessing, documenting, and managing pre-Columbian archaeological sites in

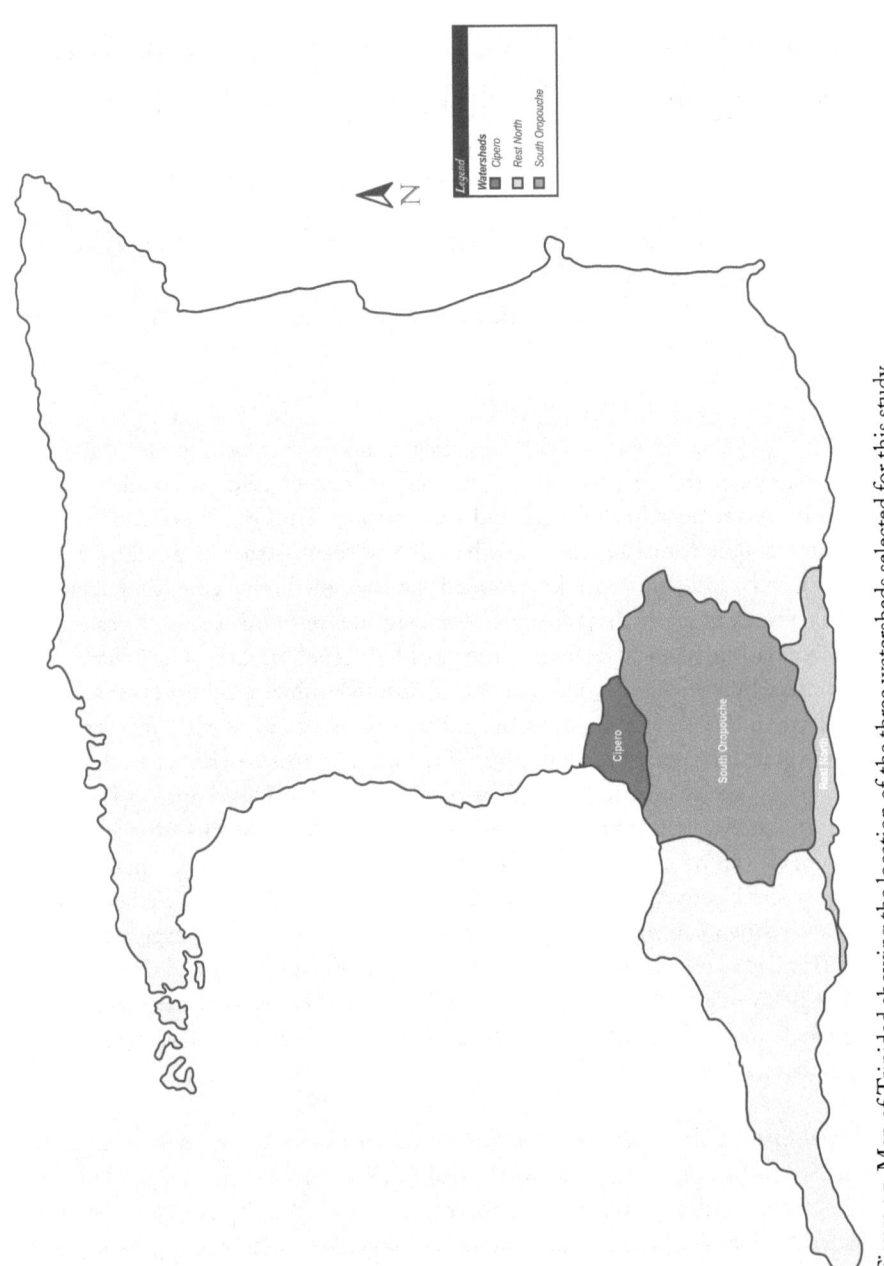

Figure 2.1. Map of Trinidad showing the location of the three watersheds selected for this study.

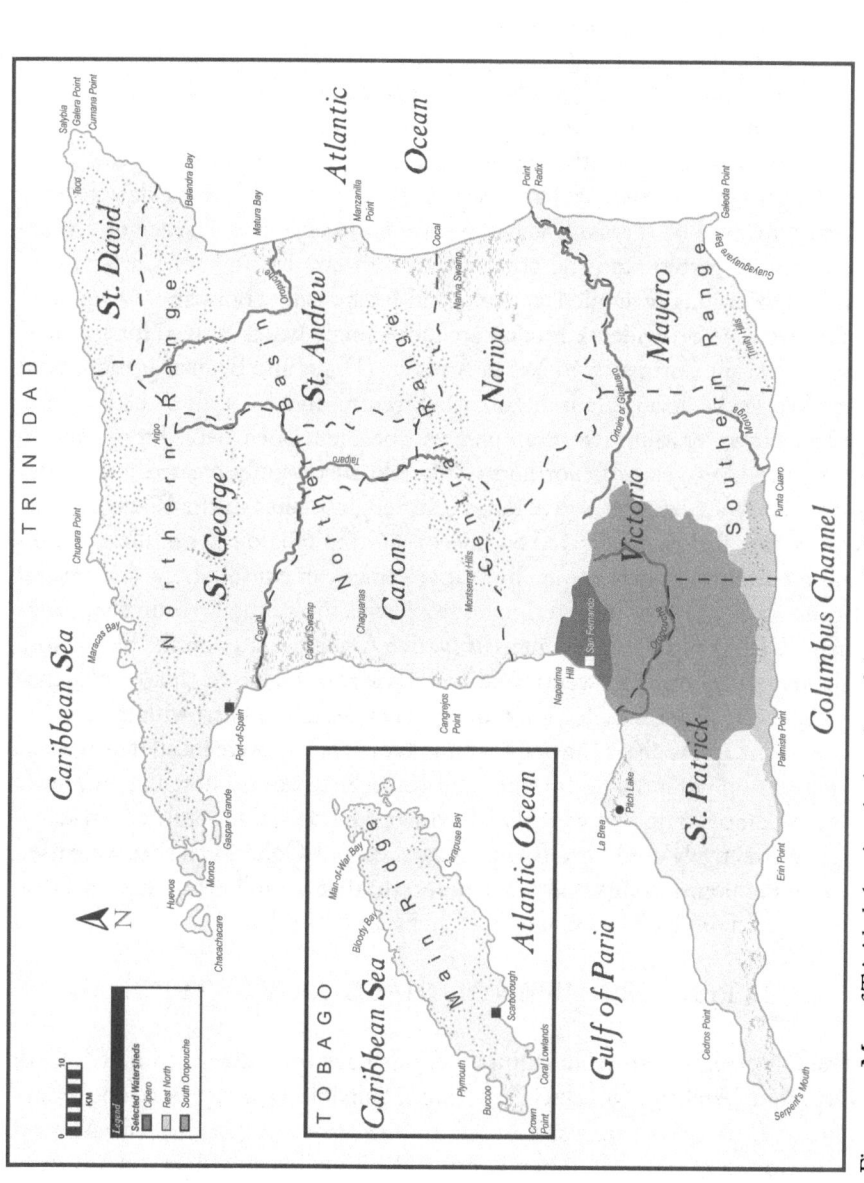

Figure 2.2. Map of Trinidad showing the location of the watersheds in relation to the island's physiography.

the Caribbean's most southerly island. The need to more effectively manage the pre-Columbian archaeology of Trinidad is pressing, given the continuing destruction and partial denudation of these sites as a direct result of agriculture, urbanization, and mining (Landell Mills Limited 1992). Locating new sites can be both time consuming and expensive. This is especially the case in tropical countries like Trinidad, where there are several challenges related to poor ground visibility and/or lack of easy access to sites (Zeidler 1995)—challenges that significantly increase time, labor, and equipment costs.

Weights-of-evidence is a Bayesian approach for combining data to predict occurrence of events. It is based on the presence and absence of a characteristic or pattern and the occurrence of an event (Bonham-Carter 1994). Although originally applied to geological prospecting (Bonham-Carter et al. 1988), weights-of-evidence models are increasingly being utilized for archaeological research, primarily in North America (Diggs and Brunswig 2006; Ford and Wernecke 2000; Hansen 2002; Schwemm and Kaberline 2004; White 2002). However, only two examples will be mentioned here. From 1998 to 2002, the University of Northern Colorado successfully created a weights-of-evidence analysis of Native American religious sites in the Rocky Mountain National Park, predicated on line-of-sight to religiously significant peaks and mountains, as determined by Native American consultations (Diggs and Brunswig 2006). Another sterling example was the cultural resource management (CRM) and risk assessment of Native American sites on the Santa Rosa Island in California (Schwemm and Kaberline 2004). The weights-of-evidence predictive model was useful, but more so when used in concert with the erosion potential map. Analysis showed that no predicted sites were located in areas of high erosion potential (Schwemm and Kaberline 2004). These two examples clearly demonstrate that weights-of-evidence models, if properly constructed, can be effectively used for CRM purposes. As pre-Columbian sites were used as training points in this study, it is important that the following summary discussion of Trinidad's pre-Columbian archaeology be given.

THE PRE-COLUMBIAN ARCHAEOLOGY OF TRINIDAD

The following Amerindian cultural periods have been identified in Trinidad: Ortoiroid (Archaic) (5000 B.C.–200 B.C.), Saladoid (250 B.C.–A.D. 600), Barrancoid (A.D. 600–A.D. 750), Guayabitoid (A.D. 750–A.D. 1300), and Mayoid (A.D. 1300–A.D. 1800) (Boomert 2000).[1] The Mayoid cultural period primarily covers the post-Columbian years and is therefore not particularly relevant to this study.

Migrating from northeast South America, early Ortoiroid (Archaic) populations settled in Trinidad around 5000 B.C. Most of the approximately 29 Archaic sites identified on the island are to be found in the southern half of the island. Ortoiroid sites can be defined by the absence of pottery and the presence of ground stones and mollusks coupled with marine-oriented subsistence that followed a terrestrial hunting-based economy (Keegan 1994:265–266). Because of its geographical situation, Trinidad is often considered to have played a crucial role as one of the first stepping-stones in the movement of Saladoid peoples from the mainland of South America to the Antillean archipelago (Siegel 1991). The Saladoids, who were the first pottery-making peoples to migrate into the Caribbean, had a mixed economy based on horticulture, hunting, and fishing. Generally considered egalitarian in their sociopolitical organization, the Saladoids lived in villages that usually coalesced around a central plaza. Trinidad was also settled by Barrancoid peoples, who considerably influenced Saladoid cultural traditions after A.D. 250. According to Rouse (1992), the Barrancoid peoples, who apparently developed during the second millennium B.C., expanded downstream at the beginning of the first millennium B.C., pushing the contemporaneous Saladero people past the delta to the coast. Between A.D. 250 and A.D. 300, a local Barrancoid complex, Erin, was established in south Trinidad (Boomert 2000:239). The possible decline of Barrancoid communities in the middle Orinoco on the South American mainland (around A.D. 650) facilitated Guayabitoid expansion from the Orinoco Delta to the Caribbean's most southerly island (Harris 1978). Guayabitoid pottery is tempered with sand, shell, and a new temper, *cauixi*, a freshwater sponge, the use of which originated in the Amazon and the Guianas. (Figure 2.3 shows a sample of pre-Columbian sites in Trinidad and Tobago.)

METHODS

Weights-of-evidence modeling for the watersheds of South Oropouche, Cipero, and Rest North was applied in seven steps: (1) selection of a descriptive model, (2) selection of exploration (evidence) themes based on the descriptive model, (3) refining the descriptive model based on the exploration (evidence) themes, (4) selection of a training set, (5) testing of the exploration themes to qualify them as viable (predictor) themes, (6) generalizing of evidential themes, and (7) consolidating the themes into archaeological site location predictive models. A generalized flow chart of these procedures is depicted as Figure 2.4. The analysis was accomplished on a personal computer using an ArcView GIS 3.1 platform with Spatial Analyst 1.1 and weights-of-evidence software. The assessment method required that all the data be analyzed in digital form. At least 20 person-days were expended by me (between October and December 2002) to prepare training points, to test exploration themes, and to produce response themes for all the selected watersheds. Analyzing response

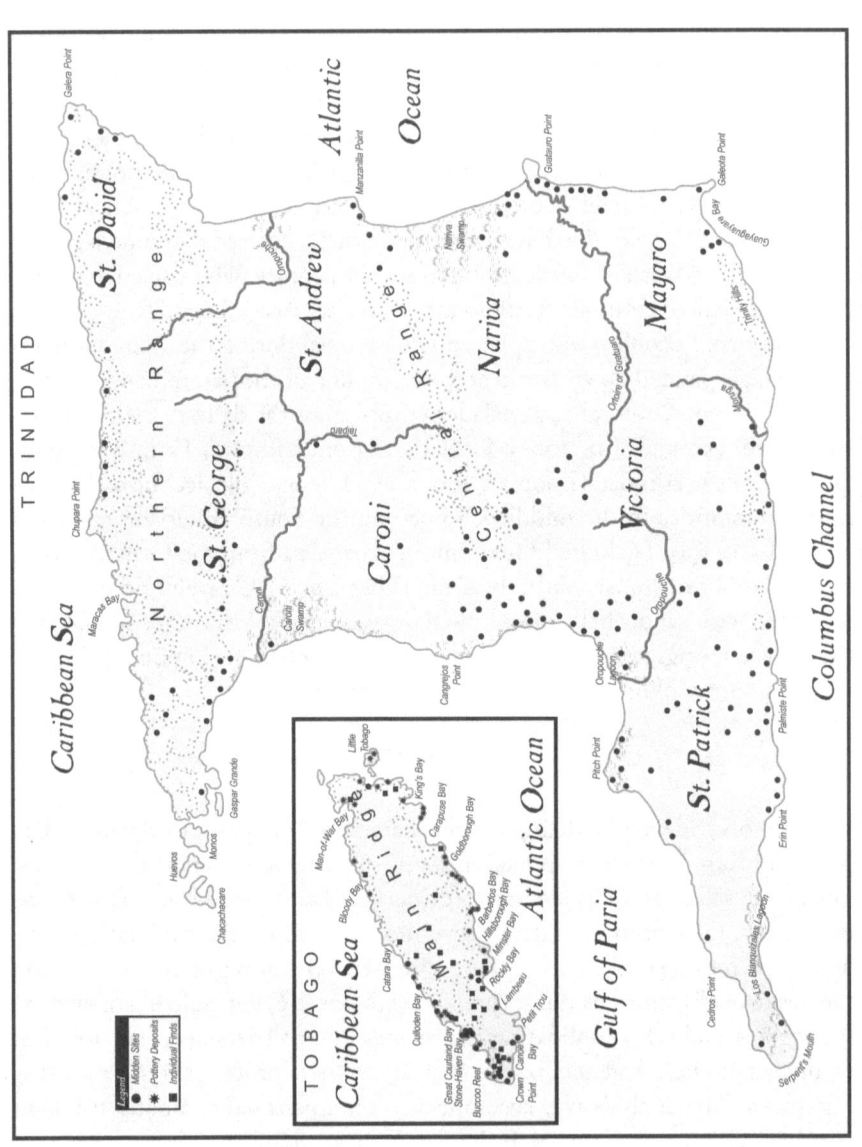

Figure 2.3. Map of Trinidad and Tobago showing a sample of pre-Columbian sites on the island.

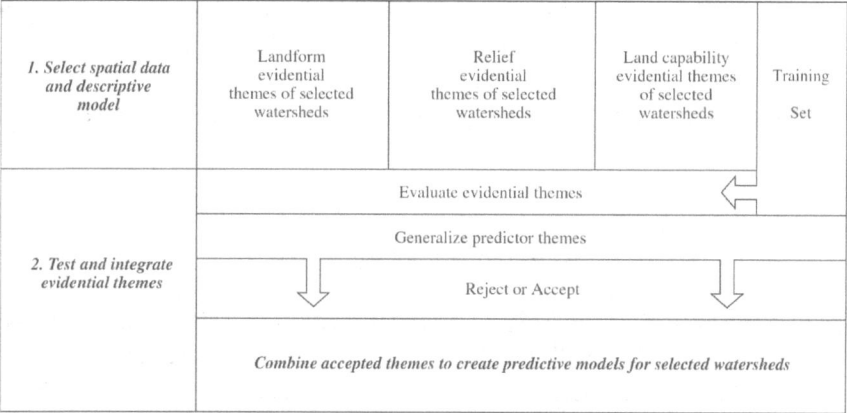

Figure 2.4. Flow chart of weights-of-evidence procedure used in this study.

themes, unique conditions tables, posterior probability maps, and other related weights-of-evidence outputs required an additional 10 person-days.

Selection of a Descriptive Model

The descriptive model is premised on the assumption that pre-Columbian settlement patterns in Trinidad and elsewhere in the Caribbean are determined by the following factors: (1) Landform, (2) Relief, (3) Land Capability, and (4) Soil Texture. Regarding the first two of these, Landform and Relief, irrespective of whether they are inland or coastal sites, a significant number of pre-Columbian sites in Trinidad, Jamaica, and elsewhere in the Caribbean tend to be situated on low-lying hills or knolls or on flat areas in foothills or mountainous regions (Allsworth-Jones et al. 1999; Boomert 2000; Curet 1992). The reasons for this are unclear but defense and health considerations have been cited (Howard 1965). Given their impact on land productivity, the factors Land Capability and Soil Texture would be especially germane to horticultural peoples such as the Saladoid and Guayabitoid (see Boomert 2000; Roosevelt 1997).

Hence, the following generalized descriptive model was devised: *Pre-Columbian sites in Trinidad are likely to be found on landforms with higher relief and in areas with favorable land capability and soil texture.*

Please note that this descriptive model was subsequently refined after the evidential themes were selected and analyzed.

Selection of Exploration (Evidence) Themes

The evidential themes of Landform, Relief, Land Capability, and Soil Texture, selected for this study, are a collection of vector data sets on Trinidad generated by the Survey and Land Information Department of the University of the West Indies, St. Augustine, Trinidad. Originally digitized from a hardcopy soils map of Trinidad (with a scale of 1:150,000), the geographic information system (GIS) data were produced in the 1990s and georeferenced in UTM (Universal Transverse Mercator) based on the coordinate system of 20N (Naparima 1955).

Refining the Descriptive Model

The disparate collection of class descriptions within the GIS evidential themes posed a considerable challenge. Relief descriptions of Trinidad are not quantitative but are loosely categorized as "flat," "low undulating hills," "rolling hills," "slightly undulating hills," "hilly," "gently slopes from hills," "hilly with mild slopes," and "hilly with steep slopes." The selected watersheds lie within the physiographic zones of the Southern Lowlands and the Southern Range—areas with either flat or gently rolling landscapes with the highest point being Trinity Hill at 303 m above mean sea level. Consequently, it was decided that the most effective way of circumventing this problem was simply to place the various "hill-related descriptions" within the general category of "hilly" and to refer to the remaining descriptions as "flat." Given the propensities of pre-Columbian peoples in the Caribbean, the "hilly" nomenclature was considered more appropriate for the refined descriptive model.

The evidential theme of Landform was less problematic, as it only contains three major classes: (1) alluvial plains and valleys, (2) terraces, and (3) uplands. Several pre-Columbian communities, especially in the larger Caribbean islands such as Jamaica, Puerto Rico, Hispañiola, and Cuba, are primarily concentrated in alluvial plains and valleys (Curet 1992; Rouse 1992). This nomenclature was therefore selected for the refined descriptive model.

Seven major classes constitute the Land Capability theme: (1) very good land that can be easily cultivated, (2) very good land, easily cultivated, for which simple protective measures are required, (3) good land that requires moderate to intensive conservation and management, (4) moderately good land that requires intensive conservation and management, (5) fairly good land that should be used for forest, tree crops, grazing, and buildings depending on the slope, (6) land unsuitable for agriculture because of slope and/or water limitations that should be left under indigenous growth or forest, and (7) land unsuitable for agriculture because of very steep slopes that should be left under indigenous growth or forest.

The Land Capability classification is a system of grouping soils primarily on the basis of their capability to produce common cultivated crops without deteriorating over a long period. Despite the fact that Land Capability classifications were crafted within the context of contemporary soil conditions in Trinidad, for heuristic purposes, it was decided to use these taxonomies in relation to pre-Columbian settlement sites. Given the importance of high land productivity among prehistoric horticultural groups, the Land Capability descriptions of "very good land," "good land," and "moderately good land" were viewed as perhaps the most relevant for the refined descriptive model.

The relative proportion of sand, silt, and clay found in a given soil determines soil texture. Similar to the Relief theme, the Soil Texture theme of Trinidad has a diverse collection of classes, which for the purposes of a descriptive model required some level of rough categorization. The classes are as follows: "sandy clay," "clay loam," "sand," "sandy loam," "loamy fine sand," "fine sandy loam," "gravelly sandy clay," "peaty clay," and "clay." Root crop agriculture, based on the cultivation of manioc, sweet potatoes, and to a lesser extent maize, was a defining characteristic of prehistoric societies in the lowland American tropics (Lathrap 1970; Roosevelt 1980). Archaeological evidence suggests that the Saladoid and Guayabitoid horticultural migrants from South America extended their root crop agricultural practices to Trinidad (Boomert 2000). Manioc, sweet potatoes, and corn generally thrive well in "free internal drainage soils" such as "sandy clay," "sand," "sandy loam," "loamy fine sand," and "fine sandy loam" (Farmer's Bookshelf 2002). However, these cultigens are not as successful in "restricted internal drainage soils" such as "clay" and "peaty clay." Therefore, on purely commonsensical grounds, the nomenclature "free internal drainage soils" was incorporated into the refined descriptive model. Hence, the refined descriptive model for the selected watersheds reads as follows: *Pre-Columbian sites in Trinidad are likely to be found in areas with hilly relief in alluvial plains and valleys, in areas with very good to moderately good land capability and free internal drainage soils.*

Selection of a Training Set

The training points used to test the refined descriptive model are all the known Archaic, Saladoid, and Guayabitoid sites within the selected watersheds. The Ortoiroid (Archaic) peoples of Trinidad were foragers, not horticulturalists (Boomert 2000; Keegan 1994). Conceivably, therefore, their settlement sites would have been more heavily determined by landform and relief rather than soil texture and land capability. However, South Oropouche is the only selected watershed with a smattering of Archaic sites, as the remaining watersheds exclusively contain Saladoid and/or Guayabitoid sites. Archaic sites were included in the South Oropouche watershed in order to create a more robust predictive model for that particular region of interest.

Archaeological site data were extracted from a compilation of site files

Table 2.1. Sites in Cipero watershed

Site Code	Site Name	Easting	Northing	County	Cultural Period
Vic15	San Fernando (Carib St.)	668850	1136425	Victoria	Saladoid
Vic13	Bontour	667375	1136575	Victoria	Guayabitoid
Vic14	San Fernando (H.P./High St.)	667825	1136600	Victoria	Guayabitoid
Vic47	Petite Morne A	672750	1134525	Victoria	Guayabitoid
Vic39	Woodlands 2	674200	1134525	Victoria	Guayabitoid
Vic20	Picton-Golconda	6741425	1133150	Victoria	Guayabitoid
Vic41	Cedar Hill A	675400	1135175	Victoria	Guayabitoid

Table 2.2. Sites in South Oropouche watershed

Site Code	Site Name	Easting	Northing	County	Cultural Period
Spa14	Lawrence Hill	671550	1124825	St. Patrick	Ortoiroid
Spa28	Banwari Trace	666400	1125000	St. Patrick	Ortoiroid
Spa13	Fyzabad	659175	1124550	St. Patrick	Ortoiroid
Vic19	Trinidad Hill	671400	1128475	Victoria	Guayabitoid
Spa2	Siparia	663075	1121350	St. Patrick	Guayabitoid
Spa25	Grant's Trace 1	671025	1116200	St. Patrick	Guayabitoid
Spa11	St. John	662275	1128475	St. Patrick	Guayabitoid

in Microsoft Excel.[2] The latter were converted into DBF files, imported to ArcView GIS 3.1 as event themes (based on their Northing and Easting coordinates), and subsequently converted to shape files in ArcView. Tables 2.1 through 2.3 list the specific sites that were used in relation to the selected watersheds.

Testing of the Exploration Themes to Qualify Them as Viable (Predictor) Themes

In step 5, the testing process involved digitally comparing the areal (or spatial) distribution of a training set with evidential themes. Prior to getting to this stage, however, several preliminary operations in ArcView were required. First, the watersheds of South Oropouche, Cipero, and Rest North were individually clipped from the Trinidad watershed theme. The watersheds were subsequently clipped from the Landform, Soil Texture, Land Capability, Re-

Table 2.3. Sites in Rest North watershed

Site Code	Site Name	Easting	Northing	County	Cultural Period
Vic7	La Lune 1	684100	1114600	Victoria	Saladoid
Spa30	Palo Seco	654400	1113500	St. Patrick	Saladoid/Barrancoid
Spa10	Quinam	661725	113650	St. Patrick	Saladoid/Barrancoid
Spa8	Palo Seco East	655525	1113625	St. Patrick	Guayabitoid
Spa26	Batiment Crase 1	671650	1113725	St. Patrick	Guayabitoid
Spa33	Guayabal River	660550	1115300	St. Patrick	Guayabitoid

Table 2.4. Details of the analysis parameters of selected watersheds

Watersheds	Unit Area (km^2)	Total Study Area (units)	Total Study Area (km^2)	Number of Training Points	Prior Probability
Cipero	0.3	165.71	49.71	5 (70%)	0.0294
South Oropouche	1.6	273.92	438.27	7 (70%)	0.0256
Rest North	0.2	403.61	80.72	9 (100%)	0.0224

Note: One hundred percent of the Rest North training points were selected because, of the nine points, only five lie within the study area. There is also no appreciable difference in prior probability and output weights between the application of 100 percent and 70 percent of the training set.

lief, and Pre-Columbian Sites evidential themes. This was designed to enable efficient processing of only those areas that fell within the physical parameters of the watersheds.

In ArcView Spatial Data Modeler, the study area is an integer grid theme that defines the regions of interest. It acts as a mask on areas of evidential themes, with training points outside the study area being ignored during processing. In order to create study areas for each selected watershed, individual watershed shape files were converted to grid themes, each with a 500-cell grid size. This grid cell size spatial resolution was selected as it was not considered too fine grained or too coarse grained.[3] Next, using Spatial Data Modeler in ArcView, analysis parameters were set for each of the selected watersheds. The details are in Table 2.4.

The weights of each evidential theme of the selected watersheds were then calculated as "free" or "categorical" data. Testing produced weights, contrast,

Table 2.5. Attributes of output weights of Landform evidential theme (Cipero)

Class	Landform	Area (km²)	Area (units)	No. Pts	W+	W-	Contrast
0	Not given	6.4422	21.4741	1	0.4510	-0.0869	0.5379
1	Alluvial plains and valleys	8.8970	29.6568	0			
3	Uplands	34.3740	114.5799	4	0.1507	-0.4445	**0.5952**

Table 2.6. Attributes of output weights of Soil Texture evidential theme (Cipero)

Class	Texture	Area (km²)	Area (units)	No. Pts	W+	W-	Contrast
0	Not given	6.4422	21.4741	1	0.4510	-0.0869	0.5379
1	Clay	43.0479	143.4931	4	-0.0816	0.4153	-0.4969
15	Sandy loam	0.2231	0.7436	0			

and other statistical values calculated for each of the various comparisons. The weights (positive weight, W+; negative weight, W-) express the degree of spatial association between the training set and the evidential themes. Selected tables and charts depicting output weights for Cipero, South Oropouche, and Rest North are presented in Tables 2.5 through 2.16 and Figures 2.5 through 2.15. The contrast values of the various classes within the previously mentioned tables and figures were used as the basis for accepting and rejecting particular evidential themes for the predictive models. The following rule of thumb for interpreting contrast values for predictor themes was applied (see Bonham-Carter 1994):

If contrast value is:	Level of prediction is:
0–0.5	Mildly
0.5–1	Moderately
1–2	Strongly
>2	Extremely

A decision was made to select only those contrast values above 0.5, as values below this threshold were not considered significant enough to produce reasonably good results.

With respect to Cipero, the evidential theme of Soil Texture was completely bereft of positive contrast values (Table 2.6 and Figure 2.6). Hence, Soil Tex-

Table 2.7. Attributes of output weights of Land Capability evidential theme (Cipero)

Class	Area (km²)	Area (units)	No. Pts	W+	W-	Contrast
0	6.4422	21.4741	1	0.4510	-0.0869	0.5379
3	8.8970	29.6568	0			
4	10.5541	35.1804	1	-0.0615	0.0160	-0.0775
5	16.3290	54.4301	1	-0.5082	0.1810	-0.6892
6	7.4908	24.9693	2	1.0292	-0.3566	**1.3858**

Class	Land Capability
0	
3	Good land, requires moderate to intensive conservation and management practices
4	Moderately good land, requires intensive conservation and management practices
5	Fairly good land, should be used for forest, tree crops, grazing, and buildings, depending on the slope
6	Unsuitable for agriculture due to slope and/or water limitations, should be left under indigenous growth or forest

Table 2.8. Attributes of output weights of Relief evidential theme (Cipero)

Class	Relief	Area (km²)	Area (units)	No. Pts	W+	W-	Contrast
0		6.6653	22.2177	1	0.4153	-0.0816	0.4969
1	Flat	8.8970	29.6568	0			
6	Hilly	24.7863	82.6211	2	-0.2264	0.1856	-0.4121
17	Rolling	9.3645	31.2151	2	0.7886	-0.3102	**1.0988**

Table 2.9. Attributes of output weights of Landform evidential theme (South Oropouche)

Class	Landform	Area (km²)	Area (units)	No. Pts	W+	W-	Contrast
0	Not given	0.0463	0.0289	0			
1	Alluvial plains and valleys	134.6719	84.1700	1	-0.7799	0.2192	-0.9991
2	Terraces	7.8339	4.8962	0			
3	Uplands	295.7162	184.8226	6	0.2464	-0.8374	**1.0838**

Table 2.10. Attributes of output weights of Soil Texture evidential theme (South Oropouche)

Class	Texture	Area (km²)	Area (units)	No. Pts	W+	W−	Contrast
1	Clay	22.8780	14.2988	1			
3	Fine sandy clay	0.4329	0.2705	0			
14	Sandy clay loam	0.1257	0.0786	0			

Table 2.11. Attributes of output weights of Land Capability evidential theme (South Oropouche)

Class	Area (km²)	Area (units)	No. Pts	W+	W−	Contrast
0	0.0463	0.0289	0			
3	78.2682	48.9176	1	−0.2285	0.0437	−0.2722
4	154.5175	96.5734	2	−0.2152	0.1010	−0.3162
5	122.2863	76.4289	2	0.0243	−0.0096	0.0339
6	73.9659	46.2287	2	0.5448	−0.1553	**0.7001**
7	9.1842	5.7401	0			

Class	Land Capability
0	
3	Good land, requires moderate to intensive conservation and management practices
4	Moderately good land, requires intensive conservation and management practices
5	Fairly good land, should be used for forest, tree crops, grazing, and buildings, depending on the slope
6	Unsuitable for agriculture due to slope and/or water limitations, should be left under indigenous growth or forest
7	Unsuitable for agriculture due to very steep slopes, should be left under indigenous growth or forest

ture was eliminated from this watershed's predictive model. The predictive model for Cipero was therefore based on the following:

1. Evidential Theme: Landform/Class Identifier: 3/Class Descriptor: Uplands
2. Evidential Theme: Land Capability/Class Identifier: 6/Class Descriptor: Unsuitable for agriculture because of slope and/or water limitations, should be left under indigenous growth or forest
3. Evidential Theme: Relief/Class Identifier: 17/Class Descriptor: Rolling

Table 2.12. Attributes of output weights of Relief evidential theme (South Oropouche)

Class	Relief	Area (km²)	Area (units)	No. Pts	W+	W-	Contrast
0	Not given	51.3436	32.0898	2	0.9300	-0.2169	1.1469
1	Flat	134.6719	84.1700	1	-0.7799	0.2192	-0.9991
5	Gently rolling	0.0094	0.0059	0			
6	Hilly	125.1215	78.2009	1	-0.7054	0.1873	-0.8926
9	Low hill	1.6351	1.0219	0			
10	Low hills	6.1132	3.8208	0			
11	Low rolling hills	7.2920	4.5575	0			
14	Mildly undulating	0.3812	0.2382	0			
17	Rolling	93.6106	58.5066	3	0.7231	-0.3265	**1.0496**
23	Undulating	10.1156	6.3223	0			
24	Undulating hills	7.9742	4.9839	0			

Table 2.13. Attributes of output weights of Landform evidential theme (Rest North)

Class	Landform	Area (km²)	Area (units)	No. Pts	W+	W-	Contrast
1	Alluvial plains and valleys	3.1795	15.8973	1	1.0795	-0.0793	**1.1588**
3	Uplands	77.5430	387.7152	8	-0.0793	1.0795	-1.1588

Table 2.14. Attributes of output weights of Soil Texture evidential theme (Rest North)

Class	Texture	Area (km²)	Area (units)	No. Pts	W+	W-	Contrast
1	Clay	61.9658	309.8291	3	-0.8470	1.0976	-1.9446
2	Clay loam	0.4556	2.2778	1	3.5355	-0.1145	**3.6501**
3	Fine sandy clay	15.5314	77.6570	5	1.1044	-0.6074	**1.7118**
5	Fine sandy loam	0.0829	0.4147	0			
7	Loamy fine sand	2.1789	10.8947	0			
8	Loamy sand	0.0346	0.1728	0			
10	Peaty clay	0.1994	0.9971	0			
14	Sandy clay loam	0.2739	1.3693	0			

Table 2.15. Attributes of output weights of Land Capability evidential theme (Rest North)

Class	Area (km²)	Area (units)	No. Pts	W+	W-	Contrast
3	2.2341	11.1703	0			
4	9.2191	46.0955	0			
5	25.6302	128.1511	6	0.7672	-0.7282	**1.4954**
6	22.3394	111.6970	0			
7	21.2997	106.4986	3	0.2397	-0.1013	0.3410

Class	Land Capability
3	Good land, requires moderate to intensive conservation and management practices
4	Moderately good land, requires intensive conservation and management practices
5	Fairly good land, requires intensive conservation and management practices
6	Unsuitable for agriculture due to slope and/or water limitations, should be left under indigenous growth or forest
7	Unsuitable for agriculture due to very steep slopes, should be left under indigenous growth or forest

In regard to South Oropouche, the Soil Texture evidential theme (Table 2.10) failed to generate any weights or contrasts, hence it was eliminated from this watershed's predictive model. South Oropouche's predictive model was therefore based on the following:

1. Evidential Theme: Landform/Class Identifier: 3/Class Descriptor: Uplands
2. Evidential Theme: Land Capability/Class Identifier: 6/Class Descriptor: Unsuitable for agriculture because of slope and/or water limitations, should be left under indigenous growth or forest
3. Evidential Theme: Relief/Class Identifier: 17/Class Descriptor: Rolling

Rest North's predictive model was based on the following:

1. Evidential Theme: Landform/Class Identifier: 1/Class Descriptor: Alluvial plains and valleys
2. Evidential Theme: Soil Texture/Class Identifier(s): 2, 3/Class Descriptor(s): Clay loam/Fine sandy clay
3. Evidential Theme: Land Capability/Class identifier: 5/Class Descriptor: Fairly good land
4. Evidential Theme: Relief/Class Identifier: 1/Class Descriptor: Flat

Table 2.16. Attributes of output weights of Relief evidential theme (Rest North)

Class	Relief	Area (km²)	Area (units)	No. Pts	W+	W-	Contrast
0	Not given	17.0415	85.2073	5	1.0055	-0.5837	1.5892
1	Flat	3.1795	15.8973	1	1.0795	-0.0793	**1.1588**
	Hilly	14.9182	74.5912	0			
10	Low hills	9.3304	46.6521	0			
12	Low undulating hills	0.8798	4.3988	0			
17	Rolling	23.2740	116.3698	3	0.1486	-0.0668	0.2154
23	Undulating	12.0992	60.4960	0			

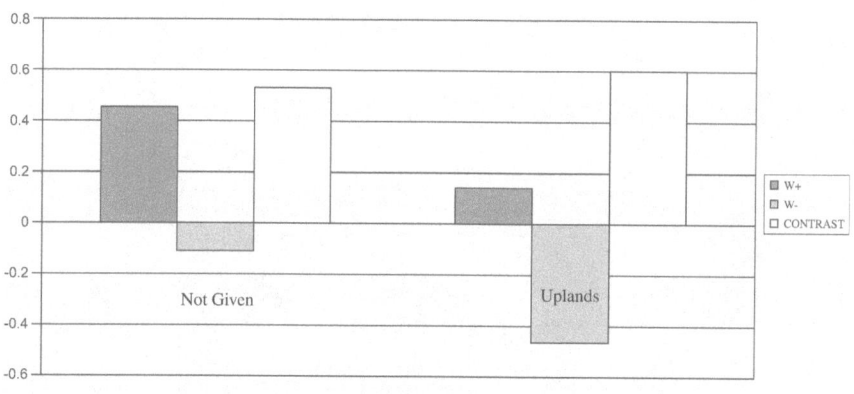

Figure 2.5. Output weights of Landform evidential theme (Cipero watershed).

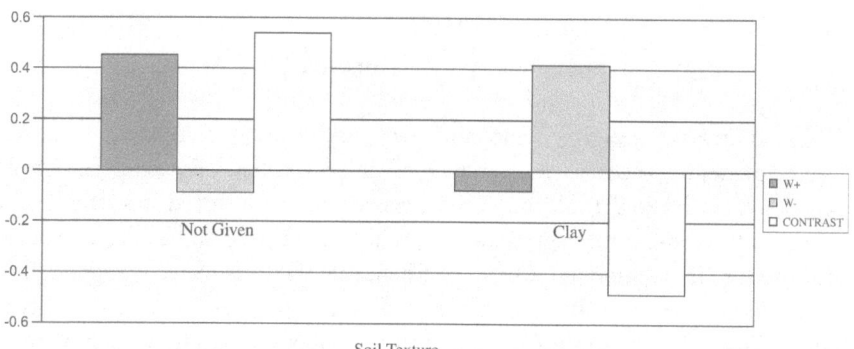

Figure 2.6. Output weights of Soil Texture evidential theme (Cipero watershed).

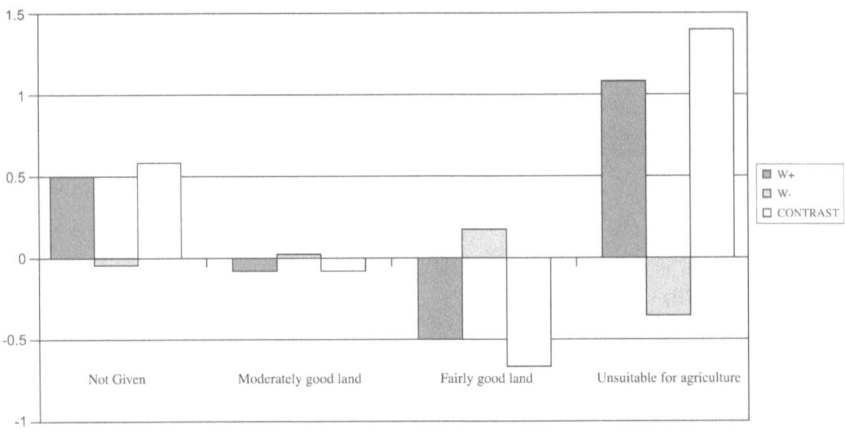

Figure 2.7. Output weights of Land Capability evidential theme (Cipero watershed).

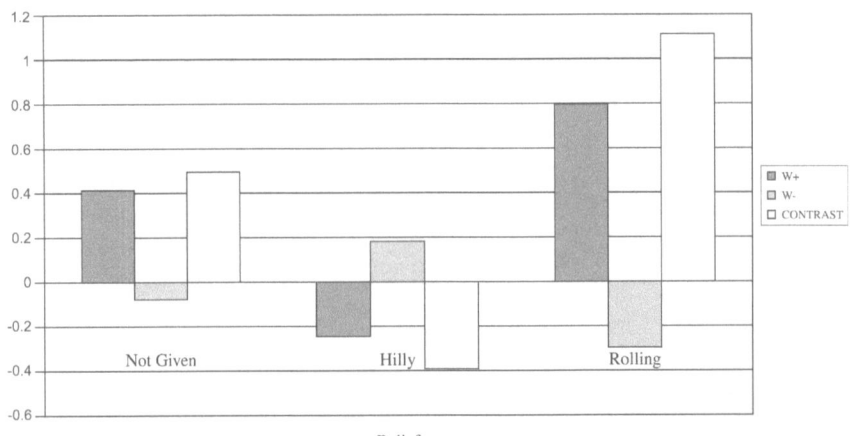

Figure 2.8. Output weights of Relief evidential theme (Cipero watershed).

Generalization of Evidential Themes

Prior to creating a unique conditions table and a response theme, all the selected evidential themes were generalized or "reclassified." By using the "group classes classification" tool, the current classes were converted into the binary classes of 1 (those not selected for the predictive models) and 2 (those selected for the predictive models). Once specified, the new classes were appended to the evidential themes' attribute tables as Landform 2, Texture 2, Capability 2, and Relief 2. For example, class 6 in South Oropouche's Land Capability evi-

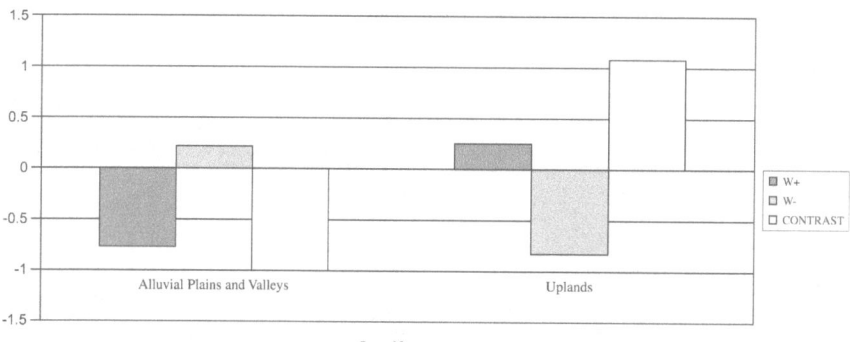

Figure 2.9. Output weights of Landform evidential theme (South Oropouche watershed).

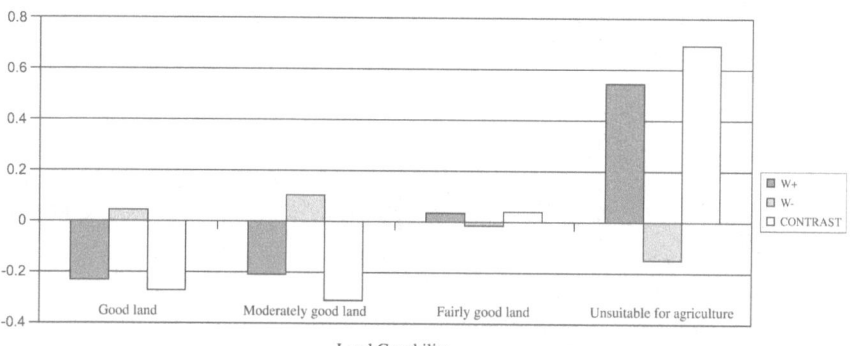

Figure 2.10. Output weights of Land Capability evidential theme (South Oropouche watershed).

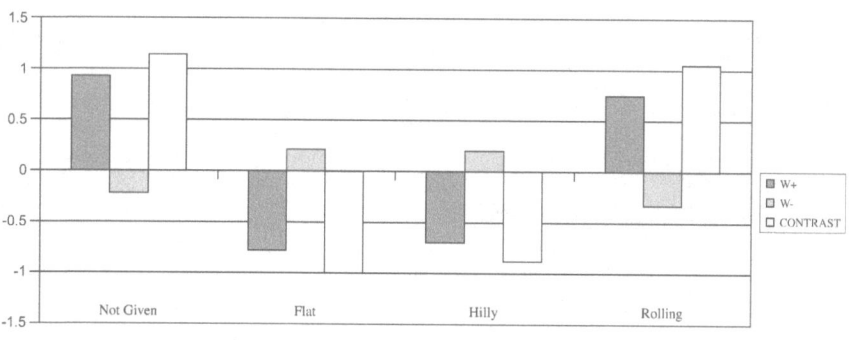

Figure 2.11. Output weights of Relief evidential theme (South Oropouche watershed).

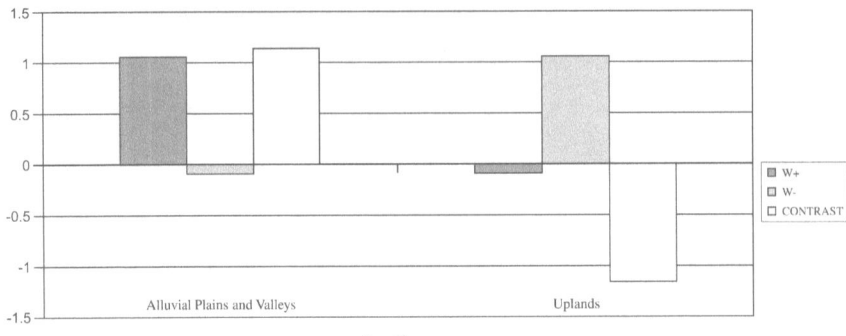

Figure 2.12. Output weights of Landform evidential theme (Rest North watershed).

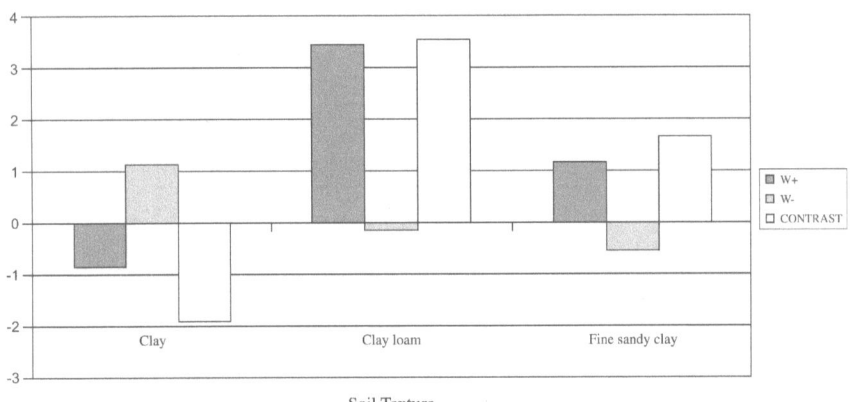

Figure 2.13. Output weights of Soil Texture evidential theme (Rest North watershed).

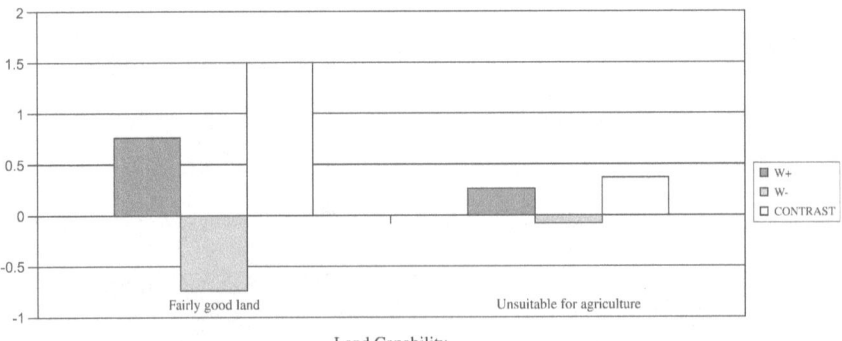

Figure 2.14. Output weights of Land Capability evidential theme (Rest North watershed).

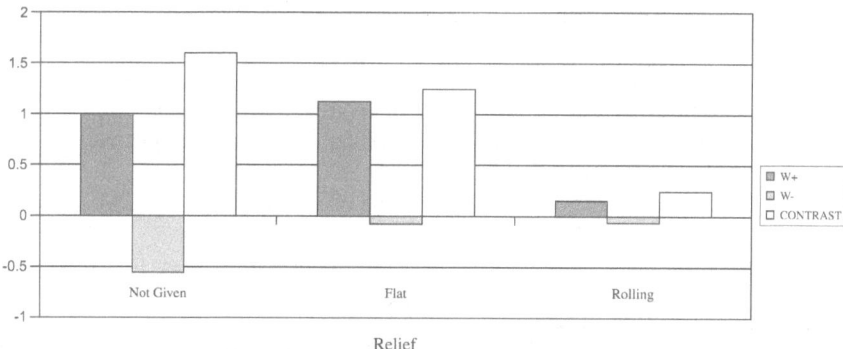

Figure 2.15. Output weights of Relief evidential theme (Rest North watershed).

dential theme was reclassified as 2 while the remaining classes in that theme were reclassified as 1. The Rest North Soil Texture evidential theme contained two very different selected classes: clay loam and fine sandy clay (2 and 3, respectively). Based on the refined descriptive model, "clay loam" is considered a "restricted internal drainage soil" while "fine sandy clay" is generally regarded as a "free internal drainage soil." Therefore, the two classes were not combined and reclassified as 2. Rather, a new class descriptor named "Texture 3" was created for "fine sandy clay" while "Texture 2" was ascribed to clay loam. As part of the response theme calculations, the two classes were subsequently run as conditionally independent entities.

Consolidating the Themes into Archaeological Site Location Predictive Models

After generalization, the selected themes were combined by generating a unique conditions grid and attribute table. The weights-of-evidence tool calculated the posterior probability, normalized probability, sum of weights, uncertainty due to weights, uncertainty due to missing data, and total uncertainty and joined these statistics to the attribute table of the unique conditions grid. The various data outputs generated by weights-of-evidence analysis, such as weights-of-evidence, attributes of response themes, posterior probability, and conditional independence, are presented in Tables 2.17 through 2.28. Figures 2.16 through 2.18 are layouts showing the posterior probability results of all three watersheds. In order to create predictive models showing areas of "high," "moderate," and "low" archaeological site location favorability, the posterior probability results of the various watersheds (Tables 2.19, 2.23, and 2.27) were ranked. Essentially, the prior probability of each watershed was used as the threshold between "low" and "moderate" favorability (Boleneus et al. 2002:31) while the highest

Table 2.17. Attributes of weights-of-evidence (Cipero)

Evidence_T	Class_Fiel	W_99	W1	W2
Cipercapa_shp	Capabil_2	0.0000	-0.3545	1.0168
Perrelief_shp	Relief_2	0.0000	-0.3149	0.8103
Iperlandf_shp	Landform_2	0.0000	-0.4430	0.1501
Sites.shp		5.0000	170.0000	0.0294

Table 2.18. Attributes of response theme (Cipero)

Value	Count	Perrelief	Iperlandf	Cipercapa	Area (m²)	Trngpoints
1	2690415	-99	-99	-99	2690415.00	0
2	14880402	1	1	1	14880402.00	1
3	17129069	1	2	1	17129069.00	0
4	8926771	2	2	1	8926771.00	2
5	7373343	1	2	2	7373343.00	2

posterior value was used as the threshold between "moderate" and "low" favorability. These unique values were subsequently reclassified in ArcView as 1 for "low" favorability, 2 for "moderate" favorability, and 3 for "high" favorability to produce layouts depicted in Figures 2.19 through 2.21.

RESULTS AND ANALYSIS

Predictive models for Cipero, South Oropouche, and Rest North were generated by summing the weights-of-evidence of the binary maps related to these watersheds. The various overlap combinations of the binary maps resulted in the highest cumulative weights in the areas where archaeological sites are likely to be found. The sum of weights for Cipero indicates that Land Capability (unsuitable for agriculture because of slope and/or water limitations) has the highest weighted value (1.0168), followed by Relief (rolling, 0.8103) and Landform (uplands, 0.1501). Cipero's "high favorability" areas constitute 14 percent of the watershed, "moderate favorability" areas 18 percent, and "low favorability" areas the remaining 68 percent (Table 2.29).

With respect to South Oropouche, Relief (rolling) has the highest weighted value (0.7274), followed by Land Capability (land unsuitable for agriculture because of slope and/or water limitations, should be left under indigenous growth, 0.5564) and Landform (uplands, 0.2514). South Oropouche's "high favorability" areas constitute 5 percent of the watershed and its "moderate favorability" areas 25 percent, while its "low favorability" areas make up the remain-

Table 2.19. Attributes of posterior probability (Cipero)

Value	Count	Perrelief	Iperlandf	Cipercapa	Area (m²)	Trngpoints	Lrpostprob	Site Favorability
1	2690415	-99	-99	-99	2690415.00	0	0.00015000	Reclassified as 1
2	14880402	1	1	1	14880402.00	1	0.01976000	Reclassified as 1
3	17129069	1	2	1	17129069.00	0	0.00000000	Reclassified as 1
4	8926771	2	2	1	8926771.00	2	0.06298000	Reclassified as 2
5	7373343	1	2	2	7373343.00	2	0.07525000	Reclassified as 3

Table 2.20. Attributes of conditional independence (Cipero)

Etheme	Perlandf_S	Ipercapa_S
Errelief_shp	0.3613	0.5762
Perlandf_shp		0.3613

Note: Values <.05 indicate some conditional dependence.

Table 2.21. Attributes of weights-of-evidence (South Oropouche)

Evidence_T	Class_Fiel	W_99	W1	W2
Ororelief_shp	Relief_2	0.0000	-0.3276	0.7274
Sorocapa_shp	Capabil_2	0.0000	-0.1576	0.5564
Sorolandf_shp	Landform_2	0.0000	-0.8475	0.2514
Sites.shp		7.0000	273.9100	0.0256

Table 2.22. Attributes of response theme (South Oropouche)

Value	Count	Sorocapa_S	Ororelief	Sorolandf	Area (m²)	Trngpoints
1	5615182	-99	-99	-99	5615182.00	0
2	40268557	2	1	2	40268557.00	0
3	69189146	1	2	2	69189146.00	1
4	158203632	1	1	2	158203632.00	3
5	133016551	1	1	1	133016551.00	1
6	9083254	2	1	1	9083254.00	0
7	22873678	2	2	2	22873678.00	2

ing 70 percent (Table 2.30). A markedly different situation exists in regard to Rest North, which has Land Capability (fairly good land) predominating with a weighted value of 1.1758, followed by Soil Texture (fine sandy clay, 0.7686). Negative values for Soil Texture (clay loam, -0.9330), Relief (flat, -2.9183), and Landform (alluvial plains and valleys, -2.9183) render them as totally insignificant as predictive themes. Rest North's "high favorability" areas comprise 4 percent of the region of interest, its "moderate favorability" areas 25 percent, and its "low favorability" areas the remaining 71 percent (Table 2.31). The conditional independence of Rest North (Table 2.28) is a perfect 1. Although this level of conditional independence does not occur in reality (Boleneus et al. 2002), it suggests that the weights-of-evidence results for this watershed are very reliable.

It could therefore be argued that Land Capability (whether land unsuitable for agriculture or fairly good land) has a significant bearing on site location in

Table 2.23. Attributes of posterior probability (South Oropouche)

Value	Count	Sorocapa_S	Ororelief	Sorolandf	Area (m^2)	Trngpoints	Lrpostprob	Site Favorability
1	5615182	-99	-99	-99	5615182.00	0	0.02106000	Reclassified as 1
2	40268557	2	1	2	40268557.00	0	0.03259000	Reclassified as 2
3	69189146	1	2	2	69189146.00	1	0.04316000	Reclassified as 2
4	158203632	1	1	2	158203632.00	3	0.02106000	Reclassified as 1
5	133016551	1	1	1	133016551.00	1	0.01049000	Reclassified as 1
6	9083254	2	1	1	9083254.00	0	0.01633000	Reclassified as 1
7	22873678	2	2	2	22873678.00	2	0.06595000	Reclassified as 3

Table 2.24. Attributes of conditional independence (South Oropouche)

ETHEME	Rorelief_S	Orolandf_S
Sorocapa_shp	0.2771	0.4945
Rorelief_shp		0.3496

Note: Values <.05 indicate some conditional dependence.

Table 2.25. Attributes of weights-of-evidence (Rest North)

Evidence_T	Class_Fiel	W_99	W1	W2
Tnortcapa_shp	Capabil_2	0.0000	-5.8465	1.1758
Tnortext2_shp	Texture_3	0.0000	-0.3057	0.7686
Stnortext_shp	Texture_2	0.0000	0.0031	-0.9330
Nortrelie_shp	Relief_2	0.0000	0.0357	-2.9183
Tnorlandf_shp	Landform_2	0.0000	0.0357	-2.9183
Sites.shp		9.0000	402.5000	0.0224

Note: See text for description of Texture 3.

all three watersheds, followed by Relief (rolling). Landform (uplands) is absent in Rest North but is present in "modest" quantities in South Oropouche and Cipero. Soil Texture (fine sandy clay), which has been described as a "free internal drainage soil," only figures prominently in Rest North.

As earlier indicated, the original refined descriptive model for this study read as follows: *Pre-Columbian sites in Trinidad are likely to be found in areas with hilly relief in alluvial plains and valleys, in areas with very good to moderately good land capability and free internal drainage soils.*

When compared with the above model, the weights-of-evidence analysis of the three watersheds, like the above descriptive model, places significant weighting on "hilly" relief. But the weights-of-evidence model places no weighting on "alluvial plains and valleys" or on Land Capability (very good to moderately good land). There is, however, some importance ascribed to "free internal drainage soils" in relation to the Rest North watershed. Landform (uplands) has some leverage in site location, as reflected in South Oropouche and Cipero. Given that the weights-of-evidence analysis was applied to only a restricted number of watersheds in south and southwestern Trinidad, the following (weights-of-evidence) revised descriptive model is hereby presented: *Based on weights-of-evidence analysis of the Cipero, South Oropouche, and Rest North watersheds in southern and southwestern Trinidad, pre-Columbian archaeological sites in this part of the island are likely to be found in areas with (a) hilly relief,*

Table 2.26. Attributes of response theme (Rest North)

Value	Count	Pilottext	Pilolandf	Ilotrelie	Pilocapa_S	Area (m²)	Trngpoints
1	8612620	-99	-99	-99	-99	8612620.00	0
2	121947458	1	1	1	1	121947458.00	2
3	31599187	1	2	2	1	31599187.00	0
4	16622668	2	2	2	2	16622668.00	6
5	16536102	1	1	1	2	16536102.00	0
6	681965	1	2	1	1	681965.00	0

Table 2.27. Attributes of posterior probability (Rest North)

Value	Count	Tnortext2	Nortrelie	Tnorlandf	Tnortcapa	Stnortext	Area (m²)	Trngpts	Lrpostprob	Site Favorability
1	5696024	-99	-99	-99	-99	-99	5696024.00	0	0.00004000	Reclassified as 1
2	37986145	1	1	1	1	1	37986145.00	0	0.00000000	Reclassified as 1
3	199994895	1	1	1	2	1	199994895.00	3	0.02913000	Reclassified as 2
4	10798247	2	1	1	1	1	10798247.00	0	0.00001000	Reclassified as 1
5	2277877	1	2	2	1	1	2277877.00	0	0.00000000	Reclassified as 1
6	16103	1	2	2	1	2	16103.00	0	0.00000000	Reclassified as 1
7	3290408	2	1	1	2	1	3290408.00	2	0.10839000	Reclassified as 3
8	79178	1	2	2	2	1	79178.00	0	0.00016000	Reclassified as 1
9	361123	1	2	2	2	2	361123.00	0	0.00000000	Reclassified as 1

Developing Weights-of-Evidence Predictive Models / 61

Table 2.28. Attributes of conditional independence (Rest North)

Etheme	Ortrelie_S	Norlandf_S	Nortcapa_S	Tnortext_S
Nortext2_shp	1.0000	1.0000	1.0000	1.0000
Ortrelie_shp		1.0000	1.0000	1.0000
Norlandf_shp			1.0000	1.0000
Nortcapa_shp				1.0000

Note: Values <.05 indicate some conditional dependence.

(b) land capability characterized by either fairly good land or land unsuitable for agriculture because of slope and/or water limitations, (c) upland landforms, and (d) "free internal drainage soils" along the south coast of the island.

Some archaeologists clearly seem to believe that the data they study are somehow directly and automatically linked with the past, and perhaps in no other area of archaeological "specialty" is this as pronounced as in predictive modeling. Little real introspection is required to arrive at the realization that the variables and correlations, which comprise the entire substance of "inductive" predictive modeling experiments, are solely contemporary (Ebert 2000: 130). In essence, predictive modeling cannot be a productive archaeological pursuit without the explicit realization that statistical tests and correlations can only inform us about coincidences in the present, which must then be linked with the past through the process of explanation (Ebert 2000:130).

There are, for example, significant challenges associated with interpreting archaeological site prediction on the basis of Land Capability classifications. This taxonomic system is based on contemporary (Hardy 1974:55, 1981:39) not prehistoric conditions, and as such applying these classifications to our interpretations of pre-Columbian landscapes may be problematic. For one thing, it seems simply incongruous associating predominantly pre-Columbian horticultural settlements with "unsuitable land for agriculture."[4] However, prehistoric inhabitants might have chosen to live in places totally unsuitable for agriculture. Not only would this have afforded them additional arable land but it would also have ensured that the hustle and bustle of village life did not interfere with nearby agricultural fields (Keegan, personal communication 2003). Moreover, what is now being described as "unsuitable land for agriculture because of slope and/or water limitations" might have been the reverse deep in time. It is possible for climatic changes to have adversely and dramatically affected vegetation, the availability of underground water, and the organic composition of soils over time. For example, around A.D. 500 there were hyperarid conditions as a result of major climatic changes in the southern Caribbean

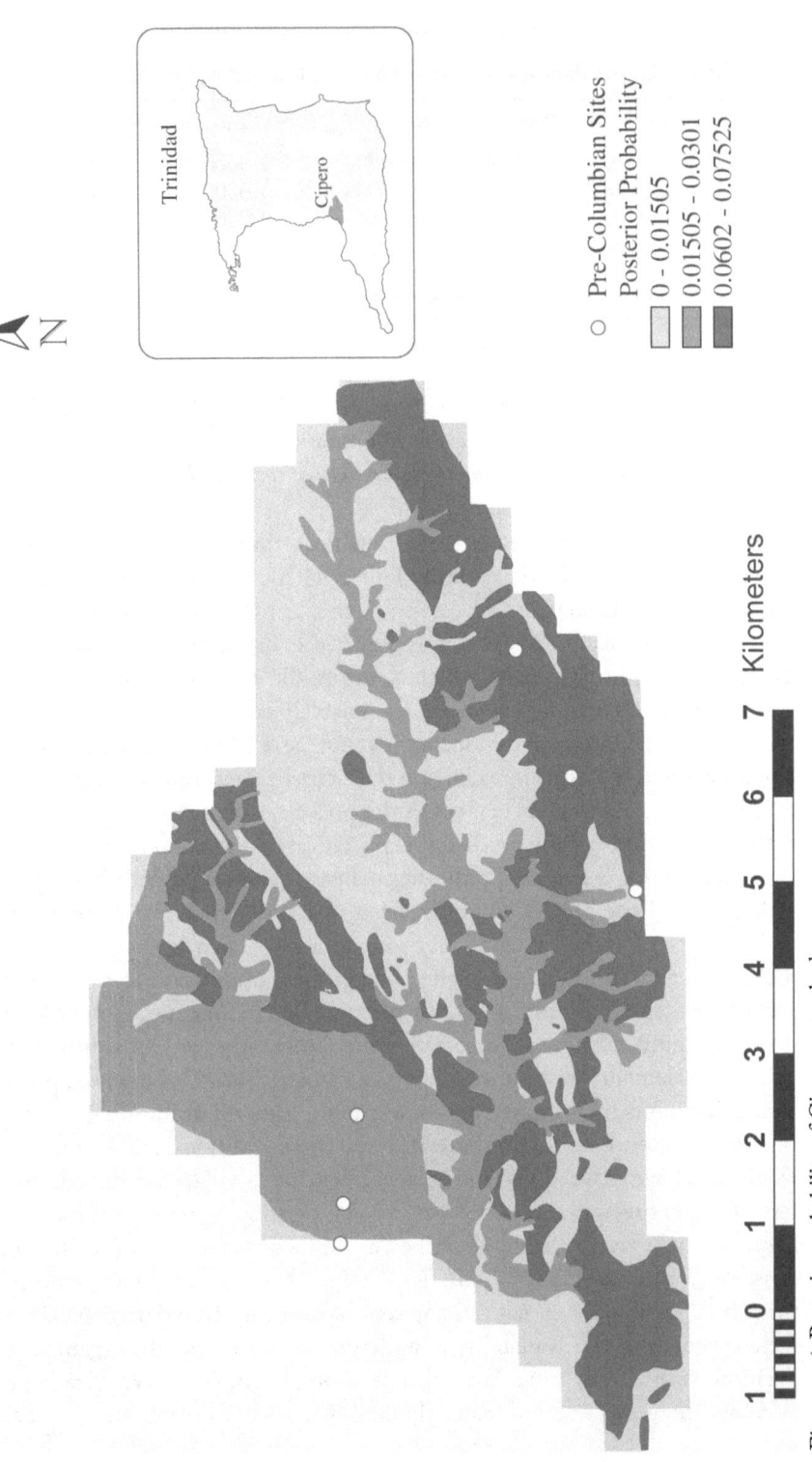

Figure 2.16. Posterior probability of Cipero watershed.

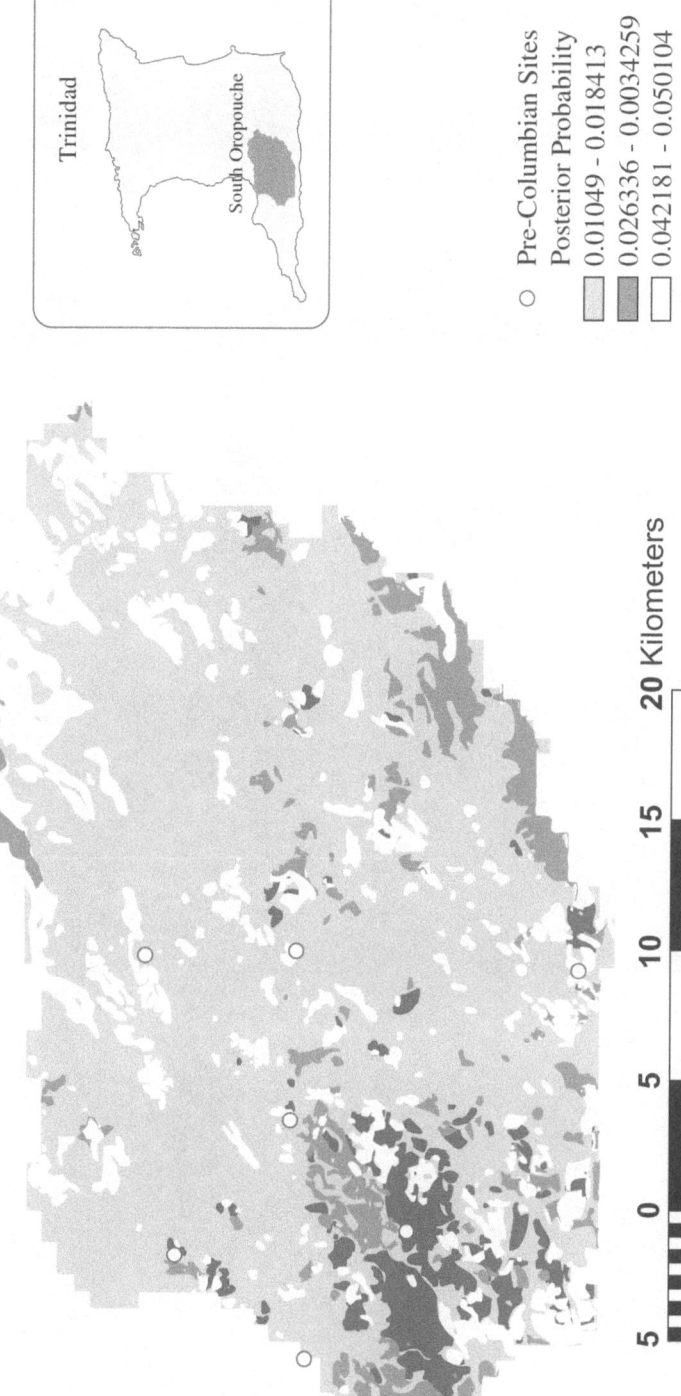

Figure 2.17. Posterior probability of South Oropouche watershed.

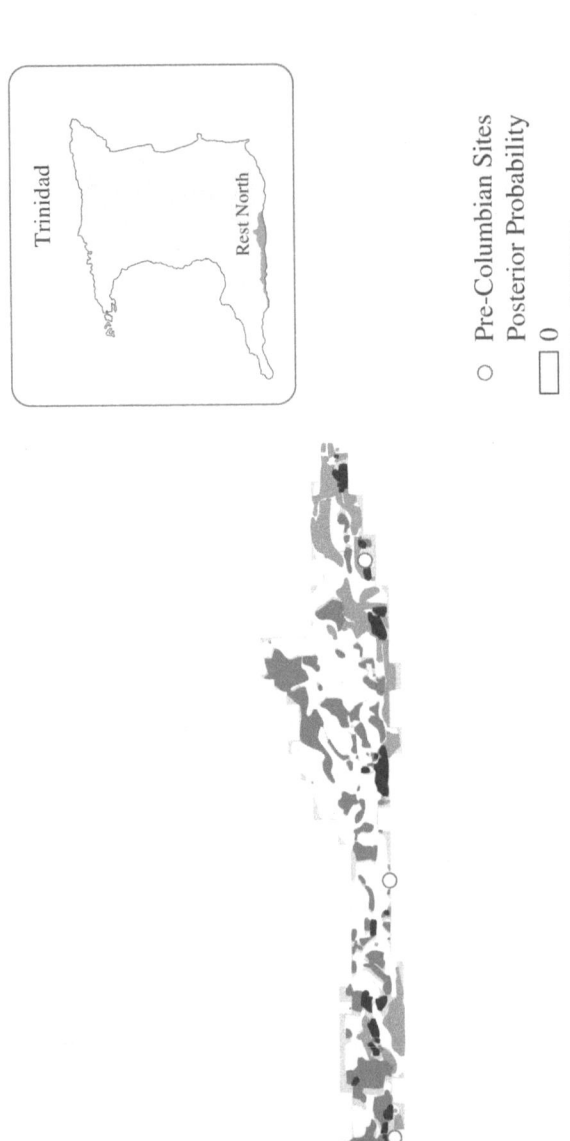

Figure 2.18. Posterior probability of Rest North watershed.

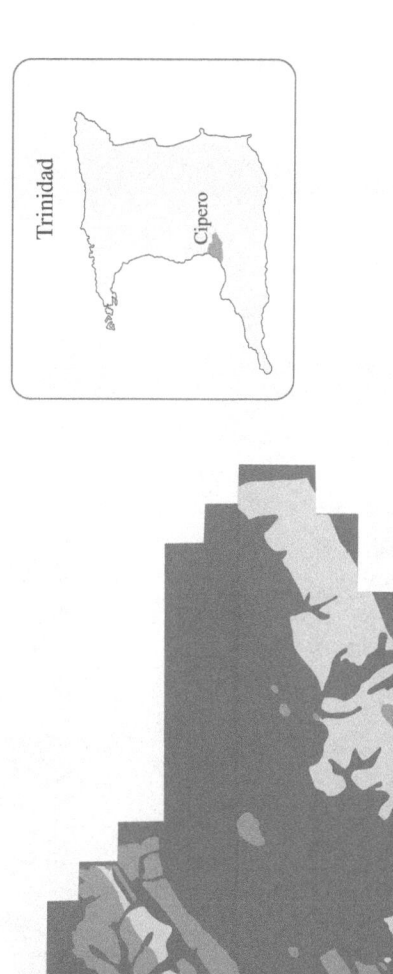
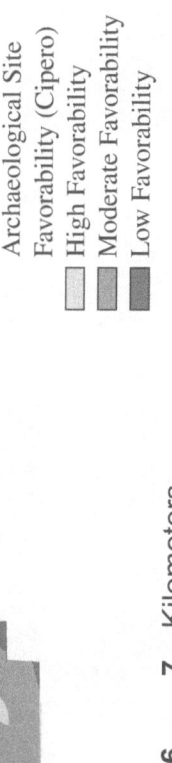

Figure 2.19. Archaeological site favorability for Cipero watershed.

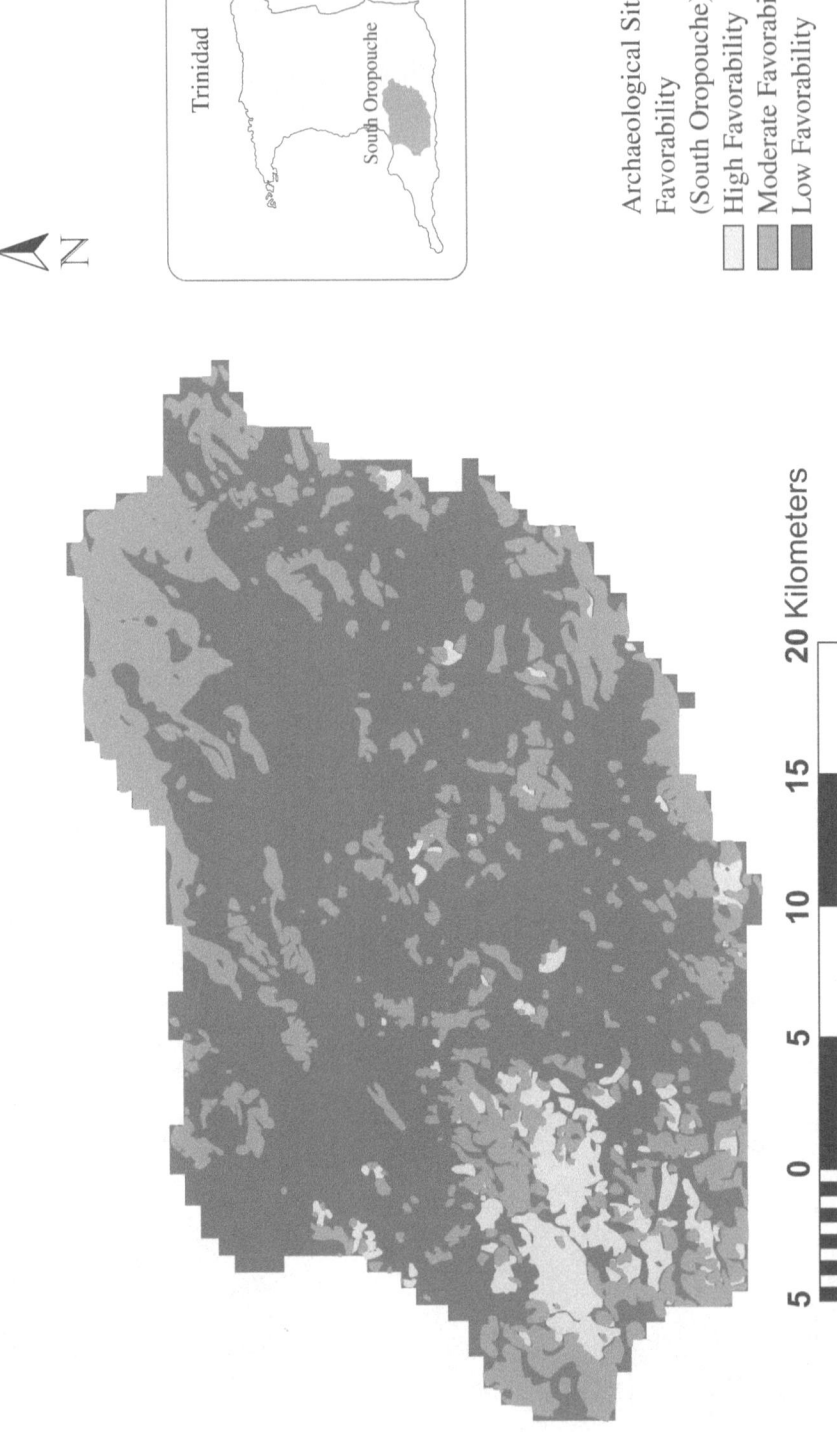

Figure 2.20. Archaeological site favorability for South Oropouche watershed.

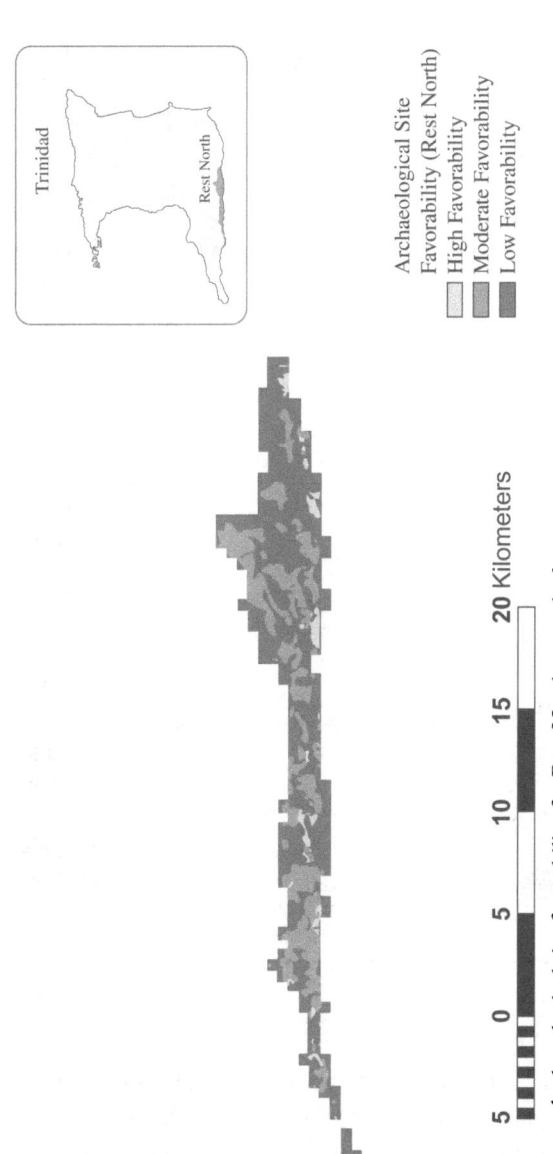

Figure 2.21. Archaeological site favorability for Rest North watershed.

Table 2.29. Archaeological site predictive model for Cipero watershed

Predictive Model	$P \geq 0.075$	High favorability 7 km² (14% of watershed)	Land Capability (unsuitable for agriculture due to slope and/or water limitations) Landform (uplands)
	$P \geq 0.0294$	Moderate favorability 9 km² (18% of watershed)	1. Relief (rolling) 2. Landform (unsuitable for agriculture)
	$P \geq 0.0$	Low favorability 34 km² (68% of watershed)	Landform (unsuitable for agriculture) and/or negative evidence

Table 2.30. Archaeological site predictive model for South Oropouche watershed

Predictive Model	$P \geq 0.065$	High favorability 23 km² (5% of watershed)	1. Relief (rolling) 2. Land Capability (unsuitable for agriculture due to slope and/or water limitations, should be left to indigenous growth or forest) 3. Landform (uplands)
	$P \geq 0.0256$	Moderate favorability 109 km² (25% of watershed)	1. Land Capability and Landform or 2. Relief and Landform
	$P \geq 0.0$	Low favorability 306 km² (70% of watershed)	Landform and/or negative evidence

(Hodell et al. 1991; Meggers 1996). In addition, deforestation and frequent indiscriminate land use during the post-Columbian era would conceivably have taken a heavy toll on the physical integrity of landscapes (Deagan 1990). However, despite their creation for contemporary use, Land Capability classifications are still important for weights-of-evidence analysis, as the location of sites cannot be divorced from their current geographical context (Barker 1982). Even though correlation does not necessarily suggest causation (Arjoon 1999),

Table 2.31. Archaeological site predictive model for Rest North watershed

	P ≥ 1.08	High favorability	1. Land Capability (fairly good land)
		3 km² (4% of watershed)	2. Soil Texture (fine sandy clay)
Predictive Model	P ≥ 0.0224	Moderate favorability	Land Capability
		20 km² (25% of watershed)	
	P ≥ 0.0	Low favorability	Negative evidence
		58 km² (71% of watershed)	

establishing clear associations between sites in Trinidad and Land Capability classes can shed light on where sites are likely to be found.

The weighted value of "hilly" Relief in both South Oropouche and Cipero accords well with general settlement predispositions among pre-Columbian peoples on some islands of the Caribbean. These settlement sites appear to have allowed a commanding view of the surrounding areas, suggesting that defense considerations might have influenced this type of settlement location. Dubbed "hilltop" settlements (Howard 1965), a significant number of Jamaica's pre-Columbian habitation sites are concentrated on the island's foothills. In his study of Kingston, Jamaica, Allsworth-Jones (Allsworth-Jones et al. 1999) cited several pre-Columbian hilltop settlements within that general area, such as Harbour View, Bellevue, Chancery Hall, Rodney's House, and Norbrook. However, there are also almost equally numerous coastal sites in Jamaica (e.g., Little River, Mammee Bay, and Port Henderson; Aarons 1984; De Wolf 1952), and coastal, low-lying sites abound in the Bahamas (Keegan 1992) and Barbados (Drewett 1991). While acknowledging that several Saladoid settlement sites in Trinidad are located inland on ridges or hilltops, Boomert (2000:264) argues that these sites are in the minority as there are several coastal Saladoid and Guayabitoid habitation sites on the island. It seems therefore that the "hilly" Relief is more specific to South Oropouche and Cipero as a predictive variable and should not necessarily be construed as reflective of a general trend in pre-Columbian Trinidad and the Caribbean. A similar scenario exists in relation to the weighted value of Landform (uplands) in both South Oropouche and Cipero (Tables 2.29 and 2.30). While it is true that Landform (alluvial plains and valleys) may be a more germane descriptive model for archaeological site prediction in some of the larger islands of the Caribbean (Keegan 2000), weights-of-evidence analysis has clearly demonstrated that Landform (uplands) is more usefully applied as a predictive theme specifically in these two watersheds in southwestern Trinidad.

The relatively strong weighted value and concurrence of a "fairly good land for agriculture" Land Capability with a "fine sandy clay" Soil Texture in Rest North (Table 2.31) suggest that the "high favorability" areas in this watershed had much potential for pre-Columbian horticultural activity. As earlier indicated, fine sandy clay is a "free internal drainage soil" and is therefore highly suitable for a variety of cultigens grown and consumed by the Saladoid, Barrancoid, and Guayabitoid peoples. Keegan (2000) and Petersen and Watters (1997) assert that the Saladoid peoples practiced a mixed economy in which root crop agriculture figured prominently. The presence of clay griddles is used to infer that bitter manioc was cultivated for cassava bread (Veloz Maggiolo 1997). Sweet potatoes also were grown at contact, but there is no archaeological evidence for root crops before the contact period such as was found at En Bas Saline, Haiti (Newson 1993). Such foods tend to thrive well in well-drained soils such as "fine sandy clay." Throughout the Caribbean, horticultural pre-Columbian populations, for example, the Tainos in Manuabo, Puerto Rico (Curet 1992), were apparently attracted to areas containing "free internal drainage soils" conducive to root crop agriculture. Anna Roosevelt (1997:168–169) provides evidence that suggests that the Guayabitoid peoples of the mainland and, by extension, the Guayabitoid peoples of Trinidad had chiefdom societies. According to Roosevelt (1997) the anthropomorphic imagery of the Guayabitoid peoples was associated with some form of a chiefly cult, glorifying the memorial images of the ancestors of an elite people. The Guayabitoid period (A.D. 600–1300) was essentially characterized by incipient maize cultivation and the emergence of ranked societies in the middle Orinoco (Roosevelt 1997:168–169). Clearly then, both Saladoid/Barrancoid and Guayabitoid peoples were engaged in horticultural activities that required "free internal drainage soils," although the Guayabitoid, being the more socially complex group, would have produced cultivars on a much more sophisticated scale. The presence of a "fairly good land" Land Capability classification in addition to "free internal drainage soils" might therefore have factored in the decision of pre-Columbian groups to settle within the Rest North watershed.

However, the scoring of an area by the model as having a very high "attractiveness" for the use of habitation sites (as is the case with Rest North) does not mean that the probability of discovering a site in that area is 100 percent. Sites are relatively rare concentrations of recoverable remains within an active landscape. Although the model may assign a high probability score to an area, it does not necessarily follow that a sufficient amount of human activity occurred at the location to have produced nonperishable and preserved remains (Duncan and Beckman 2000).

WEIGHTS-OF-EVIDENCE PREDICTIVE MODELS AND CRM IN TRINIDAD

A case will now be made for the judicious use of weights-of-evidence models in effectively managing the island's pre-Columbian sites. First, however, it is important to point out that a cultural resource cannot be managed until it is found (Drewett 2001). Conventional methods require field archaeologists to locate the resource. Because, like that of many countries of the neotropics (Zeidler 1995), Trinidad's archaeology suffers from low site accessibility and poor ground visibility, site location efforts are frequently fraught with difficulties. For example, a considerable portion of the Rest North watershed is secondary forest. A mix of sugar cane, rice, and vegetable farming as well as fairly large towns and villages characterizes South Oropouche and Cipero. Pre-Columbian sites, because they are invariably represented by pottery and stone artifacts, may be inconspicuous on the landscape. Traveling back and forth in search of sites through often difficult terrain can be both costly and time consuming. By providing predictive models of where the most favorable site location areas are situated, researchers will be spared considerable monetary costs and time wastage, invariably associated with ground surveys over large areas.

This is not to say that weights-of-evidence models will make ground surveys in Trinidad redundant. While extolling the virtues of predictive models, Zeidler (1995:19) argues that these models often need to be "ground truthed" or georegistered with global positioning system (GPS) technology, a practice that has been shown to be reasonably effective even in tropical rain forest environments (Baksh 1991; Chagnon 1991; Wilkie 1989). Precise locational information on each archaeological site can be acquired as the field survey proceeds, with all the relevant archaeological and ecological variables incorporated into a GIS format for statistical analysis and long-term data management (Zeidler 1995:19).

Weights-of-evidence models can enhance land-use planning in Trinidad. Cleere (1989) asserts that land-use planning, as practiced in most countries, relates to every aspect of the landscape. Human operations of all kinds—forestry, agriculture, road building, mineral extraction, industrial activity—can disturb the balance and degrade the aesthetic qualities of the landscape, to the detriment of future generations. Therefore, archaeological heritage management must be predicated on people working collaboratively. Trinidad, especially in the south, has a welter of oil and natural gas mining installations, owned and operated by Petrotrin as well as by a constellation of foreign-based companies. Much of the forested zone in Rest North, especially areas along the south coast from Palo Seco to La Lune, is under the control of the Government Forestry Division. Weights-of-evidence models can guide these agencies in the developing of culturally sensitive land-use management strategies, designed to protect archaeological sites in "high" and "moderate" favorability areas. However, these CRM efforts should be effectively coordinated from the center by the premier heritage management agency in the country, the National Trust of Trinidad and Tobago. The incorporation of new GIS data sets such as digital elevation models (DEMs), roads, land-use patterns, rivers, and coastlines will enable cultural resource managers to produce a slew of new weights-of-evidence models for more effective site location predictions and land-use management.

Archaeological heritage management is also designed to both protect and update Trinidad's archaeological database. Archaeologists are always avid for data, both qualitative and quantitative. Without any form of heritage management, the stock of sites would dwindle rapidly (Cleere 1989:9). Since the 1980s, Trinidad has been the scene of a number of archaeological projects, conducted mostly by expatriates (Boomert 2000; Dorst 2001). In addition, the archaeological program at the University of the West Indies, St. Augustine, in Trinidad was revitalized in 2001, with the employment of a full-time resident archaeologist. Against this background, there exists an ongoing need to develop well-integrated research designs. By digitally highlighting the most favorable pre-Columbian site locations, weights-of-evidence models will provide an important database for scholarly archaeological research. Archaeologists sometimes find hand-drawn maps in paper databases cumbersome and difficult to integrate and manipulate (Wescott and Kuiper 2000). However, the weights-of-evidence models will provide a powerful and efficient managerial tool for spatial data sets, allowing the field archaeologist the ability to access, analyze, and interpret large amounts of archaeological data in a fraction of the time previously required. New site discoveries can easily be added to the database and used to run updated probability surface models on selected areas in Trinidad. If culturally significant sites are found, their attributes can be inputted.

CONCLUSION

Generated in this study are three weights-of-evidence models designed to bolster CRM efforts in Trinidad and elsewhere in the Caribbean. If used constructively, weights-of-evidence can enhance the management of the island's pre-Columbian sites by (a) reducing the monetary and time costs of fieldwork on the island, (b) facilitating more effective land-use management, and (c) helping archaeologists and cultural resource managers to create, update, and protect Trinidad's archaeological database. It is envisaged that future weights-of-evidence analysis will be subjected to field verification and will focus on larger areas on the island, based on a greater variety of GIS data sets such as land-use patterns, coastlines, and digital elevation models.

NOTES

1. All dates herein are calibrated.

2. The site files are the product of 22 years of site inventory carried out in Trinidad by Dr. Arie Boomert, Mr. Peter Harris, and Dr. Nicholas Saunders.

3. The finer-grained resolution requires longer processing time but produces more details. The coarser-grained resolution requires shorter processing time but produces fewer details.

4. It is important to note that three out of the seven sites used for weights-of-evidence modeling in South Oropouche are Ortoiroid (Archaic) sites (Table 2.2).

3
Forward Planning

The Utilization of GIS in the Management of Archaeological Resources in Barbados

Kevin Farmer

This chapter examines the need for cultural resource management on the island of Barbados and the particular benefits to be gained from utilizing geographic information systems (GIS) in this regard. Barbados is a small, largely coral, island located to the east of the archipelago of the Lesser Antilles. Urbanization is spreading into traditional rural landscapes while redevelopment of existing urban spaces continues. The need to accurately and adequately respond to land management issues as they relate to the preservation of the archaeological landscape is important. The focus of the chapter is guided by a project to develop a Sites and Monuments Inventory System at the Barbados Museum and Historical Society through a grant from UNESCO.

Barbados is a small island situated in the west Atlantic Ocean, some 90 miles east of the archipelago of the Lesser Antilles in the Caribbean Sea. The island measures 21 miles in length by 14 miles wide and has a population of 270,000 with a population density on average of 1,626 persons per square mile. The island has witnessed some four thousand years of human habitation and continues to experience increased population pressure as urbanization encroaches on both the traditional rural and urban landscapes. With this ongoing land development, there is a need for informed planning that can be provided by a geographic information system (GIS) within a cultural resource management methodology. This chapter will focus on GIS methodology and its application in the management of sites in Barbados.

Land use on the island has reached the stage where urbanization is competing with agriculture for land. The need for additional housing means that productive agricultural land is being converted into land for housing. The rise in suburbia means that existing urban areas are increasing exponentially to provide services for the suburbs, resulting in Bridgetown's economic zone spreading north and south from its original location. Such unchecked expansion could spell disaster for known and unknown historical and prehistoric archaeological sites on the island.

Barbados, given its lack of an overarching legislative framework in which to safeguard sites and landscapes of historical, environmental, or natural heritage, is at present practicing cultural resource management based on convention and moral suasion. Planning agencies, in particular, are operating with somewhat ad hoc systems that require significant improvement. Against this background, the need to protect, preserve, and manage archaeological sites in Barbados in a systematic, structured way, taking into consideration the interests of all the stakeholders, is indeed warranted.

In 2000, the government of Barbados became signatory to the UNESCO Convention that allows state parties to nominate sites to the World Heritage Center for inscription on the World Heritage List. This convention signals to the world that Barbados has recognized the importance of its heritage and therefore believes its heritage ought to be shared with the world. The nomination process is arduous and time consuming because it places the burden of proof on the state party, which in seeking nomination must illustrate ongoing management plans for the site or monument. Management of archaeological sites can be enhanced by utilizing GIS. The GIS will form the basis for site monitoring, evaluation, and protection.

HERITAGE MANAGEMENT

At present on the island, the task of heritage management is shared by a number of government departments and nongovernmental organizations (NGOs). The built environment is overseen by the Town and Country Planning Department, under which legislative policy is enforced and directed, with its NGO counterpart (with no legislative power) being the Barbados National Trust. The protection of the island's coastline is handled by the Coastal Zone Management Unit, with its NGO counterpart being the Barbados Marine Trust.

The archaeology of the island, as it relates to legal archaeological excavation and the management of excavated material culture, is managed by the Barbados Museum and Historical Society (BMHS), an NGO, which the government has recognized as the official repository of all excavated material culture on the island. Both the BMHS and Barbados National Trust act as technical advisors to the government but neither has legislative enforcement powers. Legislative jurisdiction, as it relates to archaeological resources found in caves or on the beach, resides with the National Conservation Commission, which is a government agency. A single institution with a comprehensive legislation and enforcement arm is needed. At the time of writing, an antiquities law was being drafted by the Attorney General's Office in Barbados.

It is therefore necessary to examine the various stakeholders directly involved in the management of the island's cultural patrimony in order to understand the necessity for a comprehensive management plan. The first phase of such a plan is to ask questions such as "What is there to preserve?" "Where is it?" "What is its condition?" and "Who is the owner of the site?" As an early sugar island, the majority of the land in Barbados is in private hands, unlike the later new sugar islands of the eighteenth and nineteenth centuries. The later sugar islands such as St. Lucia, Dominica, and St. Vincent had land designated as either natural reserves or as tracts of land belonging to the Crown, thereby ensuring that early in their development as colonies an ethos of conservation was built into the system of land management. It is therefore imperative that steps be taken to protect and preserve archaeological sites in Barbados, given these continuing threats to the physical environment.

A BRIEF HISTORY OF LAND USE IN BARBADOS

In order to create a clearer understanding of the need for a GIS-based heritage management system in Barbados, it is important that we present a brief land-use history of the island, which includes human settlement and its impact on archaeological sites.

From Ichirouganiam to Barbados

The Amerindian place name for Barbados is *Ichirouganiam*, which means "red land with white teeth." Archaeological research has put Amerindian settlement of Barbados from about 1750 B.C. to about A.D. 1500 (Drewett 1991). Amerindian settlements were mainly along the coast, in close proximity to potable water and natural wetlands, with some inland sites (Figure 3.1). Agricultural practice utilized a system of slash and burn usually based on the clearing of virgin forests. Areas were cut, trees and shrubs left to dry were then burned, and this provided fertilizer for the planted crops. In these cleared plots, multicultivation was practiced. Overall, the prehistoric landscape was characterized by selective small-scale land clearing with much of the surrounding virgin forest left intact. Protein was obtained mainly from the sea because of the paucity of large land animals for hunting. However, the landscape was to change with the arrival of the Europeans and the introduction and subsequent development of the plantation system in Barbados.

European Expansion

Early European settlement can also be referred to as frontier settlement, which involved limited deforestation for the creation of small landholdings based on such cash crops as tobacco, cotton, and indigo (Watts 1980). Linear settlement was the initial pattern practiced, with settlements hugging the western and southwestern coastlines and with some inland forays undertaken. This settle-

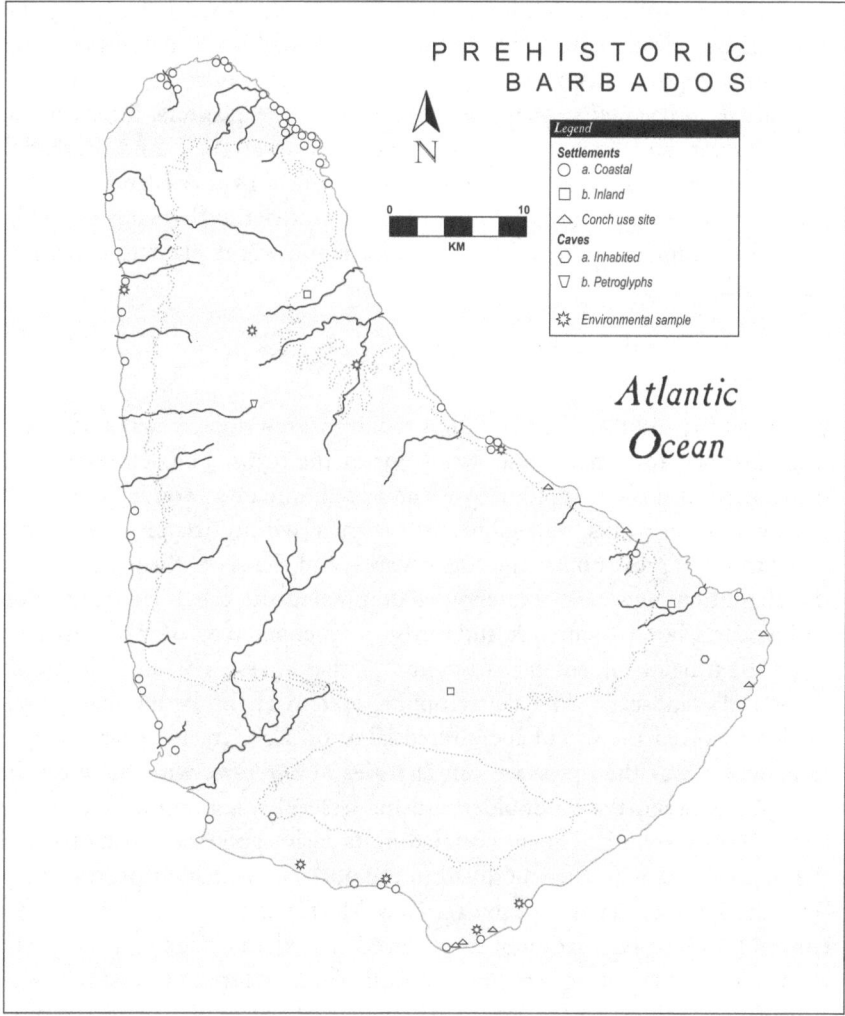

Figure 3.1. Map of Barbados showing prehistoric site locations. From *Prehistoric Barbados* by Peter Drewett. Used with permission.

ment type was determined by the limited land needed for the cash crops being grown as well as the difficulty encountered in clearing virgin forests, owing to scarce manpower. This type of land use was changed with the demise of tobacco as the main cash crop. Surging production and desire for Virginian tobacco heralded the demise of the island's planting of that particular crop, leaving behind fragile and increasingly infertile soils unable to sustain the growth of the other cash crops—cotton, indigo, and ginger. There was a need for a new cash crop and it was found in sugar.

Experimentation with multi-crops for export was to cease with the introduction of an exploitative mono-crop—sugar. Change was rapid. By 1665 sugar was king and firmly entrenched in the island. It had led to deforestation, exorbitant land prices, displacement of small farmers, the introduction of slavery, new floral and faunal species, and wealth for some planters, infrastructural development, and new settlement in the interior of the island. Barbados's success at sugar cultivation made it the blueprint for other islands to follow, and during the eighteenth and nineteenth centuries the Barbados model became the template upon which the transatlantic world plantation economy was based.

The Landscape of Sugar

Between 1665 and 1834 the plantation economy grew and created a new landscape distinct from the frontier landscape of the 1630s. The deforested landscape, with its growing road network and predominantly wooden houses and nucleated sugar works, evolved toward "islands" within "islands." Three main structures, the great house, the sugar works, and the slave village, dominated the plantation landscape. Warehouses dominated the urban landscape along with taverns, hotels, churches, and yards (or tenements) used by the enslaved.

At the time of full emancipation in 1838, the processes of sugar dominated the island's landscape. The sharecropping system of the Pernumbuco model (which involved the use of indentured labor on large tracts of land, reaping cane, which was then processed in factories or *engenhos*, with the profit being split between the landholder and his lessees) was reintroduced in Barbados. This system had been modified in its early application to Barbados in the 1640s and was further modified in the post-emancipation period of 1838. Sharecropping under the guise of a New Master and Servant Act sought to control the freed population of ex-enslaved. The slave village that was part of the nucleated plantation settlement was displaced, its space turned into sugar fields, with new villages for freedmen being established on the periphery of the plantation land-tenantries. These tenantries provided rented space on which to erect a house and with some land for subsistence farming, in lieu of rent, tenants worked on the plantation. Such tenantries occupy the landscape to this day.

Although the Barbadian landscape has increasingly become urbanized—stereotypical of "urban drift"—it can be aptly described as an urban drift influenced by the plantation system. The architecture of the great house with its Caribbean vernacular dominates the landscape along with the architecture of the chattel houses, the latter of which were created after emancipation to house the landless free. Sugar fields that have subsequently been bought to provide housing for the middle class still retain the plantation names as their place names. Essentially, Barbados is the land that sugar made—a transplanted landscape created for economic exploitation.

Given the history of land use in Barbados, it is clear that there is a pressing need to manage the island's archaeological and historical heritage, as many sites have either been destroyed or are under serious threat because of encroaching urbanization. This clearly underscores the need to develop an inventory of these resources. The management of this body of information (within the context of Barbados's demography and built environment) is best handled by an integrated GIS system.

GIS AND HERITAGE MANAGEMENT

There is a need for an archaeological inventory monitoring system, which will allow for the development of a Historic Sites and Monuments Record (HSMR). Integrated within the HSMR system are planning guidelines that would allow for the monitoring of sites during the various stages of development and land-use planning. The system should be able to address issues of site modeling and potential damage to sites caused by development. Such issues will be addressed by the information entered into the system as well as by the type of system being developed to manage archaeological resources. An important component of this system would be the use of global positioning satellite (GPS) technology to map and locate sites on the ground, with the site information being subsequently entered in the GIS database.

This GIS system, by facilitating an integrated and interactive mapping program for sites and monuments on the island, will enable informed decision making in the planning stages of urban and rural development. The GIS system will utilize either raster or vector data models to store its information.

The GPS system can be used to locate sites accurately both within the GIS environment and in the real world, especially as there is no accurate digital map for the island that relates to WGS (World Geodetic System) 1984 parameters. With the aid of GPS, sites can be located according to their longitude and latitude, thereby making it easier to locate them within a proposed development area. Conversely, field mapping can be applied to the GIS in the office to highlight potential sites within a proposed planning area.

Another potential use of GIS is in the construction of historic base maps, thereby enabling the perusal of one map comprised of several layers of digital historic maps. This facilitates quicker access for GIS users as they do not have to wade through a series of paper maps possibly housed in different locations. This historic base map can then be employed to locate sites that might not be visible, therefore pointing to potential areas for archaeological excavation.

SITES AND MONUMENTS INVENTORY SYSTEM AT THE BMHS

The project being undertaken by the BMHS is a pilot project designed to create a database of archaeological sites on the island based on GIS and GPS. The project proposal submitted and approved by UNESCO states: "This project will involve the development of a comprehensive electronic information management system that will integrate the data pertaining to sites and monuments on the island. The development of this system will require the examination, recording and data entry of sites on the island as well as a refinement of current cataloguing process and the development of a database application. This centralized system will enable the Museum to better fulfill its mandate and the island to have a centralized database of its important sites and monuments."

This project, which relates to land-use management in Barbados, is ambitious in its scope and therefore necessitates a comprehensive centralized automated data bank.

Audit of GIS on the Island

Presently, there is no accurate or adequate national GIS mapping of Barbados. However, this has not prevented government and private agencies on the island from using GIS for mailing and tracking deliveries of goods, locating utility poles, and locating planning areas or areas designated as coastal infrastructure. The major problem is that Barbados does not have a National Grid, which precludes the island from having a centralized standard for GIS/GPS application. The existing Barbados National Grid was scrapped because it did not conform to the WGS format, which is the base of all GPS mapping. Both the lack of a National Grid map and the presence of only one GPS base station have severely limited the utilization of GIS on the island. The existing base station, operated by the Coastal Zone Management Unit, has a coverage problem because while accurate mapping is possible in the south of the island, this accuracy decreases as one travels north.

A second problem is the absence of transitional data sets for the use of GPS on the island. This means that the use of GPS is somewhat curtailed in the application of GIS. This is perhaps due to the traditional Ordnance Survey of the island utilizing a local datum that is not internally consistent and therefore difficult to readjust when one wishes to use a geocentric datum point. These limitations on the use of GIS in Barbados have influenced our decisions in terms of the type of equipment and data-capture systems considered most appropriate for the proposed GIS project.

Project Implementation and Methodology

Utilizing satellite imagery of the island as the base map was the solution to the foregoing problems. Satellite imagery, both panchromatic (to a scale of 12 feet) and polychromatic (to a scale of 20 feet), was utilized to provide imagery for a base map of the island. With this imagery, feature data sets were gathered that included (1) geological information such as rock type and formation, (2) pedological information such as soil type, (3) topographic information such as contour lines, (4) parish boundaries, (5) road network, and (6) place names.

The HSMR project utilizes a multiple comparative analysis to ensure accurate data capture of site and monument locations. This comparative analysis takes the form of using UTM (Universal Transverse Mercator) georeferenced satellite imagery of the island to determine site location. This information is then evaluated against scanned maps of the island georeferenced to WGS 1984 North, the latter of which are now the coordinates for Barbados. These readings are then compared and analyzed against GPS readings taken in the field. The comparison helps to determine the accuracy of the recorded location. If one wishes, further comparisons with the location coordinates from the sole base station on the island can then be taken. Initially, a second GPS unit was considered for determining a datum point. However, such a system is only practical where there is an accurate extant digital base map and base stations. Once it was ascertained that neither existed on the island, a different approach was needed. It must be noted that a revision of the digital base map of Barbados was being developed at the time of writing, with no firm date set for completion.

The project will be based on ESRI's ArcView 9.0 as its GIS platform. The relational database being used is being supplied by Exegesis, a United Kingdom–based firm working in conjunction with the BMHS to customize their product to our specifications. UNESCO has been funding the project and the expected benefits of the latter are as follows:

1. Greater access for the people of Barbados to their heritage records,
2. Implementation of a program that will ensure the sustainability of sites records for future generations,
3. Protection of the cultural/natural environment,
4. The presentation of Barbados's archaeological and historical heritage through interactive media aimed at educating both adolescent and adult students,
5. Policy papers with well-documented information on sites,
6. Enhanced application of the World Heritage Convention as it relates to site management, and
7. Sustainable, functioning cultural/natural heritage tourism sites.

Such benefits will be made possible through the creation of an inventory of archaeological sites within parishes, which will begin with an examination of current records at the BMHS and other nongovernmental and governmental agencies. The compiled list of sites will then be cross-referenced with a systematic search for extant documents on sites. Following this background search, an organized and orderly field reconnaissance will be initiated. The field reconnaissance will significantly increase the number of known sites across the island and, with the data collected, will contribute to the creation of site location models that will greatly benefit future land-use planning. In addition, the success of the pilot project will be used to garner support from and provide service to both the public and the private sectors. Funding by and linkages with these sectors will enable the sustainability of the project and ultimately the creation of a GIS department at the BMHS within the next four years.

As earlier indicated, the creation of the database involves the ability not only to locate and store attribute data for the various sites but also to record this body of information and create data sets that can be used to determine predictive modeling for the island. These data sets on the island's geology, topography, parish boundaries, road networks, place names, sites, and monuments will form the basis for determining site location and use. These attribute data were defined in order to provide the end users with information that could be easily understood and effectively utilized.

The attribute data include the following: (1) site location, (2) site name, (3) site use (what was the site utilized for, such as prehistoric habitation, industry, settlement, slave resistance, and worship), (4) site type (relates to the time line of the site, that is, prehistoric or historic), and (5) materials, namely artifacts or features found at the site. These classifications were further standardized by using certain definitions designed to enable consistency of use as well as to differentiate between a historical site and an archaeological site. The following definitions were used in this classification refinement exercise.

Definition of Terms

Historic sites are places where significant past events have occurred or areas in which there are properties or monuments utilized for celebrating or commemorating such events or persons associated with these events.

Historic monument is an immovable property utilized in the interpretation of past events, thereby encompassing statuary, or other such objects or depictions used to celebrate or commemorate a person, event, idea, or site where a historical event occurred or where there are buildings, districts, or landscapes.

Archaeological site is a place where there is material evidence of past human life and activities.

For the purpose of the project, sites have the potential to contain both archaeological and historical remains. The application of the foregoing definitions in the construction of the database will allow for systematic data entry, which will lend itself to usable query reporting. This in turn will allow for the making of more-informed decisions with respect to site management and land-use issues.

Ultimately, the development of the GIS system in Barbados will facilitate the asking of questions such as "What are the cultural characteristics of certain sites?" and "Where may certain sites be located on the landscape?" Questions such as these will enhance the level of archaeological research on the island. With this system, the past 20 years of professional archaeological enquiry and excavation can now be digitally managed, facilitating a more-efficient retrieval of information and, most important, a greater understanding of our past. GIS can be also utilized for predictive modeling. The employment of a graphical approach coupled with a weighted value method of predictive modeling will enable the discovery of anomalous sites.

Predictive Modeling

Predictive modeling is to be one of the primary uses of the proposed GIS for Barbados. This technique is necessary given the rapid land-use developments on the island. Though predictive modeling has been criticized for being too environmentally deterministic, it should not be summarily dismissed in light of its potential to facilitate informed decision making in relation to land use and site identification. As with all automated techniques, the effectiveness of predictive modeling is based on the range of data inputs coupled with the types of queries made by the end user.

The construction of the predictive model may be inductive, based on observed data, or deductive, based on theory, or it can be premised on a combination of inductive and deductive approaches. The analysis of inputs such as spatial parameters, physical and environmental characteristics, and economic indices as well as cultural traditions can lead to the following outputs (see Wheatley and Gillings 2002:168): (1) presence/absence of sites/artifacts, (2) site class, (3) density of sites/artifacts, (4) sites of significance, and (5) site probability.

The importance of predictive models in enabling archaeologists, town planners, and cultural resource managers in Barbados to make informed decisions should not be underestimated. Essentially, these models will enable the foregoing individuals to develop comprehensive research designs for archaeologically sensitive areas thereby becoming more proactive to archaeological site management rather than simply "reacting" by engaging in rescue digs as the need arises. However, the project time frame of 10 months did not allow for data capture in the field and hence the creation of predictive models, as much time was spent in resolving the issues of lack of a digital base map and the selection of a relational database.

Despite this, the project's strength is to be found in the creation of a relatively sizable database involving approximately 64 prehistoric sites in Barbados. These pieces of information have duly been entered into the GIS database and can be searched to determine type of site, site use, event date, occupation date, location, and site description. Limited GPS readings are available, but, as discussed above, issues of conversion and accuracy of base-station data have been problematic. Suffice it to say, however, that the results clearly suggest that the pilot project is viable and will form the basis for the development of a sustainable archaeological and historical sites inventory for Barbados.

Preliminary Project Activity and Issues

Though the project has been able to gather information on the known prehistoric sites on the island, the use of that information is, at this stage, somewhat limited. Such limitations occur because of the dearth of accurate information for the creation of coverages relating to geology, soils, vegetation, land allotments, utility infrastructure, and topography. These issues will be addressed in 2007 when the Department of Lands and Surveys produces a digital base map for the island, which will allow for a GIS database for archaeological purposes. The project will be further sustained by the ongoing training of archaeologists and GIS technicians in the use of the system. This will ensure that whatever information is added to the system is processed for accuracy and relevance.

Further, as a pilot project, information on Bridgetown, the capital of Barbados, will be the basis for the GIS database. This proposal is timely given that Bridgetown is proposed as a World Heritage site based on the UNESCO Convention. The pilot project for the city will enable the development of a much-needed management plan for the historic city in keeping with UNESCO's World Heritage specifications. At the same time, the project will provide the requisite attribute data for the creation of a map suitable for the cultural resource management of the city. Bridgetown, being a highly developed urban center in the Caribbean, has extant records relating to land allotment, land ownership, soil profiles, and contemporary as well as historic maps and it is envisaged that this array of data will aid in the creation of an accurate digital map of the city. The various surveys carried out by town planners and disaster mitigation managers will further enhance the attribute data for the city. Finally, these data will enable the GIS to be used to determine buffer zones for development, as overlaying old historic maps may reveal historical and archaeological sites, streets, and other places of interest that should be protected for posterity. These are some of the applications for which the GIS system could be judiciously used in the future.

CONCLUSION

The development of a GIS system for the creation of a sites and monuments register is important for sustainable environmental management and land use on the island of Barbados. Undoubtedly, such a system is necessary if issues of land use and cultural resource management in a small island, developing state in the Caribbean, like Barbados, are to be effectively tackled. The development of the pilot project for an HSMR system in Barbados, utilizing both GPS and GIS, is the initial step in the creation of such a system. There is, therefore, the need for efficient training of personnel in the creation of this system so as to enable its sustainability and utilization in the future.

4
Developing an Archaeological Information System for Trinidad and Tobago

Bheshem Ramlal and Basil A. Reid

Researchers and the general public often find it extremely difficult to gain access to information on archaeological sites in Trinidad and Tobago. Most of the records available for these sites are stored as paper copies at the Archaeology Centre at the University of the West Indies, St. Augustine. The conditions of these records necessitate minimum handling so that the paper records do not fall apart or become lost forever. In addition, the paper-based method has also made it cumbersome to update information on new site discoveries. To address these and other issues, the Department of Surveying and Land Information and the Archaeology Centre of the University of the West Indies undertook the design and development of an Archaeological Information System (AIS) that would provide not only a means for accessing information but also a digital database that may be maintained and updated with new information as it becomes available. The AIS was developed using ArcView GIS 3.2 (ESRI) and Microsoft Access software and was designed for national use. However, this system may be easily migrated to the Internet to provide international access. This chapter summarizes the existing situation and highlights the major limitations of the existing paper-based system. It provides details of the design and application of the AIS and discusses potential benefits of using geographic information systems (GIS) tools in archaeology.

Archaeological remains may be seen as finite and nonrenewable resources that are in many cases highly fragile and vulnerable to damage and destruction. They may contain irreplaceable information about our past and therefore may increase our potential for further knowledge in the future. In Trinidad and Tobago, there are many archaeological sites where extremely valuable remains were found. These sites are not properly maintained and are being slowly lost to development. The remains that were found at these sites are housed at the Archaeology Centre of the University of the West Indies, St. Augustine, at the

National Museum of Trinidad and Tobago, or at the Tobago Museum. While these remains are well documented and are kept in reasonably good condition, access to view and use the material is quite limited. This devalues the usefulness and benefit of having such a collection.

The University of the West Indies and the National Museum both saw the need to provide access to the material to the academic community as well as other stakeholders. This must be achieved while ensuring that the integrity of the archaeological collections and sites is safeguarded. The strategy adopted to realize this objective was the design and development of an archaeological information system that will eventually be web accessible. The first step, however, was to use geographic information systems (GIS) technology to create appropriate databases to store, manage, and display comprehensive data sets on archaeological sites. This chapter describes the process used in developing this system and presents the major results of the project. Detailed discussions of GIS, its components, and applications are provided in Burrough and McDonnell (1998), Bolstad (2001), and Longley et al. (2001) and need not be the subject of discussion in this chapter.

METHODS

The Archaeological Information System (AIS) was developed using a system development methodology (Calkins et al. 1989; Turner et al. 1987) that entailed the following major steps: (a) performing a user needs assessment and (b) using the information obtained to undertake a conceptual design for the AIS. The design was then tested by developing a prototype using Microsoft Access and ArcView GIS 3.2 software. Several data sets were used to test the system to ensure that all requirements were met.

User Needs Assessment

To effectively design an information system, it is necessary to determine requirements of the proposed system (Calkins et al. 1989; Huxhold and Levinsohn 1995; Tomlinson 2003). A detailed user needs assessment was undertaken to identify the requirements of the proposed AIS. This involved the identification of the goals and functions of the organizations that intend to implement the system, the types of data that are needed, and the GIS functions needed by potential users of the system. A start-up session was held to ensure that potential users were aware of what GIS is and how it may be used in the context of the management of archaeological information. A questionnaire was administered to as many persons as possible in each organization. This took the form of face-to-face and telephone interviews. At the end of the assessment, all the

Table 4.1. Major applications of the AIS

Application Description	Type
Identify sites—simple "point and click" query to display the attributes of a feature	Browse
Find site records—perform simple query functions to locate	Browse
Find sites (spatial query)—perform simple find function to locate a record on a map	Query and display
Site inventory map—display all sites	Display
Site/land-use map—display of sites by land-use types	Display
Site/county, ward, regional boundary maps—display of sites by region	Display
Site characteristics map—display of sites classified by characteristics	Query and display
Site age or other attribute map	Query and display
Aggregate sites with respect to polygon themes	Map analysis

data and other needs to plan and implement the proposed system were identified. These are grouped into four categories of requirements: functional, data, technical, and institutional. Each of these is described here.

Functional Requirements

The functional requirements consist of a list of the GIS functions that are to be used in the proposed AIS. In most cases, users were unable to identify the type of analysis functions that were needed. This required a translation of the needs of users into five major categories: (a) browse—perusing the data similar to manual means, (b) simple display—preparation of maps, (c) query and display—querying the database and presenting the results in map form, (d) map analysis—use of analytical capabilities of the GIS, and (e) spatial modeling—developing scenarios using GIS. See Calkins et al. (1989) for a detailed discussion on each of these categories of GIS functions. Table 4.1 provides a list of the applications compiled from the needs assessment and the major category for each.

Data Requirements

Several data sets were identified for inclusion in the AIS. These are listed in Table 4.2. It may be noted that while not all of these data sets would be directly used in the applications, they are needed as a framework for presenting the results of queries.

The levels of detail needed were also identified in the needs assessment.

Table 4.2. Data required for the AIS

Feature	Scale	Object Types	Description	Characteristics/Attributes
Site data	1:25,000	Point	Archaeological site description	Site number, name, county size, character, series, age, site chronology, classification year, year of discovery, map scale, map number, location, class, site description
Buildings	1:25,000	Point	Important buildings	Building name, address, description, importance
Roads	1:10,000	Line	Roads	Road name, type, class, length
Rivers	1:25,000	Line	Rivers	River name, class, type
Soils	1:25,000	Polygon	Soil type	Soil code, class, characteristics
Coastline	1:25,000	Polygon	High-water mark	No attributes
County	1:100,000	Polygon	County boundaries	County name
Wards	1:100,000	Polygon	Subsets of counties	Ward name
Parks and protected areas	1:100,000	Polygons	Boundaries of protected areas	Name, type
Land use	1:100,000	Polygons	Land-use/land-cover classification	Land-use class, area
Elevation	1:25,000	Points	Elevation points	Elevation in meters

It was agreed that maps at a paper scale of 1:25,000 will provide adequate detail. However, this was not easy to achieve in some cases. The scales of data sets available are also provided in Table 4.2. The major focus of the AIS is that of archaeological site data. The attributes for these sites are described in Table 4.3. It may be noted that in addition to the data provided below, the site data collected included photographs, documents, and other historical information available for the site. Available documents and photographs are included in the initial design of the AIS. However, detailed historical information will be added later.

Table 4.3. Major attributes stored for archaeological sites

Attribute	Description
Number	Each site is given a number prefixed with the county in which it is located. For example, a site in the county of Caroni is numbered CAR 1.
Name	Site names are assigned based on recognized geographical or cultural features in the general location of the site.
Character	Sites are classified according to the general character found upon site inspection. Seven types are documented in the archive: 1. Middens—refuse heaps that may contain shells and other food remains, fragments of pottery, or bone and shell artifacts. 2. Middens with burials—middens in which human interments have been made. 3. Pottery deposits—ceramic and other artifacts. 4. Flint deposits—refuse or workshop areas with no pottery and negligible food remains found. 5. Burials—individual or collective interments outside of midden areas. 6. Caves—caves with pottery remains and/or stone, bone, or shell artifacts. 7. Petroglyphs—Amerindian rock drawings.
Complexes	Sites are also classified according to the cultural relationships of their former occupants. This is done using complexes, series, and subseries. Two complexes exist for Trinidad: Archaic age and Ceramic age.
Series	Complexes are broken into series. For example, the Ceramic age complex may be classified into Saladoid, Barrancoid, Guayabitoid, Sauzoid, and Mayoid series.
Subseries	Series are further subdivided into subseries. For example, the Ortoiroid series comprises the Banwarian and Ortorian subseries.
Age	The prehistory of Trinidad and Tobago may be divided into four main ages: Lithic, Archaic, Ceramic, and Historic.
Location certainty	The certainty of site location is classified according to the precision at which the site is referenced: well known, generally known, and unknown.
Class	Sites are classified according to their importance in terms of cultural resources management criteria: A—Extremely significant site. To be protected forever from any interference. B—Considered to be sufficiently significant for protection as long as controlled archaeological investigations have not taken place. C—Considered insignificant regarding the need for actions to be taken toward its protection. D—Site is completely destroyed. No protection needed. ?—Site cannot be located, so no classification is possible.
Size	Areal extent of site. May range from less than 100 m^2 to greater than 500 m^2 in 100 m^2 increments.
Carbon date	Chronometric dating of material and site.

Technical Requirements

The major technical requirements to be identified for the AIS pertained to hardware and software systems considered most appropriate to the task at hand. Since most of the applications needed to be performed by the AIS will employ simple querying and map display, ArcView GIS 3.2 (ESRI) was identified as the most appropriate GIS software package for developing the AIS. The package allows the handling of spatial data sets along with the hot linking of images and other documents, report preparation, customization, and the linking to database management systems software. In addition to the GIS software, a database management system was required for storing descriptive data. It was therefore decided to use Microsoft Access to manage the attribute database. This package is easily accessible and relatively simple for users to learn quickly. In addition, Microsoft Access may be customized as a stand-alone option for executing attribute queries and analyses. Software for web page design will be needed later to create the appropriate documents for Internet service provision. The major hardware components required for implementing the AIS were a desktop computer, a scanner for inputting maps, and a printer for generating maps and reports.

Institutional Requirements

Institutional requirements are necessary to ensure that the proposed system is maintained and utilized in an optimal manner. Several strategies were developed for achieving this. These included the creation of a data entry form in Microsoft Access, manuals on how to update both the graphic and the attribute components of the spatial database, and strategies for checking and controlling the quality of the data being entered.

Conceptual Design

The first step in the database design was to complete the conceptual design. This involved the development of a data model using the entity-relationship (ER) diagramming technique. The ER diagram describes the relationships present in the proposed AIS among the spatial entities. The attributes are not included in the diagram to avoid clutter. Attribute information may be found in the master data list provided in Table 4.2.

In Figure 4.1, the rectangles represent entities and the elongated hexagons represent relationships. An indication of whether the entity is geographic (G) or nongeographic is also included in the symbol. In addition, the presence or absence of topology (T) is included in the entity symbol. The double hexagon represents relationships where spatial overlay functions are required.

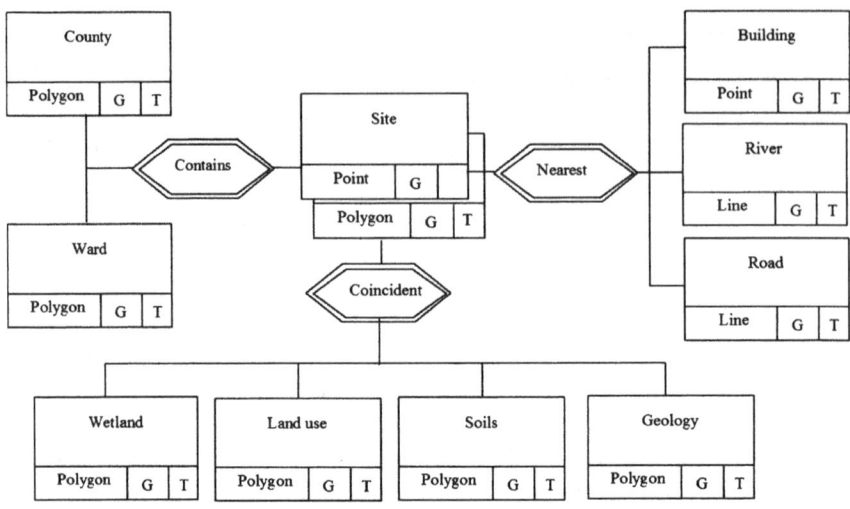

Figure 4.1. Entity-relationship diagram of conceptual model.

System Development

The conceptual design was used to create the relational database in Microsoft Access and the spatial database in ArcView GIS 3.2. The relational database design also included the development of a form that allowed the input of site data. This is shown in Figure 4.2.

The major steps in developing the spatial database for the AIS involved acquiring data sets that were available in digital form, creating the spatial data themes that were only available in paper form, and inputting these data to the GIS software. The data were edited to ensure consistency and correctness. The spatial database was then connected to the relational database using Structured Query Language (SQL) linking. Sample spatial data sets are shown in Figures 4.3 and 4.4.

GIS ANALYSIS USING THE AIS

Several analyses may be executed using the completed AIS. Examples of applications that may be generated are presented here. Many types of queries are possible, the most obvious being the identification of sites that meet single or multiple criteria. Examples of this are the identification of all sites made up of middens, sites belonging to the Ceramic age, or sites that are greater than 500 m² in size. However, the AIS allows for more complex queries, such as the identification of sites that may be located 500 m from a river or the coastline. Figure 4.5 shows the results of such a query.

In addition, sophisticated queries that involve the overlay of several themes

Archaeological Database: Data Entry Form

Site_No	SGE-1	SIte / Project Centriod Coordinates.	X	669229.29391
Site_Name	Perriquier Bay		Y	1177911.13963
County	St. George		Class	Cannot be Relocated
Char	Individual	Year Discovered		1978
Series	Saladoid	Site Description		Sample point 1. This is a fictional point.
Age	Ceramic	A brief Description of Site.		
Site Chrono	25500+/- 100 BP			
Calender Year	805 - 520 BC			
Site size	100 - 200 sq.m	Site Rep_File		sge-1.htm
Map Scale	1:250000			Site reportfile name e.g. sge-1.htm
Map	11	Date Entered		20/05/02
Loc	0-Generally Known	Last Updated		20/05/02

Save Form   Exit Form

Record No. 1

Figure 4.2. Attribute data entry form.

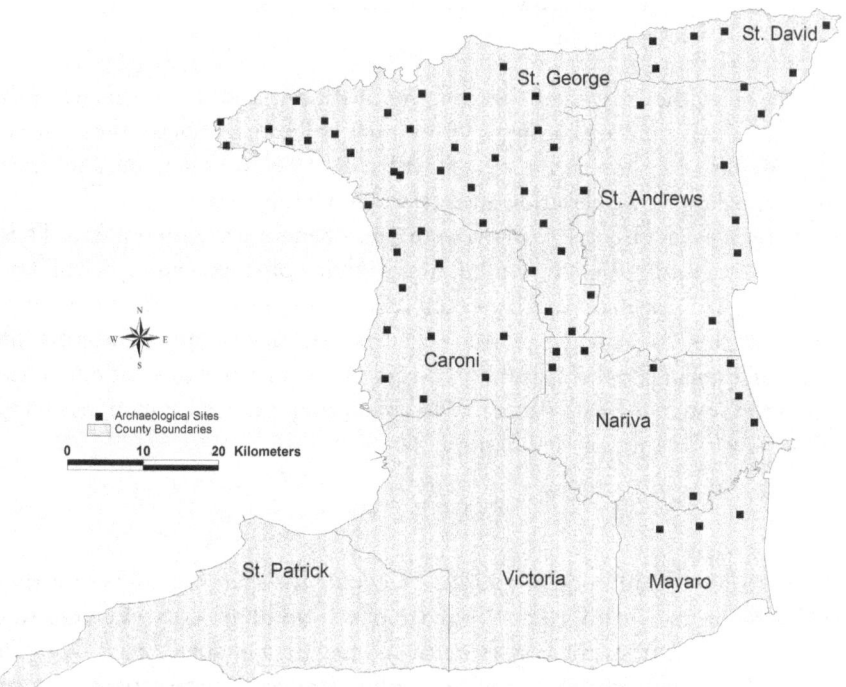

Figure 4.3. Map of Trinidad created using the archaeological sites data set.

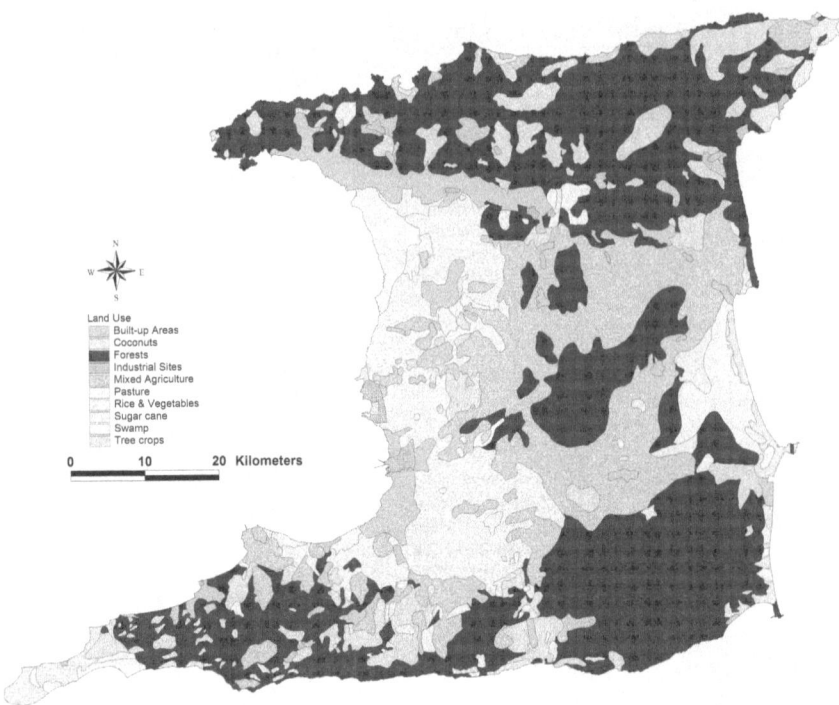

Figure 4.4. Map of Trinidad created using the land-use data set.

of data allow the analysis of sites in terms of the physical characteristics of the area in which they are located. For example, Figure 4.6 shows the archaeological sites after they are intersected with a digital elevation model and classified according to the elevation level at which they are located.

Several other GIS applications were developed for use with the AIS. These included analyzing the location of sites in terms of slope and aspect of areas where sites are located. Another example is the intersection of the site location theme with soils, geology, and river themes that may yield new insights into pre-Columbian peoples' reasons for placing sites at particular locations. These allow the system to be used as a tool to obtain simple as well as complex details about any of the sites stored in the system.

CONCLUSION

GIS provides a multitude of tools that facilitate the spatial analyses of various phenomena that are influenced by geography. In addition, GIS provides a suitable environment for the easy retrieval and mapping of spatial data. The proposed AIS described above provides a sound strategy for the capture, storage, management, analysis, and dissemination of archaeological data. The design

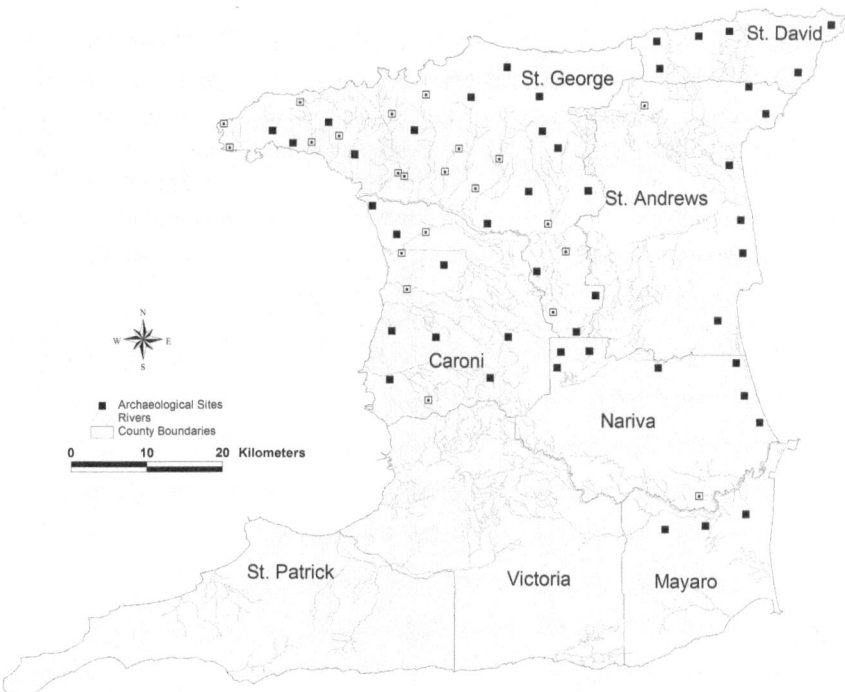

Figure 4.5. Selected sites (shown as dotted boxes) that are within 500 m of a river and/or the coastline.

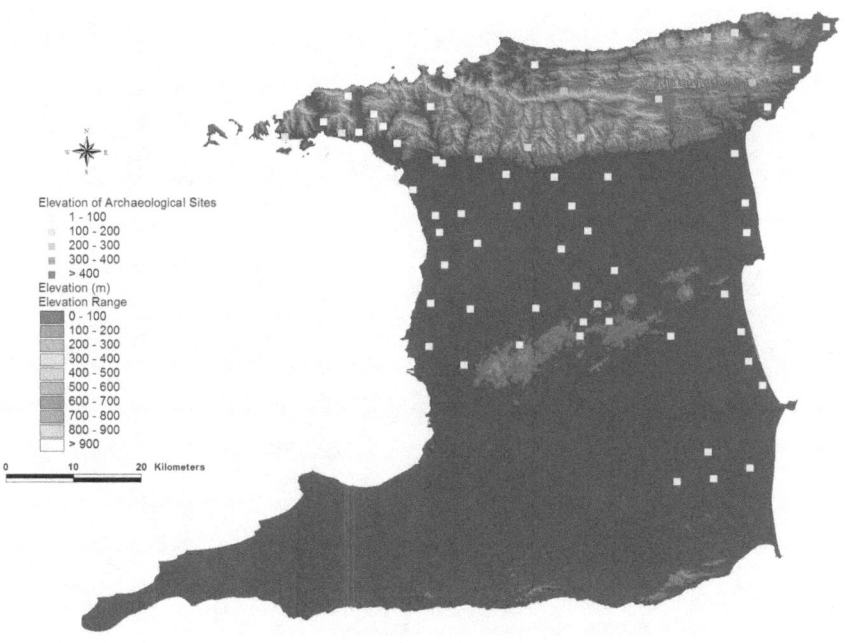

Figure 4.6. Sites intersected with digital elevation model.

facilitates the easy access of detailed information that would not normally be available to the many potential users. The AIS may be used as a tool to inform and educate both students and visitors about the cultural history of Trinidad and Tobago. Making the AIS web accessible may also be valuable to serious researchers from other geographical locations around the world who seek data sets on the country's archaeology that are both wide ranging and easily retrievable. These are some of the significant benefits that can be derived from the proposed AIS, while simultaneously protecting the integrity of archaeological collections and sites in Trinidad and Tobago.

III
Archaeology, GIS, Cartography, GPS, Satellite Imagery, Aerial Photography, and Photogrammetry

5
Maps, *Matricals*, and Material Remains

An Archaeological GIS of Late-Eighteenth-Century Historic Sites on St. John, Danish West Indies

Douglas V. Armstrong, Mark W. Hauser, David W. Knight, and Stephan Lenik

The steep and rugged landscape of St. John along with its irregular rainfall made it marginal to the capital interests of the Danish West Indies. While mercantile trade was central to the economy of St. Thomas and the plantation economy was well suited to St. Croix, the setting of St. John contributed to its peripheral role as a mixed plantation and provisioning economy. This marginality, in combination with the mixed motives and objectives of the Danish colony, produced a setting for social relations that have been described as an incomplete hegemony. This landscape facilitated the development of negotiated freedom for persons of color. In this chapter, we use GIS to integrate the documentary and archaeological records in order to reconstruct the social context of ownership and control in eighteenth-century St. John, Danish West Indies. We found that in the late eighteenth century, free persons of color on St. John took advantage of the relative flexibility in the Danish land-tenure system to establish informal and formal landholdings for themselves and their families in the less contested lands of St. John. This study uses historic maps and tax records (*matricals*) along with the material remains and ruins of archaeological sites to reconstruct cultural transitions and emerging venues for freedom.

The island of St. John, Danish West Indies (now United States Virgin Islands), is an ideal setting to apply geographic information systems (GIS) to the reconstruction of past cultural landscapes. This archaeological study makes use of detailed maps, historic details recorded in tax records (*matricals*), and the rich array of structural and material remains that survive on St. John to reconstruct the island's late-eighteenth-century cultural landscape.[1] In 2004, as the first phase of a detailed diachronic study of St. John, we chose to focus on sites dating to the era of Peter L. Oxholm's maps of the island (1780–1800; Figures 5.1 and 5.2). This study examines the historical context of these maps and conditions pertaining to their production to assist in interpreting the cultural landscape.

Peter Oxholm's works are the only complete maps of St. John dating to the Danish colonial period on the island (1718–1917). The fact that these maps are keyed to the island's tax records makes them a pivotal link between our archaeological survey data and the combination of economic and demographic information in archival records. The in-depth reconstruction of the historical landscape of St. John is dependent on not only material footprints of sites but also the type and quality of information recorded on the maps. Oxholm's maps provided the interpretive key to spatial and geographic reconstruction by allowing us to link space and place (confirmed through archaeological survey) with the people and general economic parameters recorded in the island's tax records.

An understanding of Oxholm's objectives in mapping the island, as well as of details pertaining to the conditions and limitations of his mapping effort, is essential to our reconstruction of the late-eighteenth-century cultural landscape. Because of St. John's steep slopes and poorly defined plantation boundaries, Oxholm had a difficult time completing the task of mapping this rugged island. The present survey has the advantage of global positioning systems (GPS) and elegant GIS computer programs. With these tools, we were able to find and efficiently plot sites and relate ruins to cultural and economic systems of the late eighteenth century.

With respect to interpretive analysis, our findings provide insight into social relations within St. John, a setting of distinct variation, yet still embedded within the social construct of the broader "slave society" of the Caribbean (see Goveia 1965:vii). Through our analysis we found that beginning in the late eighteenth century, more than a half century prior to emancipation, a portion of the rural population of people of color took advantage of the ambiguities of Danish colonial administration, the small size of the island, and the presence of lands marginal to agro-industry to gain access and title to lands—and a margin of freedom. Moving forward in time from this era, land ownership was to become a basis for African Creole community formation, and freedom, on the island (Armstrong 2003a, 2003b; Olwig 1994).

A HISTORIC SITES GIS FOR ST. JOHN

St. John affords an unusually rich setting of environmental and site preservation that allows a remarkable level of site identification and reconnaissance.

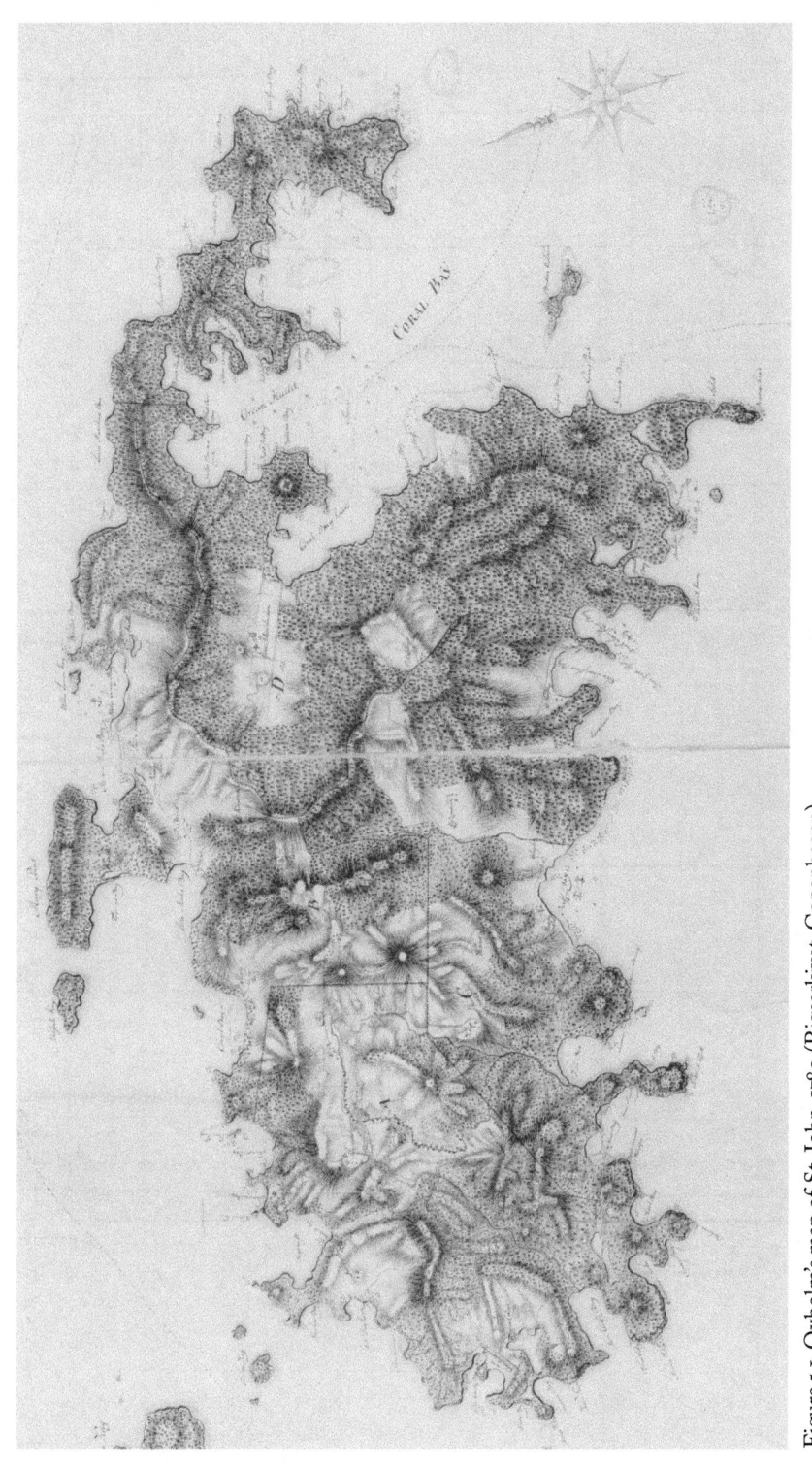

Figure 5.1. Oxholm's map of St. John, 1780 (Rigsarkivet, Copenhagen).

Figure 5.2. Oxholm's map of St. John, 1800 (Rigsarkivet, Copenhagen).

However, the island is rapidly changing and its sites are increasingly at risk. The population on St. John decreased dramatically over the last half of the nineteenth century and remained sparsely populated through much of the twentieth century; thus until recently sites remained relatively undisturbed. Beginning in the mid–twentieth century large tracts of lands were acquired and preserved in what would become the Virgin Islands National Park. Now nearly two-thirds of the island is protected within the Virgin Islands National Park, operated by the National Park Service of the United States. However, over the past few decades the island has become a tourist and real-estate investment hot spot. Land outside of the park boundaries is rapidly filling with houses perched precariously on hillsides and beachfronts. Meanwhile, the park itself has seen a significant increase in tourists. Many visitors participate in two- to three-hour excursions from cruise ships stopping at Charlotte Amalia on St. Thomas; others spend a day to a week at hotels, resorts, and guest houses. As a result, archaeological sites, both in and out of the National Park, are being dramatically impacted by this more intensive land use. Ruins of old abandoned settlements had for decades been left relatively undisturbed, with artifact scatters and architectural elements exposed in situ and undisturbed on the surface. Today the surface artifacts are rapidly disappearing and sites across the island are at risk from both casual disturbance and destruction associated with construction, development, and looting (Freehill 2006).

Initiating a historic sites GIS for St. John involved a GPS survey and the gathering of information including data from previous archaeological surveys, excavations, and studies. Our objectives of this study (first phase of the historic sites GIS) were to (1) locate historic sites dating to the 1780–1800 period on St. John; (2) translate Danish tax records (*matricals*) and create a database linking the demographic and economic records found in them; (3) plot these data on GIS map coverages for the years 1780 and 1800; (4) analyze changes in the cultural and economic landscape; and (5) use our findings to relate St. John to the broader social and economic landscape of the Caribbean.

A complex array of data was collected, including multiple GPS points per site, cross-referencing with previous survey work, and the integration of an array of documentary materials and details from archaeologically defined contexts. We were able to spatially link demographic and economic information available in the island's tax records. The data are organized around three scales of information (including both points and polygons): (1) *site:* specific information on individual sites (individual land holding, parcel, estate, or plantation); (2) *quarter:* grouped data for each of five geopolitical divisions of the island defined by the Danish, which are recorded in the *matricals* by quarter (these data yield summarized comparisons of production and demographic data)[2]; and (3) *island-wide* trends based on the synthesis of site and quarter data.

Each level of interpretation, plus the intersection of multiscalar analyses, provides significant insight into the island's cultural landscape and perspective on cultural and economic changes that had never been systematically explored. Subtle, yet pertinent, information on significant cultural changes is represented in the intersection of these data sets and through the multiscalar analysis of these data. The data can be combined and compared in order to explore local and island-wide trends in demography and land use.

Starting from the strength of the combined spatial and documentary data represented on the Oxholm maps of 1780 and 1800, we were able to achieve our initial goal of establishing a solid baseline of site location. The data combine demographic and economic production information with site location. This not only allows us to look in detail at land use and changing cultural landscapes for this initial period of study (1780–1800) but also provides a valuable baseline for future longitudinal studies that deal with earlier and later periods. This baseline of GIS data both will be useful for academic research and will facilitate resource management by National Park and territorial archaeologists. In fact, the GIS survey files have already been incorporated into a cultural resource management plan by the National Park Service to amplify monitoring of sites and by the Virgin Islands Department of Planning and Natural Resources in supporting a study documenting burial location and practices on the island (Kenneth Wild, personal communication 2005; see also Ebert 2000; Farley et al. 1990).

In the process of documenting sites associated with all of the properties on St. John for the period 1780–1800, we were able to define heretofore unrecognized transitions taking place that reflect dynamic cultural and economic change within Danish West Indian plantation society. The St. John historic sites GIS is generating a body of data that is useful in answering an array of research questions and for strategic site management and preservation.

PERSPECTIVE ON ST. JOHN AND THE DANISH WEST INDIES

St. John was one of three principal islands of the Danish West Indies (along with St. Croix and St. Thomas), an island group acquired from Denmark by the United States in 1917. St. John, along with other islands in the Virgin Islands group and the neighboring Lesser Antilles archipelago, represents an element of diversity in scale within the Caribbean region. As Barry Higman pointed out for the Lesser Antilles as a whole, the smallness of scale and economic scope of the smaller islands of the Caribbean have led to distinct variations in the overall pattern of land use from island to island in the region (Higman 1995:8). In contrast to larger islands in the Caribbean like Hispañiola (Haiti and the Dominican Republic), Jamaica, Cuba, Puerto Rico, or even

Guadeloupe, where an array of environmental zones, soils, and climatic conditions produces a wide range of settlement types and economic production systems, St. John's environmental setting provided a limited range of options.

While St. John was suited for provision production (foods to coal production) and maritime trades (fishing to the harvesting of coral reefs), its landscape and irregular rainfall yielded land that was only marginally suitable for the production of sugar, particularly as compared with the scale of economic production of its larger neighbors throughout the Caribbean—including the Danish island of St. Croix. Moreover, its undulating shoreline and steep slopes tended to enhance isolation and worked against controls that could be enforced by colonial regulation. Added to this is the fact that the Danes were only a minor player in the colonial arena and their interests, although tied to plantation-based agriculture, were more strongly tied to maintaining a foothold for mercantile trade on a global scale and less to land-based expansionist or imperial designs. Their agenda was to sustain a neutral base for trade within a sea controlled by naval powers including the British, Spanish, French, and, later, the United States.

Thus, St. John and many of the smaller islands of the eastern Caribbean, including its near neighbors Tortola, Virgin Gorda, and Peter Island, as well as Anguilla, Saba, and Nevis, represent settings of microdiversity within the broader Caribbean. On these islands, the narrow range of economic options combined with the smallness of scale to produce very distinct settings of insular diversity. St. John was at once an element of the broader social and economic structure of slavery, colonialism, and imperialism (Goveia 1965:52–53) and also an example of the fragmentation and idiosyncratic nature of local social and political interaction (Hall 1985; Higman 1988, 1996:1; see also Higman 1995:9).

CARTOGRAPHY OF THE DANISH WEST INDIES

A fascinating aspect of Danish West Indian history is that no formal set of maps was produced until 1780. When a set of maps was finally commissioned, the cartographic objectives for the island of St. John remained peripheral to the central goal of generating maps and plans of harbors and fortifications in order to evaluate defense systems for stable trade for the Danish foothold in the region.

In 1776, a Danish ship was seized by a British naval vessel at anchor in front of Fort Frederiksted, St. Croix (Hopkins 1993:29). The Danes were outraged, but, more important, they felt threatened by the implications of the ease of which their multinational trading system could be interrupted by a foreign power. As a consequence, the Danish government began to investigate the colony's defenses. As part of this exploration, a series of maps was commissioned by the Chamber of Customs upon petition to the King's council. In a report to the Chamber of Customs, General Huth indicated that the islands were "of all together too great commercial importance for the colonial administration to be without accurate maps of them" (Hopkins 1993:30, after Huth in DVFV-I 1777a). Huth recommended that the survey job should be carried out by Lieutenant Peter Lotharius Oxholm, who had worked with him on the Eider Canal Project in Denmark (DVFV-I 1777b).

Funding was approved to send Oxholm "to survey the island's defensive works and prepare maps of the island" (DVFV-I 1777b). The request acknowledged the existence of a detailed map of St. Croix by Jens Beck (1754; Figure 5.3). Beck's map provides remarkable detail of plantation layout and illustrates the very structured rectangular plantation layout of St. Croix. However, the map did not contain information on topographic relief or hydrographic detail. These latter details were, by the 1770s, considered essential to withstand a siege on relatively dry islands.[3] For St. Thomas, the Chamber noted the existence of a 1719 map by van Keulen with information on relief and defensive structures, but argued that it was "old and in certain respects unreliable" (DVFV-I 1777b; Hopkins 1993:30). As for St. John, the Chamber simply reported that "there is nothing beyond what is depicted on said v. Keulen," a map that provides no details on the cartography of St. John (DVFV-I 1777b). In fact, soon after the formal settlement of St. John by the Danish in 1718, a French team had produced a map of the settlement and fort at Coral Harbor (Figure 5.4).

The dominant theme in Oxholm's orders was the need for details on defense against possible attacks by other nations or raids by privateers. They were also concerned about the possibility of rebellion of slaves and the protection of water supplies in the event of a siege. Oxholm was given explicit orders to document and evaluate each island's fortifications (Hopkins 1993:33). He was to draw all forts and batteries, "together with the harbors and stretches of land lying immediately adjacent, all in plan and profile, so that such maps and drawings could always be available here at hand in the future and so that one could know and judge of the defense works' form, situation, and strength" (DVFV-I 1777c).[4] Thus along with the maps, Oxholm was ordered to report on conditions, including detailed suggestions for improvements. These instructions ultimately resulted in detailed notes on the cultural setting and conditions on St. John. The notes, written in association with the production of the 1780 map, are of considerable value to the interpretation of the island's cultural landscape and provide vivid detail of the problems encountered that encumbered production of a map as detailed for St. John as he was able to produce for St. Croix.

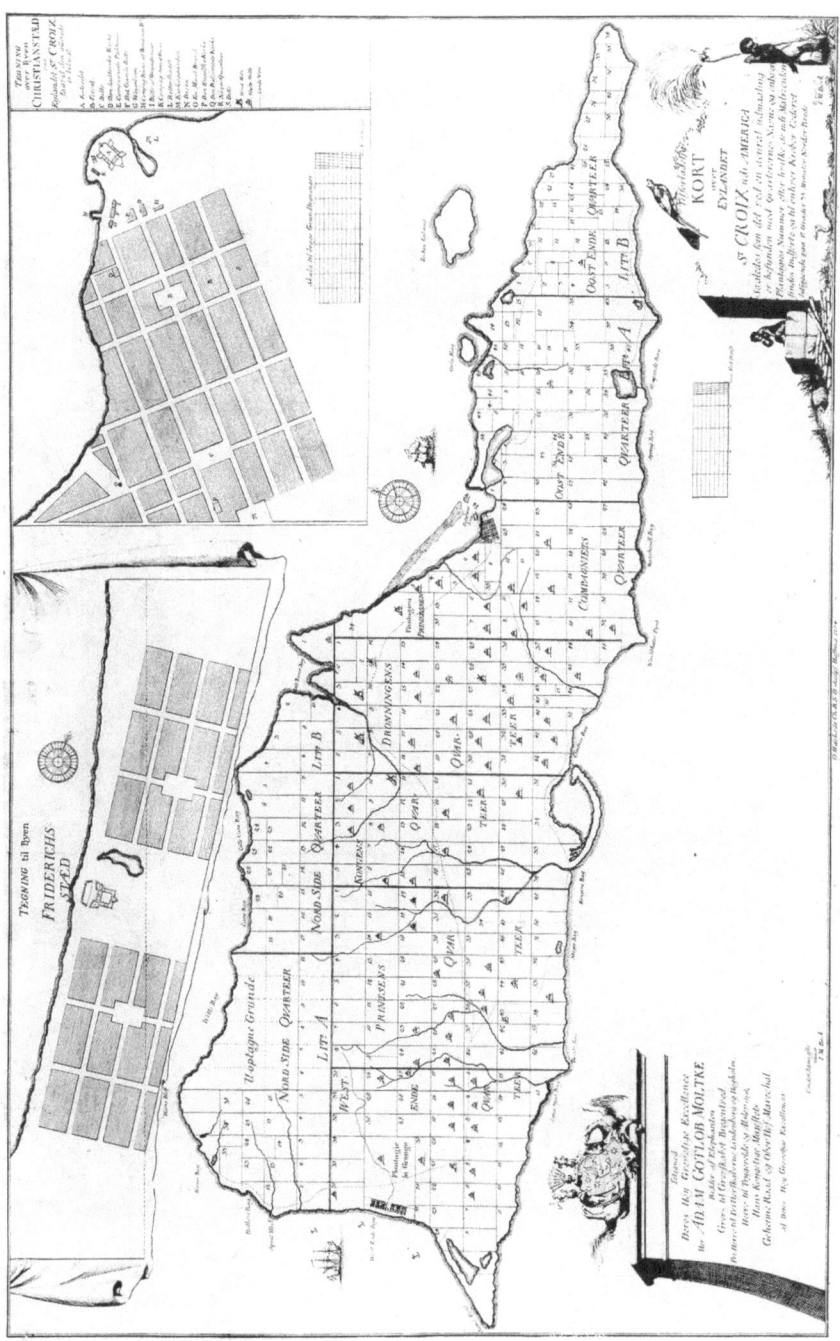

Figure 5.3: Beck's map of St. Croix, 1754 (Rigsarkivet, Copenhagen).

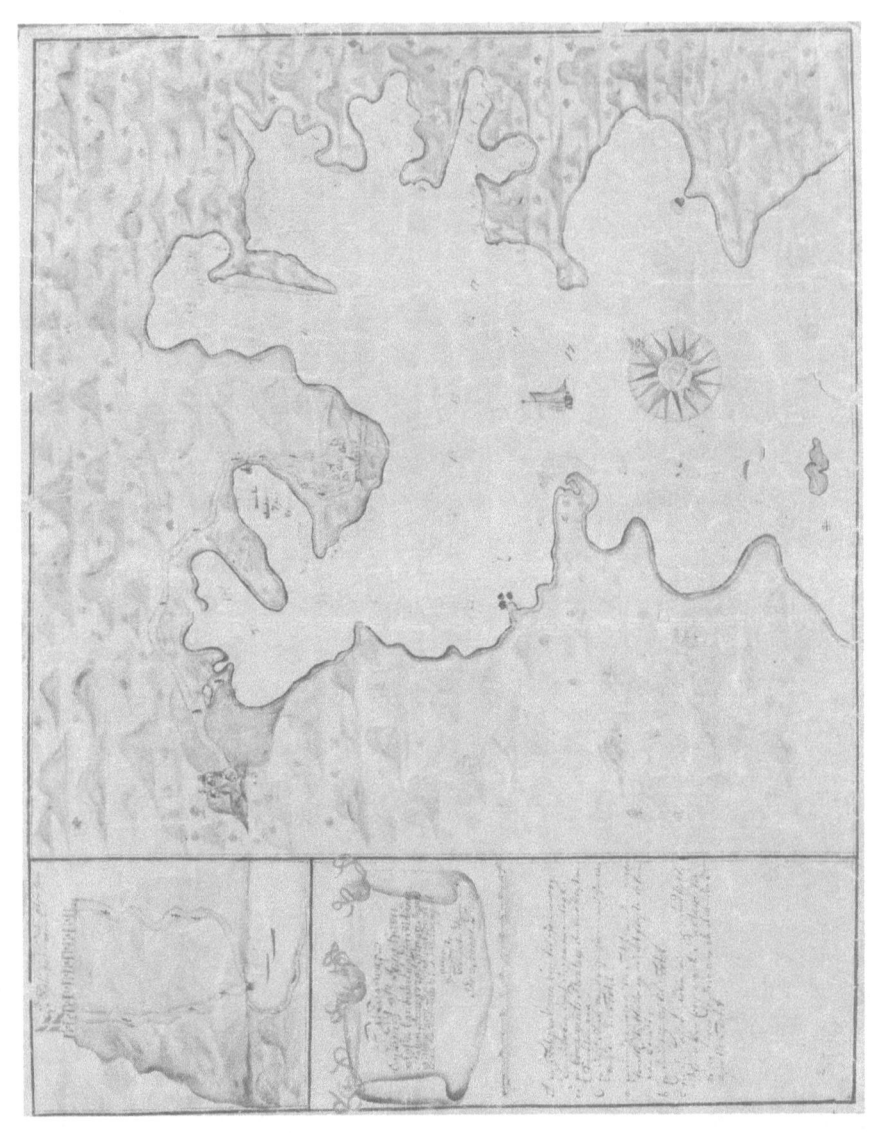

Figure 5.4. Map of Coral Harbor, 1720 (Rigsarkivet, Copenhagen).

Peter Oxholm arrived in the Danish West Indies on March 14, 1778. In the Danish West Indies he found a setting that was far different from that which he had encountered in mapping canals in the relatively flat and open landscape of Denmark. He was confronted by a multitude of languages, including Dutch and English, all spoken in local Creole dialects. He quickly determined that Beck's map was relatively accurate and that resurveying the whole of St. Croix was unnecessary, and too expensive, so he focused upon drawing plans of fortifications and harbors.

In contrast to the relatively flat lands of St. Croix, St. Thomas and St. John represented perplexing cartographic problems. Oxholm's initial notes include the observation that these islands are "nothing but mountains and cliffs, where it is almost everywhere impossible to survey or prepare a geographic large-scale map before one has first cut lines and ways through the bush to get through on" (Hopkins 1993:36; VIFR 1777–1778). He therefore asked for permission to finish work on the forts and return home. He amplified his argument by adding that if he were "to remain here longer for the sake of surveying the islands, the forts and buildings would become even more dilapidated, and thus cost even more to repair" (Hopkins 1993:36; VIFR 1777–1778). Fortunately for us his request was rejected and he continued on to map St. John.

Daniel Hopkins points out that the Danish Royal Court's response was direct and to the point. The Court wrote: "We wish that Lieutenant Oxholm shall remain in our West Indian islands until he has also attended to the geographic mapping, required of him in his orders, of St. Thomas and St. John." Hopkins asserts two key reasons for the court's insistence. The first was that the Crown had invested heavily in the expansion of free trade and anticipated the opening of world markets—and particularly expanding North American markets—through its Caribbean holdings at the conclusion of the American Revolution. The second, more whimsical, reason related to Prince Frederik's, son of Frederik V, being enamored with maps. He would ultimately accumulate one of the finest collections of historic maps in the world. His collection was compiled in a 55-volume atlas housed in the Danish National Library (Hopkins 1993:37).[5] Hence, it can be said that maps—for the sake of maps—were in vogue within the Royal Court and Oxholm was thus ordered to continue on in his work.[6]

MAPPING ST. JOHN (1780 AND 1800)

Peter Oxholm's two detailed maps of St. John were used as the basic geographic guide to the estates, roadways, customs houses, towns, and general landscape of the island (Oxholm 1780a, 1800). It was not until after the 1917 transfer of the Danish West Indies to the United States that a new U.S. Geological Survey (1918) map was made. The history of these maps reveals much about both the history of the island and the difficulty of mapping this island in the era prior to aerial photographs and GPS.

Through the centuries, St. John's steep slopes and dense vegetation (both verdant foliage and impenetrable xerophytic cacti and acacia, depending on where you are on the island) have turned away surveyors—before and after Peter Oxholm. In submitting his 1780 map of St. John, Oxholm noted that "[t]his island has hitherto been only very little known, and no survey or map of any part of it has yet been done, before the present one, which lacks nothing except each plantation's particular boundary lines, which because of the shortness of time, as well as its virtual impossibility, I have not been able to include in the drawing" (DVFV-I 1780, in Hopkins 1993:43).

Oxholm's notes and letters reflect the difficulty that he had with the terrain and in reconciling information on landownership (tax records), estate boundaries, and survey access. He stated: "I made the most of the small time I had left to at least in some regards fulfill the demand for a map of this island.... for had I completed the most accurate large-scale survey, a period of many months, perhaps even years, would have been demanded, as most of the whole island is still in bush." Oxholm's observation is critical to our understanding of the late eighteenth-century landscape, as it presents a vivid picture of an island that was made up of a series of plantations that, in theory, more or less covered the extent of the island but for which boundaries were impractical if not impossible to fully define. Oxholm chose to settle on a topographic map that was far less detailed than that of St. Croix but that he felt was sufficient to show the character of the whole island. However, he also went on to provide written descriptions of the setting he encountered, which project the image of a rough and overgrown landscape.

Oxholm's records are replete with details pertaining to the cultural landscape of St. John. Included among the documents he submitted to the Crown was a draft map of the island dated 1777 (Figure 5.5). This map includes information from Oxholm's initial coastal survey and schematic representations of fortifications and a detailed listing of names of harbors, bays, and moorings. Each of these variables was explicitly defined as priorities for evaluating the defense of the island (and perhaps more importantly the defense of the port of Charlotte Amalia on St. Thomas). Oxholm's most detailed drawing is of the fortification at Cruz Bay (Figure 5.6). This was a newly constructed battery, completed at a cost of 9,000 Riksdaler, but funds had not been sufficient to complete the guard house. Oxholm suggested that completion of the project could be funded by selling the barracks to a private individual for use as a storehouse. With respect to the old fort at Coral Bay, Oxholm commented that the location of this fort was good for defense but that the remains of the building he visited were inadequate (Figure 5.7). He went on to lament the recent

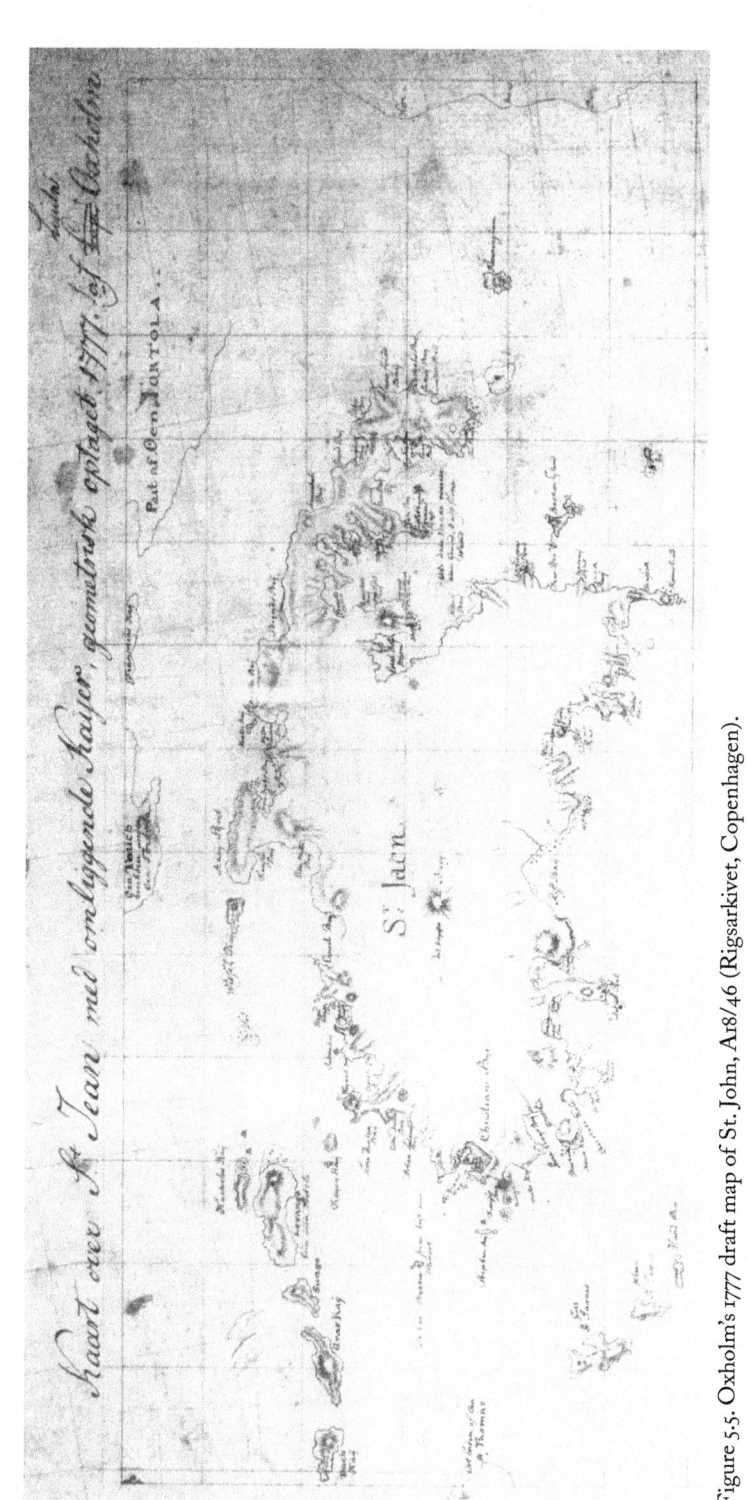

Figure 5.5. Oxholm's 1777 draft map of St. John, A18/46 (Rigsarkivet, Copenhagen).

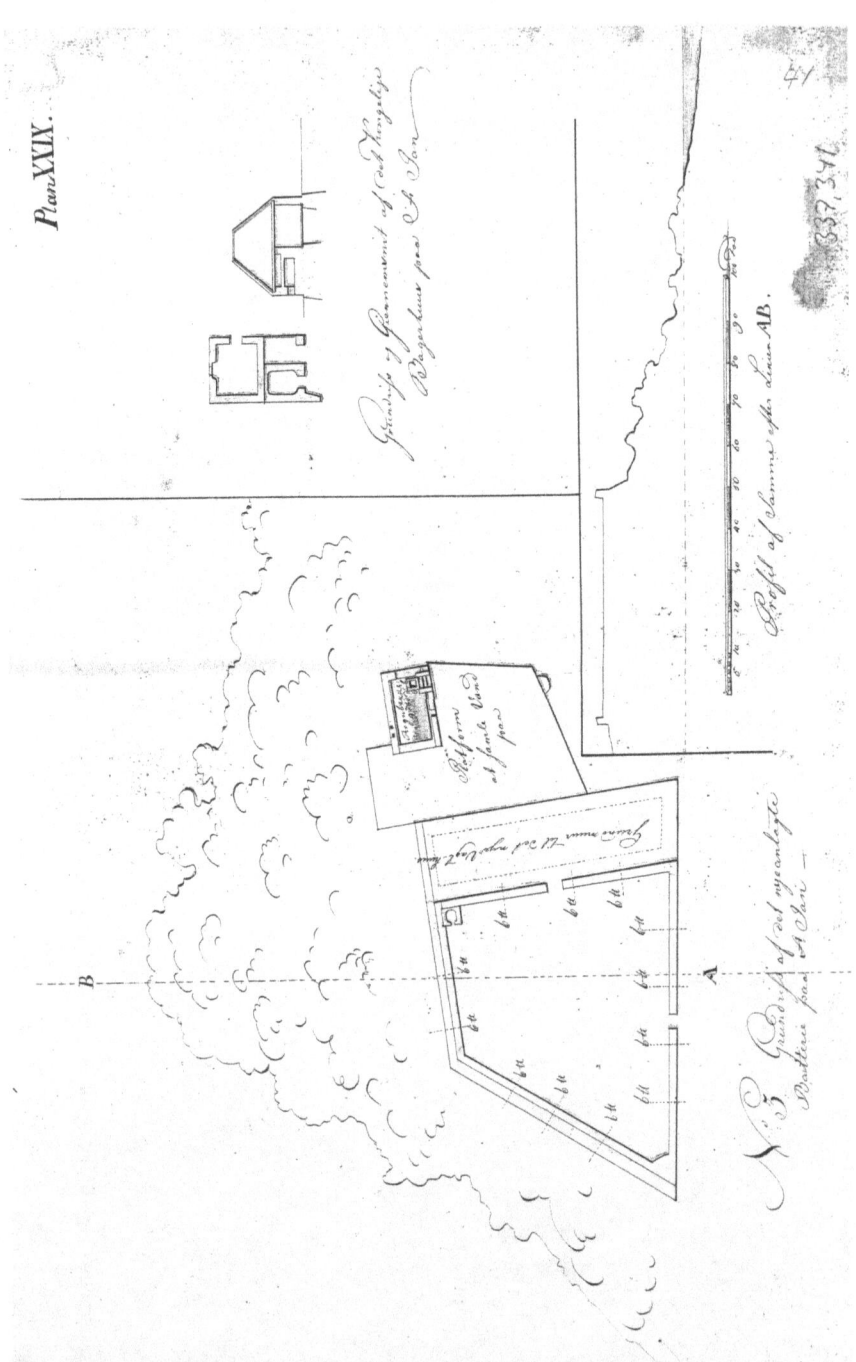

Figure 5.6. Fortification of Cruz Bay (Oxholm 1780b, Rigsarkivet, Copenhagen).

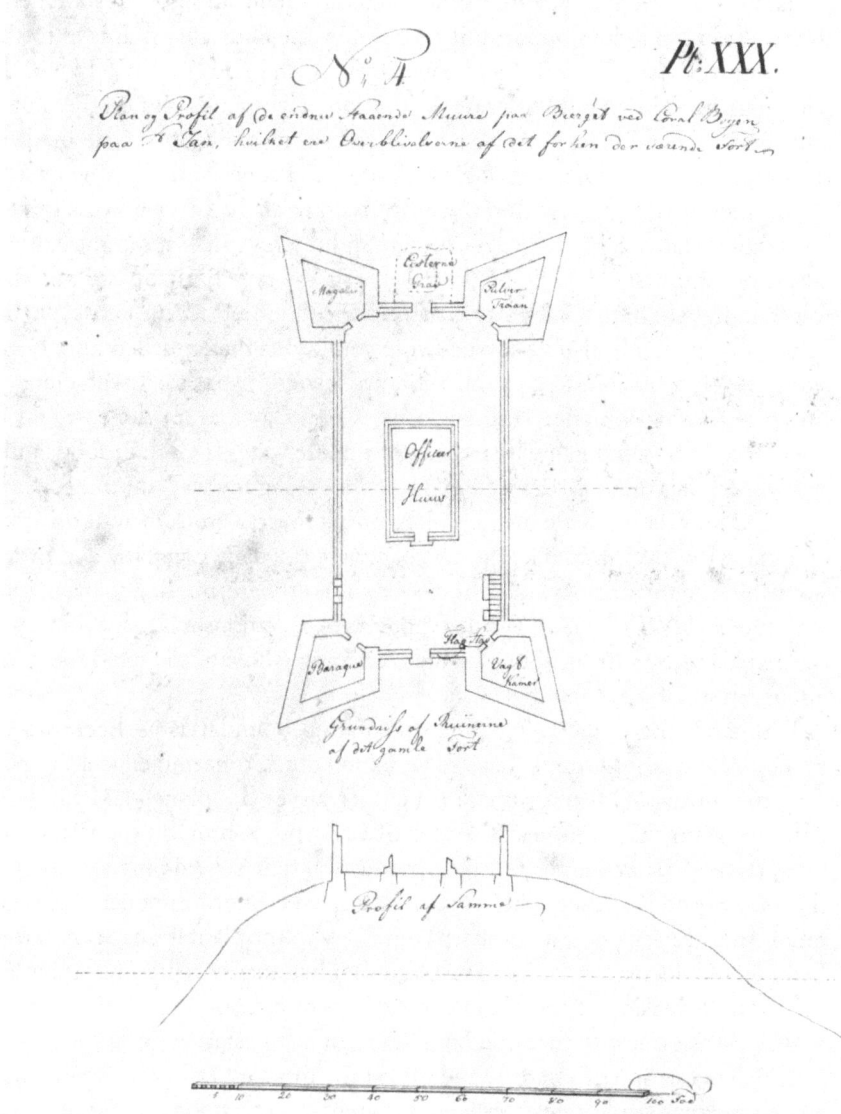

Figure 5.7. Fort at Coral Bay (Oxholm 1780c, Rigsarkivet, Copenhagen).

expenditure of funds on the less strategic fort at Cruz Bay while the fort overlooking Coral Bay remained in a state of ruin.

These maps and their accompanying commentary demonstrate the priorities of Oxholm in pursuing his mapping. Moreover, his notes repeatedly indicate that he was at best unsold on the economic viability of the island and he qualified his recommendations for enhanced fortifications with statements such as "[a] tremendous opportunity is given by the numerous points to fortify and defend St. Jan, if it will ever be worthy of such plans" (DVFV-I 1780). In particular, he pointed out the strategic location of Turner's Point on the southeast entry to Coral Harbor. In fact, no significant modifications were made to the infrastructure of fortifications, a lack of action consistent with the relative importance of the island within the infrastructure of the Danish West Indies.

Oxholm's notes regarding his survey of St. John say much about the cultural landscape of the island. Oxholm described a survey expedition on St. John that was fraught with hardships relating to the difficult terrain of the landscape that he was mapping. He also described living conditions that appalled him. In his survey work, he encountered almost totally isolated "fisher folk" who clung to existence on the points of land enclosing Coral Bay and on the east end of the island: "Yams and fish with a drink of puddle water is all their food, and a stranger among them is regarded as a wonder. Along my way out there, where I roamed for 5 days, a little bread, a piece of salt meat, a crock of water, a crock of wine, with my hammock and my coat, were my daily company and provision; not even my negroes could find nourishment there, but had to bring food with them" (DVFV-I 1780). While Oxholm's observations relate specifically to the eastern section of St. John, for the island as a whole he depicted the ubiquitous nature of impenetrable bush.

Ultimately, he opted not to map plantation boundaries as Beck did on St. Croix, as it would simply have required too much time and expense to perform the cutting of bush required for a proper survey (Hopkins 1988). From his notes we learn that even near the apex of sugar production on the island, the proportion of cleared lands for sugar production represented only a small portion of the overall acreage. The overall landscape was one of impenetrable vegetation and steep slopes—all in sharp contrast with the plantations of St. Croix. Oxholm did document the location of quarter boundaries representing the administrative division of the islands into groups of estates.

The decision not to map the boundaries of each estate reflects the lack of formal demarcation of estate boundaries at the time of Oxholm's survey. General boundaries between estates were apparently understood among the owners, but in many cases the interior boundaries were forested and within difficult terrain and thus never formally defined—at least through survey. This lack of finite boundaries indicates the lack of relative economic importance for such specific divisions and demarcation on St. John. Ultimately, the fact that these boundaries were not documented by Oxholm, as they had been on St. Croix, limited our ability to generate property-based polygons in our GIS database for each estate defined by Oxholm. However, ruins and tangible evidence of archaeological sites were defined for virtually all of the sites recorded by Oxholm. The lack of information on property boundaries led us to emphasize the location of ruins, as they are tangible points associated with activity areas relating to habitation and production. This study examines these site-based data and uses grouped spatial data at the quarter level. Grouped comparative analysis of spatial trends by quarter allows for detailed comparisons of economic activities and demography across the island.[7]

In submitting his 1780 map, Oxholm noted that it was not quite finished but that "the work on paper corresponds in every way to the endless difficulty I had with the surveying" (VIJ 1780). While Oxholm might not have been satisfied, the Royal Court gave praise to this effort noting: "In particular, the large topographic map of St. John, which is the first single map available of this island, distinguishes itself among this handsome collection of maps." Hopkins's examination of Danish records indicates that in addition to his agreed-upon salary and expenses, "the King rewarded Oxholm with a douceur of one thousand rigsdaler" (VIFR 1781–1782).

The history behind the 1800 map is not as clear and concise. We know that Oxholm had married a daughter of a St. Croix planter.[8] The 1800 map appears to have been a self-published version perhaps, as was customary at this time, on a contracted subscription basis for planters, businessmen, and island administrators. However, we do know that this new map reflected a detailed revision of land ownership that is accurate and consistent with the formal taxed properties that correspond with the 1800 tax list. In addition, the map reflects a significant change in the definition of properties that is probably linked to a rapid turnover in plantation ownership in the 20 years between the first map and its successor. The index to the 1800 map is keyed to plantations that are defined by geographic place names rather than owners, as it had been in 1780. This is an important shift that is a key element of our interpretive examination of the island's changing cultural landscape.

The details relating to the production of Oxholm's maps are essential to the understanding of the cultural landscape of St. John in the era in which the maps were produced. From this record, it is clear that the primary reasons motivating the construction of maps were (1) the need to document defenses and fortifications and (2) the need to obtain a more complete picture of land use than could be gained by simply reading the tax records. The late-eighteenth-century setting defines limitations in data collection that impact our ability to generate explicit site boundaries. Hence, while quarter boundaries are clearly depicted and can be used to generate polygons for direct comparison, for this era we cannot rely on maps to generate accurate, time-specific polygons for each individual estate. In fact, later mapping done to define lands for tax purposes at the time of transfer of lands to the United States provides a fairly accurate set of estate boundaries for most of the island. However, in initially focusing on the 1780 and 1800 maps we have not fully incorporated these polygons as we have yet to calibrate the records from the period of transfer (early twentieth century) with the estates of the eighteenth century. Such refinements are planned for follow-up projects as we focus on thematic questions relating to issues such as the social impacts of the transition from the Danish administration to the United States administration (one of several thematic studies that are now under way).

THE PRESENT GIS STUDY: RECONSTRUCTING CULTURAL LANDSCAPES

The island of St. John, United States Virgin Islands (formerly the Danish West Indies), presents an excellent opportunity to use advances in technology and knowledge of archival sources to compile archaeological and historical data in a unified GIS. The advantages of carrying out a whole-island archaeological and historical GIS on St. John (see Cowen 1990; Kvamme 1995) include (1) excellent, but previously untapped, archival resources, (2) the preservation of a significant portion of the island in Virgin Islands National Park, (3) the general preservation of sites throughout the island linked with a relatively small island population through much of the twentieth century (until the rapid expansion of tourism and settlement beginning in the 1970s), (4) the fact that nearly all sites are easily defined on the surface using standard walking survey technique, and (5) progressive resource managers who would like to expand and enhance the information in the island's archaeological site inventories to make these data more useful in preservation planning.[9]

The St. John GIS yields a synthesis of spatially linked GIS data for St. John for the era of Oxholm's maps (1780–1800). This study represents a transition from focusing on individual sites—in isolation—to an integration of a multiscalar examination of the cultural landscape of St. John using GIS. The study goes beyond simply recording the largest and most obvious sugar estates and attempts to identify the full range of living settings including small-scale settlements, freeholdings, and post-emancipation inholdings.[10]

ANALYSIS AND FINDINGS

We created a GIS base map using a combination of aerial photographic maps of the island. We then plotted all data on a 1994 color mosaic image and ESRI overlays (Figure 5.8). This GIS map allows us to "bridge" between historically defined space (from the Oxholm map), actual site location (GPS points generated from survey; Figure 5.9), and documentation of land use from the *matricals* and other sources of historic information.[11] We began by locating and

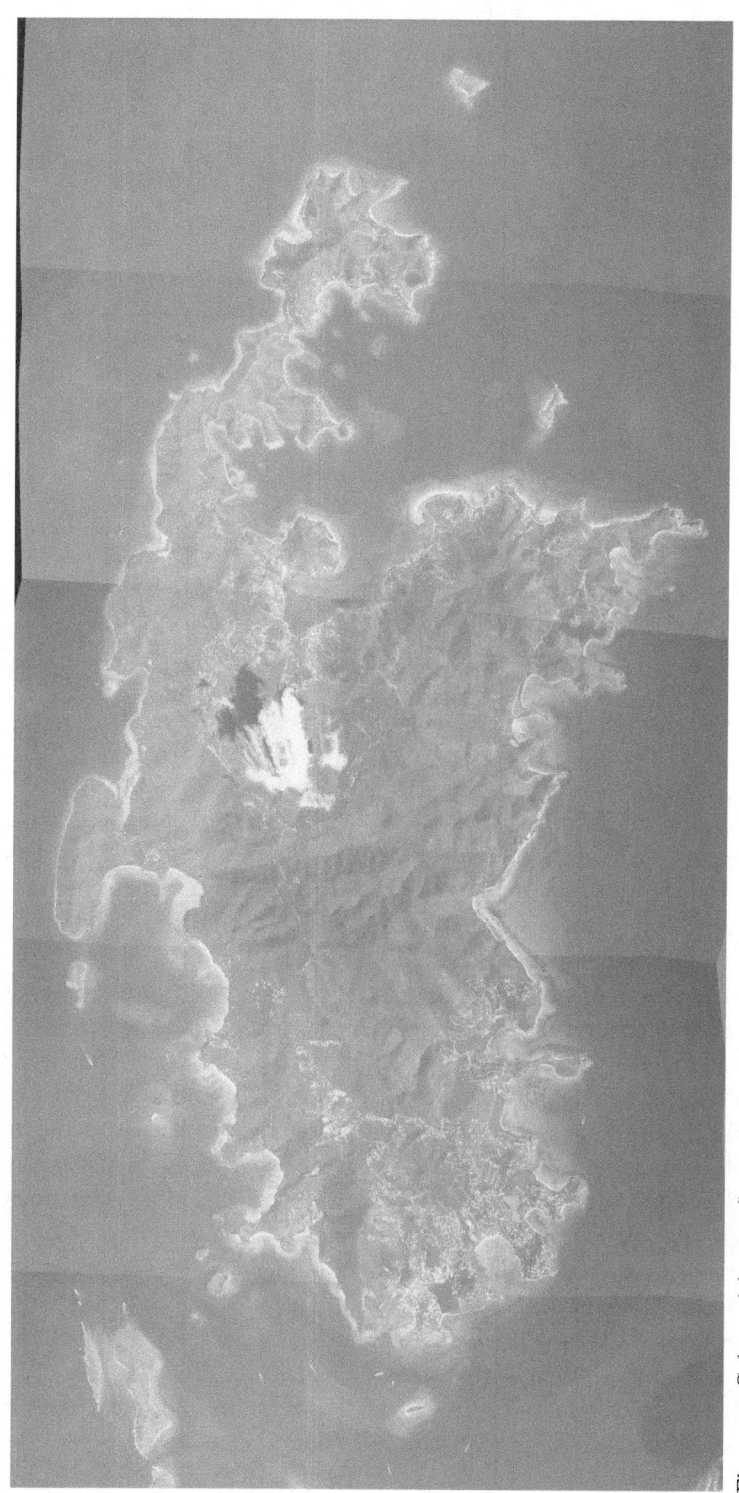

Figure 5.8. Color aerial survey/base map, 1994.

Figure 5.9. Field survey: Mark Hauser using GPS to locate sites.

plotting sites on the calibrated overlay of 1780 and 1800 data onto a base map (Figure 5.10). The information from the *matricals*, as well as other data sets (historical information, archaeological studies, Historic American Buildings Survey/Historic American Engineering Record [HABS/HAER]), was then linked to points defining each individual site.

A comparison of data from 1780 and 1800 allows us to explore trends and changes in the cultural and economic landscapes. As part of this survey, we gathered more detailed information on a group of six estates (Annaberg, Cinnamon Bay, Reef Bay, Browns Bay, Caneel, and Concordia). The data generated for these estates include detailed documentation that spans the history of each estate (details on findings relating to these estates are in the National Park Service database and are reported elsewhere, including Armstrong and Hauser 2005; Armstrong et al. 2006). The data include multiple GIS points (reflecting the overall layout of ruins and middens), as well as more detailed historical documentation and archaeological reconnaissance (including information from National Register nominations, HABS/HAER documentation, site reports, and detailed historical assessment).

The GIS allowed us to graph trends and patterns and to show their distribution in space (Figure 5.11). The GIS plot of sites shows a wide distribu-

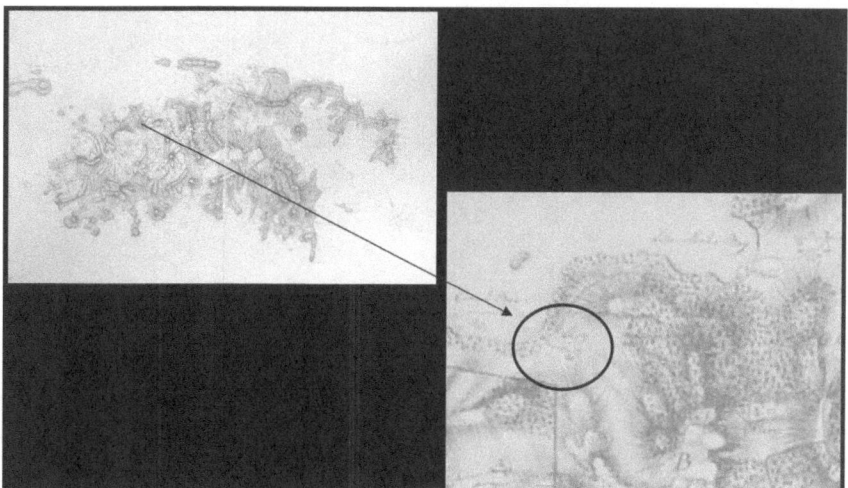

Figure 5.10. Identification of historic sites (illustration is Cinnamon Bay Plantation).

tion of historic sites across the landscape of St. John. The physical distribution of sites changes little during the period from 1780 to 1800. This is because all of the lands on the island had been formally distributed among landowners and the estates identified by Oxholm represent the habitation sites associated with each taxable property on the island. Nearly all of the parcels defined on the 1780 map are still extant, at least in terms of taxable purposes, in 1800. However, a close examination will show that in fact there are a few more points represented on the 1800 map. Note also that Oxholm keyed his map to the tax records for the time at which his map was produced. Not only are estates and parcels indexed numerically by quarter but also the respective quarter boundaries are drawn on his map and could be reconstructed in the GIS. Hence, we not only are able to plot sites but also can group clusters of sites according to the quarter of the island in which they are located.

Once all of the sites were defined through archaeological survey and plotting into the GIS we could integrate information from the tax records. The first variable that we examined was how each parcel was being used. The tax records from this era generalize production into a range of categories relating to the primary crops that were grown. Thus, each site was designated as a sugar, cotton, or provisioning estate. In essence, any estate on which sugar was produced was defined as a sugar estate for taxation purposes, even if cotton was produced and part of its land was used for provisioning. If no sugar was being produced but cotton was grown it would be defined as a cotton estate, again for tax purposes even if provisions were grown. The final category was a provisioning estate, which in essence indicated that no taxable commodities were

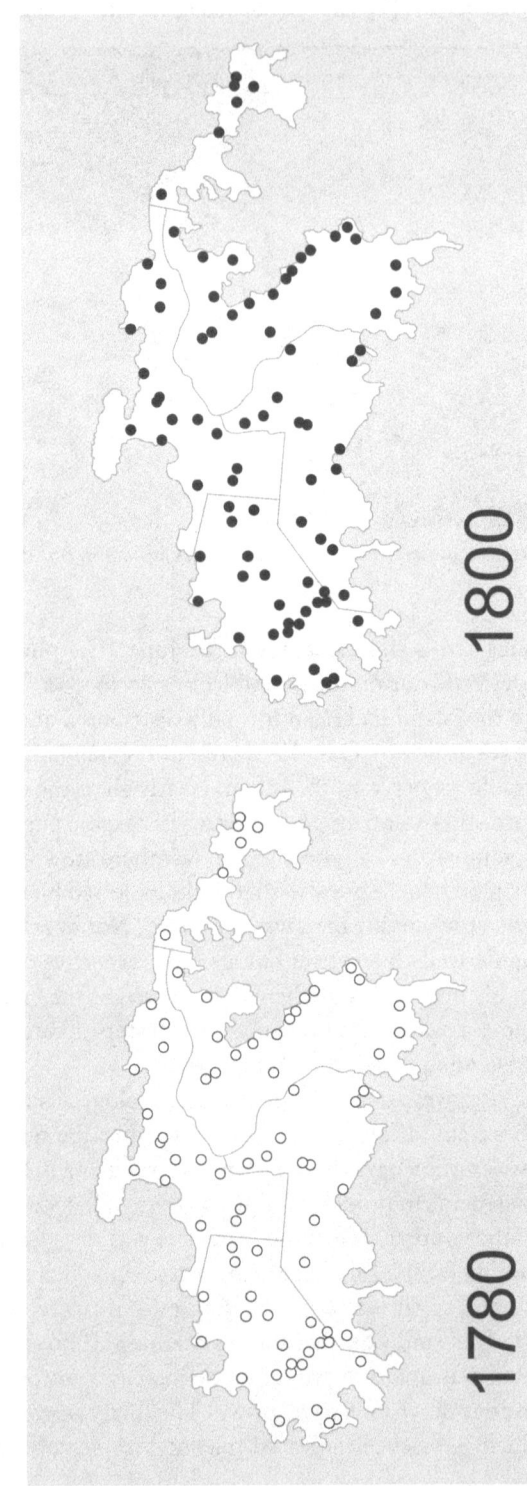

Figure 5.11. GIS plot of sites dating to 1780 and 1800 (quarter boundaries also shown).

being produced on the property (hence, no recorded production of either sugar or cotton). Using the GIS we were able to code and plot the primary economic production indicated in the tax records for each estate associated with 1780 and 1800. These data showed significant trends in the distribution of production across the island with sugar estates concentrated on the north coast and central segments of the island. The grouped quarter data allowed us to present summary pie charts of the relative proportion of each type of agricultural production across the island. Among other things, these pie charts show a trend toward even more substantial use of the Maho Quarter for sugar production in 1800 and an overall higher proportion of provision estates throughout the rest of the island for this latter period (Figure 5.12). This change in crop production can be correlated with other variables including the distribution of unfree (enslaved) laborers across the island. Between 1780 and 1800, there was a significant shift in laborers to the Maho and Reef Bay quarters of the island. Figure 5.13 illustrates this change using grouped polygon data plotting the number of enslaved laborers for each quarter of the island.

We found that, even within the limited 1780–1800 time frame of this initial study, we were able to document significant, heretofore undocumented, transitions taking place that reflected dynamic cultural and economic change within Danish West Indian plantation society. While this study focuses on the basic integration of maps, *matricals,* and material remains, our analysis has generated significant findings on trends in land use that because of space considerations must be discussed in detail elsewhere (see, for example, Armstrong and Hauser 2005, Armstrong et al. 2006, and Armstrong et al. 2007). The data indicate that a shift was taking place in the cultural landscape of the island. We have described this shift as reflecting a dual divergence. Not only were sugar estates consolidating (as indicated in the pie charts of Figure 5.12 and the demography of Figure 5.13) but also the non–sugar estates either were being abandoned or were being taken up by a growing number of free persons of color. The Danish tradition of openness to planters and traders of many nationalities, and the pragmatic recognition of any persons opting to settle the island along with the paucity of regulations for conditions on plantations, provided the ambiguous opening that allowed free colored, many of whom were the mulatto sons and daughters of plantation owners, to acquire property including both lands and enslaved laborers (see Armstrong et al. 2006).

The data illuminate an interesting duality and divergence within the cultural and economic landscape, clearly reflected in (1) the consolidation of sugar estates under a few key planters and (2) the early emergence of a free colored group who became owners of both land (cotton and provisioning estates) and slaves. The two findings appear incongruent, reflecting movement in two directions at once. The evidence for consolidation was expected and reflects the

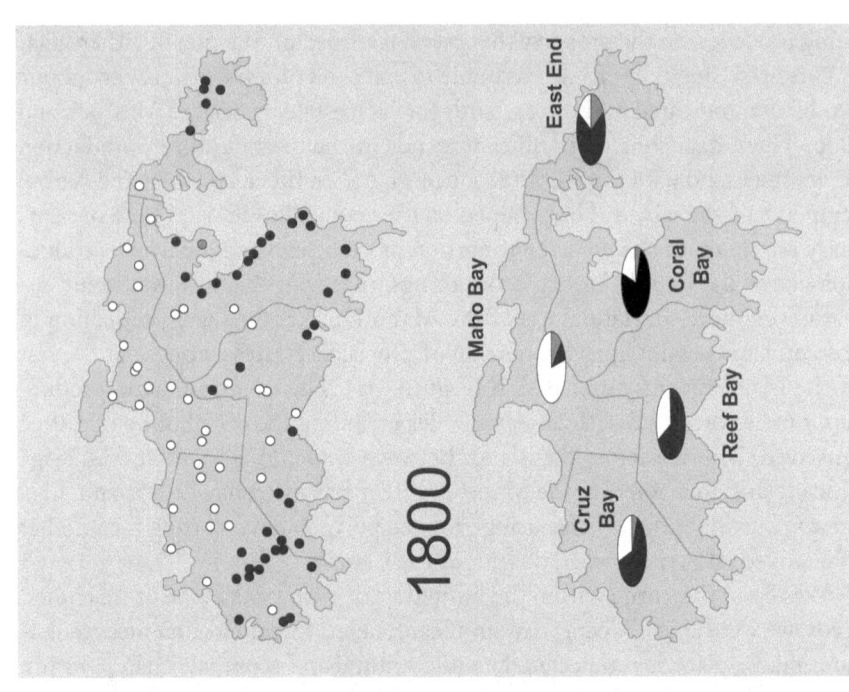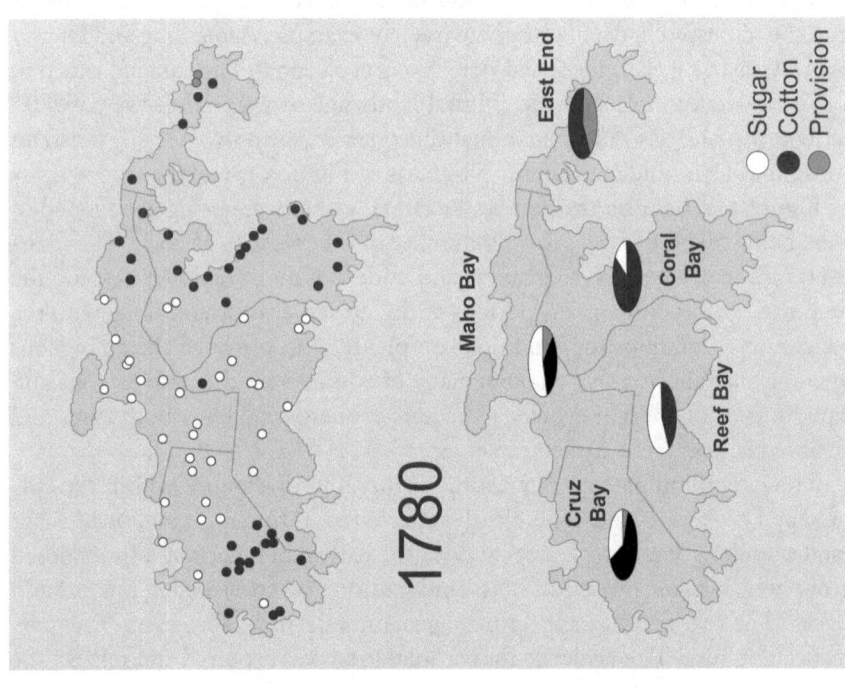

Figure 5.12. Plantation production by estate and quarter (sugar, cotton, provision), 1780 versus 1800.

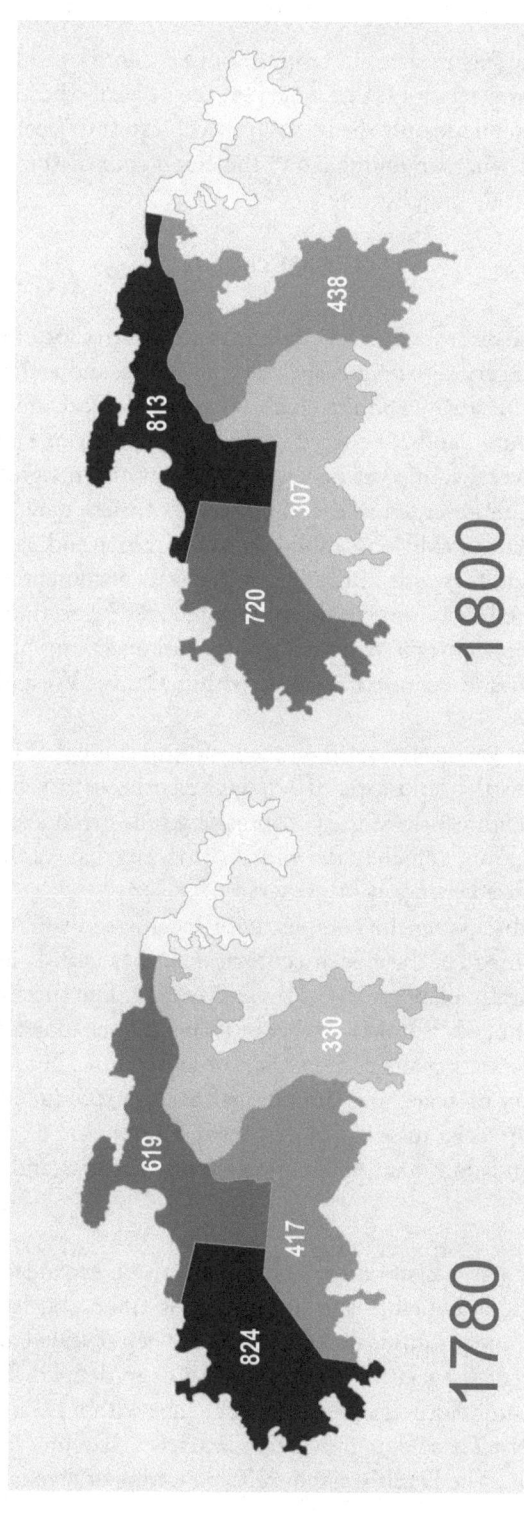

Figure 5.13. Change in distribution of unfree (enslaved) population from 1780 to 1800.

dominance of the sugar estates in terms of both economic production and demography of power relations. We came into the project expecting that during this period we would see only the initial traces of a shift to freeholdings on the island. However, what we found shows the emergence of this pattern earlier and more extensively than expected.

CONCLUSION

This study uses data from Peter Oxholm's maps (1780–1800) in combination with satellite imagery, documents such as tax records, and archaeological survey information on site location to create an archaeological and historical GIS of St. John's cultural landscape for the years 1780 and 1800. The examination of these data reveals subtle yet pertinent information on significant cultural changes that are represented in the intersection of these data sets. The study achieved its goal of establishing a solid baseline for longitudinal studies working backwards and forwards in time from this well-documented era. In addition, we discovered that even within this limited 1780–1800 time frame we see significant, yet previously undocumented, transitions taking place that reflect dynamic cultural and economic change within Danish West Indian plantation society.

In this chapter we have focused on the historical context of Oxholm's maps in relationship to the landscape of late-eighteenth-century St. John. Information on late-eighteenth-century mapmaking tells much about the cultural landscape of St. John, a small island with an economy that was marginal to the primary sugar-based economy of the region.

Higman, in discussing the complexity of local island variation and diversity within the broader Caribbean context, describes islands like St. John as a "laboratory within a laboratory" (Higman 1995:9). The specific historic trajectory of St. John, while linked to that of its neighbors, took a different path. In this particular setting the combination of ambiguities in Danish administration, smallness of scale, and limitations for sugar production opened the door to forms of social interaction that were at once part of and in variance to the formal and dominant economic systems of sugar and slavery in the region.

St. John now has a historic sites GIS that can be expanded upon to deal with the time periods before and after the 1780–1800 era. Even though its time frame is limited, significant patterns have been revealed and new, previously undocumented social relationships have been defined. The transitions seen reflect dynamic cultural and economic change within Danish West Indian plantation society. These data provide an important baseline for comparisons within the region. The Danish islands reflect a setting of diversity and variance within the broader regional economy that should be considered when addressing the overall pattern of plantation and slave economies in the region.

The project addresses questions that bridge intellectual pursuits with sound preservation practice. It brings together university (Syracuse faculty and student) and agency (National Park Service and United States Virgin Islands territorial archaeologists) personnel to generate a versatile GIS database that can be used by scholars, students, preservation planners, and the local community to expand our understanding of the networks of social interaction that were in play in eighteenth-century to early twentieth-century St. John. The initial phase of this project has already dramatically improved the quality of site file data for cultural resource management on the island. From our perspective as researchers, it is our goal to use these data to address significant questions on African Creole land use. This initial study demonstrates both the utility and complexities of the cultural landscape and the compilation of spatially integrated data. As an expression of interest and support for this project, both agencies provided seed funding used in the preparation of this proposal and for initial tests of survey strategies and both will incorporate the data generated into preservation planning.

As the project moves forward, examining new data sets and expanding its time frame and base of research questions, the island-wide archaeological and historical GIS will provide a unified database for the cultural landscape of St. John. The baseline data generated for the GIS will expand and be an excellent means of solving research problems while assisting in the preservation of the full spectrum of historic sites on the island.

NOTES

1. *Matricals* are detailed land tax records recorded annually by the Danish colonial government and housed in the Rigsarkivet in Copenhagen, Denmark. These records were transcribed and translated by David Knight. This project was funded in part by grants from the National Park Service, the Friends of Virgin Islands National Park, Syracuse University Continuing Education and Summer Sessions, and the College of Arts and Sciences of Syracuse University.

2. A "quarter" represents an administrative division of the island that is roughly equivalent to a county or parish. For this chapter, we will focus on a comparison of the Maho and Coral Bay quarters.

3. In fact, a manuscript relief map of St. Croix had been produced by Johan Cronenberg in 1750, but it was held by the Danish Admiralty and was apparently unknown to the Chamber of Customs.

4. As an indication of priorities, "situation maps" of forts and harbors were to be done first.

5. This map collection is currently housed in the National Library and is one of

the finest in the world. The Oxholm maps are housed separately in the Rigsarkivet in Copenhagen.

6. While awaiting orders, Oxholm traveled through the Lesser Antilles and was expelled upon arrival in Martinique for being a spy. Apparently, they were concerned about his keen interest in fortifications. On the way back to the Dutch West Indies Oxholm's vessel and possessions were taken by British privateers. As a consequence he asked for a significant retroactive increase in pay in compensation for his losses and for the cost of appearing before the British Admiralty court at Nevis and for the looting of his baggage. He described himself as nearly ruined and in his correspondence to the Chamber he stated that "he would prefer to be relieved of his position, while yet strength and years allowed him to seek his bread elsewhere" (VIJ 1779).

7. We anticipate generating parcel-specific polygons once we have incorporated the tax map records associated with transfer of the Danish West Indies to the United States. Using this information we can then generate a series of hypothetical estate boundaries by integrating spatial data from tax maps dating to the early twentieth century with the Oxholm maps and relative spatial information recorded in the *matricals* that span the history of Danish colonial occupation.

8. Correspondence shows that in 1784 he received word that the Chamber had mislaid all his drawings and wished to be provided with a new set and that the effort to redraw these maps resulted in a renewal of survey work on his part over the next two years. Oxholm and his supporters attempted to have his map formally published by the Crown but this effort was not successful.

9. Kenneth Wild (National Park Service, Archaeologist for the Virgin Islands National Park) has built the construction of this type of database into the park's planning and has already begun the process of carrying out GPS surveys of known ruins within the park. David Brewer (Territorial Archaeologist, with the Department of Natural Resources and Planning—State Historic Preservation Office) has provided us with encouragement in the initial planning phases.

10. For instance, we can create data categories to account for individuals whose names appear on the tax list as owners of property other than real estate (non-landed holdings may also include slaves and animal stock).

11. In fact, the data presented here represent only a historical slice of the overall historic sites GIS that is being constructed for use by the National Park Service and the territorial archaeologist; this GIS will be used as a database in which to compile all historic and prehistoric sites on the island.

6
Understanding Nevis
GPS and Archaeological Field Survey in a Postcolonial Landscape

Roger H. Leech

An archaeological perspective is used to better understand the settlement and subsequent exploitation of colonial Nevis, to provide an understanding of a period of history studied largely by historians working from documents. The island of Nevis presents particular problems to the archaeologist studying the colonial landscape. Most of the earliest land records for the island were destroyed by the French in 1706. The earliest adequate maps are of the mid-twentieth century, by which time much of the landscape laid out and farmed in the colonial period had been re-enveloped in forest and scrub. Archaeological field survey making use of handheld GPS provides a means of recording this abandoned landscape. Research in progress is now providing a new understanding of the transformation of the island. It is possible to see now a more complex variability of plantations and estates, from the seventeenth century onwards. Field survey and the use of GPS have been especially informative in revealing the abandonment of plantations or absence of investment on the cleared uppermost slopes and in providing insights into the process of estate consolidation.

The Nevis Heritage Project was initiated by the Department of Archaeology at the University of Southampton, England, in 1999 (see Nevis Heritage Project 2007). Archaeological field survey utilizing GPS has proved to be critical to meeting one of the research aims of the project: to understand better the settlement and subsequent exploitation of colonial Nevis, from the seventeenth century onwards.[1] Current understanding of the colonization of the English Leeward Islands in the seventeenth century is based almost entirely on documentary research. Historical studies point to the need for an archaeological perspective. Dunn's single chapter on "life in the tropics" highlights the lack of archaeological data: "nearly all the early houses on the islands have long since disappeared, victims of storms, fires and tropical rot" (Dunn 1972:287). On Nevis the early abandonment of sugar or any other cultivation on much of the island has ensured the preservation of early landscapes susceptible to archaeological field survey. An archaeological perspective is intended to provide new insights into a period of history until recently studied largely by historians working from documents.

Nevis presents particular problems to the landscape archaeologist. Maps of the colonial landscape are conspicuous by their absence. Maps of Nevis were certainly made in the seventeenth century, but they do not survive (Leech n.d.). One such map must have formed the basis of the subdivision of the island into parishes and divisions and may have formed the basis for the map referred to in 1678 as Mr. Hilton's map (Hilton 1678). Iles's map of 1871, the first to show the settlement of the island in detail (Iles 1871), shows many plantations in what is now forest. However, Iles's map does not show land divisions and boundaries, and overall the cartography is grossly inaccurate. It is best described as an armchair map, drawn at home from recollection. Burdon's map of 1920 is similarly inaccurate, being derived from Iles's map (Burdon 1920). The map of 1848 by Captain Barnett is much more accurate, but it does not show land divisions (Barnett and assistants 1848). There is no mapping of Nevis comparable to that for St. Kitts, where McMahon's maps show all land divisions and the sites of all the slave villages (see McMahon 1828). The earliest island-wide maps to show land divisions are of 1959 and of the 1970s, by the Directorate of Overseas Surveys; the settled parts of the island were mapped at 1:2,500, the remaining areas at 1:25,000. At both scales, these map series depend heavily on aerial photography of areas often largely concealed by the forest canopy (Directorate of Overseas Surveys 1959, 1975). By these dates forest and scrub covered much of the former plantation landscape. To reconstruct the estates and enclosed fields now concealed by forest it is necessary to turn to documentary research, aerial photography, and archaeological field survey.

ARCHAEOLOGICAL FIELD SURVEY USING GPS

Archaeological field survey has here been of particular value, notably for the majority of former estates for which no detailed estate maps survive. We have used a combination of methodologies for field survey. Reconnaissance has been through systematic quartering of the ground for the identification of earthwork and stone-walled features and sites. For the survey of plantation centers, planters' houses, works, farms, and slave villages, survey has been based on the use of total stations and/or baselines and offsets using optical squares for the establishment of right angles, following European traditions of archaeological field survey as exemplified in Britain through the work of the Royal Commissions on Historical Monuments (English Heritage 2002). These methodologies are, however, inappropriate for many of the features to be recorded, which are often widely spaced within dense woodland, notably roads, tracks, field boundaries, and the occasional boundary markers. Locating these archaeological features within the landscape and within the known geodetic framework would be a major problem without GPS, requiring complex survey and much clearance—as is conventionally undertaken for cadastral land survey today. GPS has provided the solution to these problems, and without GPS and President Clinton's removal of selective availability we could not be undertaking this survey.

Financial constraints and practical considerations have led to the use of navigation-grade GPS for survey (English Heritage 2003). Mapping-grade and survey-grade GPS have not been used on account of expense, weight in the field, and the added difficulties of using this equipment within a heavily forested environment. We have found that handheld navigation-grade GPS works well in forest, often supplemented by a handheld aerial.[2] In the Caribbean, the Wide Area Augmentation System (WAAS) differential satellite is accessible and generally the satellite coverage seems much better than in Europe, possibly because of the United States's defense interests in the Caribbean or because of the proximity of the equator. The accuracy of the handheld navigation-grade GPS when tested against known Directorate of Overseas Surveys triangulation stations reaches 1–2 m. For the survey of landscapes, to be examined in print at scales of 1:1,000 or less, this is very adequate.

For the downloading of data we have used the software supplied by Gartrip, which was developed, in the first instance, for the German hiking community (Gartrip 2007). In particular, this software meets the need to be able to download the data in a format in which it can be used in conjunction with the available government mapping at 1:25,000 and 1:2,500, based on the relevant map grid and datum.[3] The Gartrip software was selected after a review of the software for downloading then available. What this software has lacked is the capability to download the data in a format suitable for CAD and GIS software, in formats such as industry-standard AutoCAD DXF.

RESULTS

Analysis of the colonial landscape using archaeological field survey has contributed to answering a series of questions: Was there an overall plan for the subdivision of the island by the first English settlers? Were all plantations centered on "great houses" (the "*Gone with the Wind*" stereotype) and, if not, what was the variability of wealth across the planter community? How extensive was the clearance of the indigenous vegetation?

Mapping estate boundaries from cartographic, aerial photographic, and field survey data indicates that the island was subdivided into a series of divisions (Figure 6.1). These were known in the seventeenth century as "divisions" and were possibly first mapped from the sea. The enigmatic Mr. Hilton's map noted above was possibly a scenographic map similar to those that survive for Montserrat. The first settlers then followed compass directions to set out boundaries between one estate and the next. This use of compass directions helps to explain the extreme regularity of the layout of the estates on the island. The divisions then formed administrative units for the organization of the militia and were utilized for the formation of ecclesiastical parishes.

Detailed mapping has been undertaken of the plantation at Mountravers (Figure 6.2). Documentary evidence indicated that this plantation was extended in the mid-eighteenth century with the acquisition of a smaller plantation known as Woodland. The site of Woodland was discovered in the course of field survey and the detailed plan of the plantation is located in the wider landscape using GPS reference points. Survey indicates that the site of the plantation house, a small dwelling 43 feet in length by 15 feet wide, was emphatically not a "great house."

GPS mapping facilitated the survey and planning of a plantation named by us "Upper Woodland," one of a number of abandoned plantation centers above the 1,000-foot contour (Figure 6.3). The identification of these abandoned plantation nuclei, all with structures characteristic of the eighteenth century and earlier, enables us to construct a hypothetical model for the ebb and flow of plantation agriculture on these higher slopes.

To illustrate: in the second half of the seventeenth century, the rapid growth of a sugar-based economy spurred settlers to clear lands for sugar cane cultivation to the highest points possible (Dunn 1972:19–25). With the onset of erosion, from hurricanes and tropical storms, the upper limit of cultivation then gradually dropped, leaving an abandoned landscape of the seventeenth century to be mapped by GPS as part of the Nevis Heritage Project. Currently, one such plantation, Upper Rawlins, is being investigated through further survey and excavation.

A second aspect of past land use identified through field survey has been the construction of out-of-town villas by the wealthier planters and merchants in the colonial period. On the slopes above Charlestown a number of such dwellings have been identified, often characterized by attached planned formal gardens and by being separate from the sugar works. Once such sites have been surveyed, GPS has situated their location within the wider landscape, for instance, Parris's Garden (Figure 6.4), the villa of one Edward Parris, whose plantation and works were lower down the slopes of the mountain.

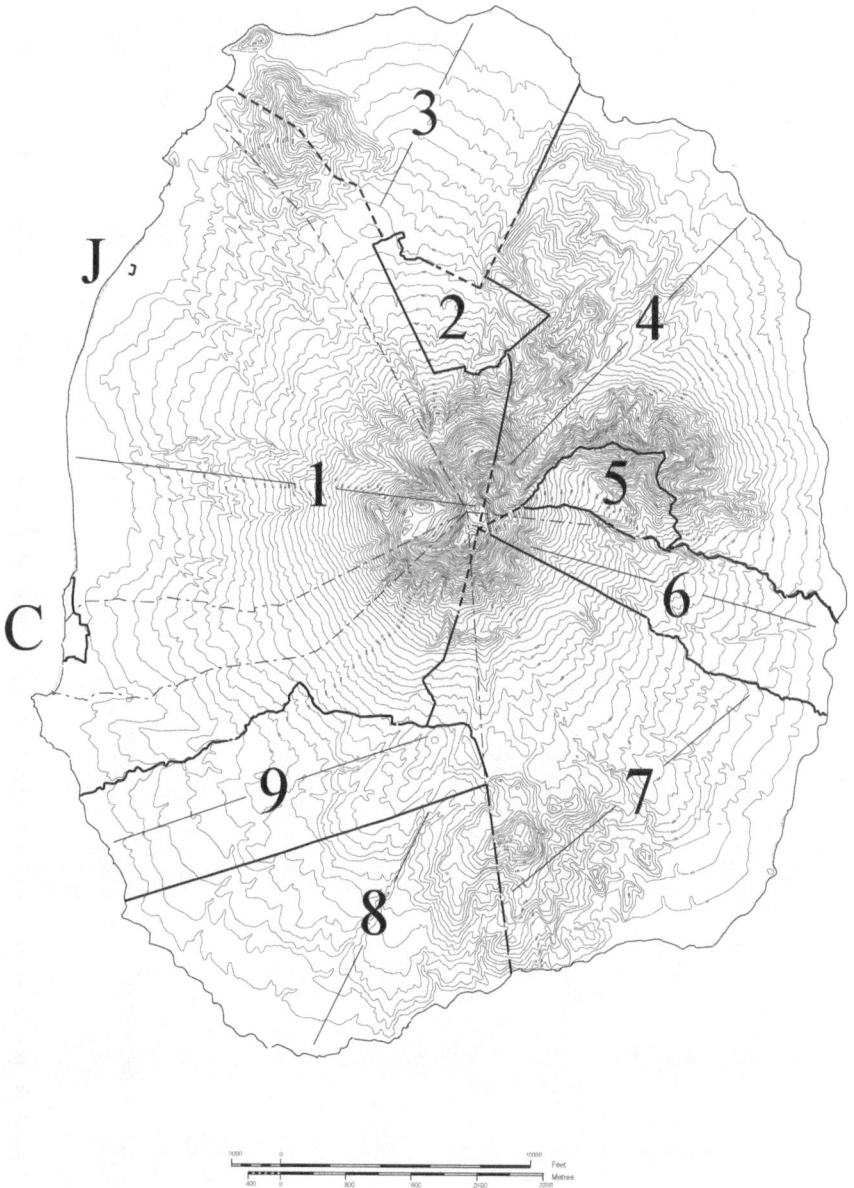

Figure 6.1. Map of Nevis showing the "divisions." J, Jamestown; C, Charlestown.

Figure 6.2. Mountravers: the plantation landscape. Features on the map of 1879 augmented by features located by GPS survey.

UPPER WOODLAND NW, NEVIS

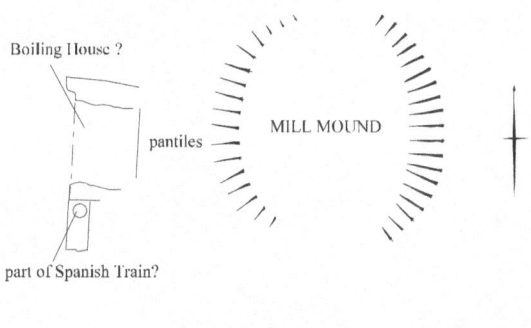

UPPER WOODLAND SE, NEVIS

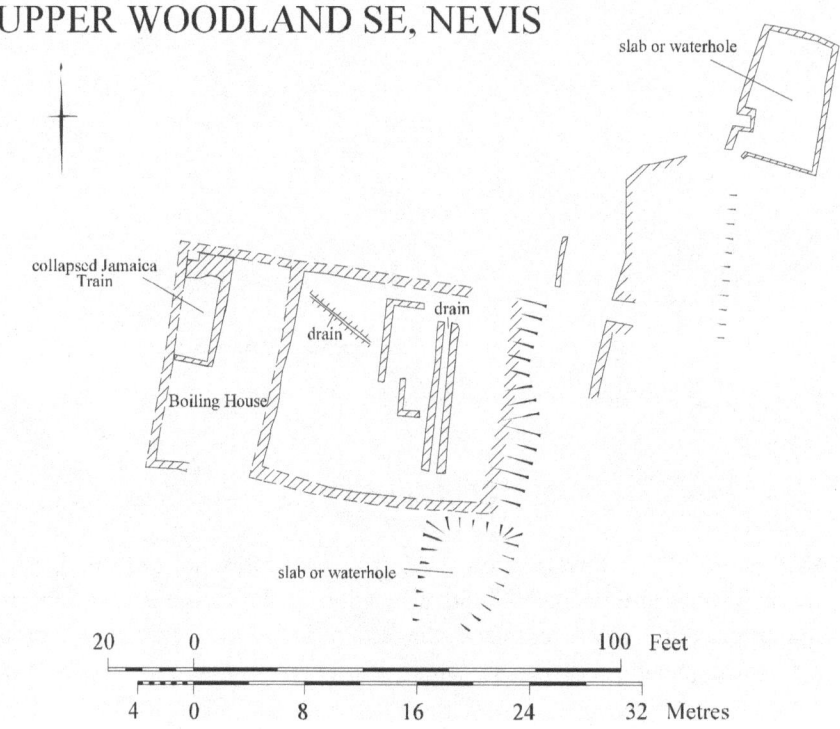

Figure 6.3. Upper Woodland plantation, plans from archaeological survey.

PARRIS'S GARDEN, NEVIS

Figure 6.4. Parris's Garden, an eighteenth-century villa.

CONCLUSION

Without GPS and the relaxation of selective availability, none of this research would have been possible.[4] The identification of the divisions that form the framework of the colonized island, the recognition of the retreat of cultivation from the higher ground, the location of abandoned plantation centers here and on the lower slopes, and the location of villas have all been much facilitated through the use of GPS.

A useful development for the future would be to move away from navigation-grade to mapping-grade GPS. At first sight the move of GPS to PDA-type pocket computers holds out one such possibility, since the PDA can be much more easily loaded with existing mapping, but I have to date agreed with the Gartrip web site, which warns against the use of these devices on account of their poor weatherproofing (Gartrip 2007). The Garmin handheld receivers used on this project are aimed primarily at dingy sailors and are able to float. This has not yet proved necessary, but these receivers have proved ideal for use in the tropical storms and showers that intermittently sweep across Nevis Peak. It is, however, clear that there will be a convergence between PDA and GPS technologies, and already the manufacturers of GPS devices are moving toward offering PDA devices that have the necessary weatherproofing.[5]

ACKNOWLEDGMENTS

I wish to thank the following: The British Academy, Morning Star Holdings, and Vince Hubbard for financial assistance; Nicole Smith for web-site assistance; staff of the Nevis Court House for assistance in research; Mrs. Pamela Leech for much help in the preparation of the manuscript; Dr. Elaine Morris and other staff of Southampton University for project support; Dr. Rob Philpott and Mr. Edward Herbert for assistance with fieldwork.

NOTES

1. For help with GPS-based survey, I must thank especially Mr. Russell Fox, formerly of the Ordnance Survey, for all his assistance; also President Bill Clinton for the removal of selective availability; and also Heinrich Pfeifer of Gartrip and staff of Garmin (U.K.) based in Romsey, Hampshire.

2. We have used handheld Garmin receivers, the 12XL and Map 76.

3. The British West Indies Grid data are printed on the published maps; the data for the map datum, Clarke 1880 (Modified), were obtained from the Overseas Survey Section of the Ordnance Survey (1984), Southampton, United Kingdom:

DA   −112.145 m
DF   −0.000054750714
DX   +9 m

DY   +183 m
DZ   +236 m

4. *This research would have been impossible without President Clinton's removal of selective availability in 2000.*

5. At the time of writing, Trimble is offering a weatherproof handheld GPS that runs Archpad in a Windows Mobile environment.

7
The Use of Imagery to Locate Taino Sites in Jamaica in a GIS Environment

Parris Lyew-Ayee and Ivor Conolley

The Tainos, formerly referred to as Arawaks, developed within the Greater Antilles roughly 1,000–1,500 years ago and were the primary inhabitants of Jamaica prior to Columbus's arrival in 1494. Over 23 Taino settlement sites have, to date, been accidentally discovered in Trelawny, a parish located in north-central Jamaica. The following study will utilize aerial photographs, photogrammetry, multispectral satellite imagery, and three-dimensional images within a geographic information systems (GIS) environment to create a physical profile of Taino locations in Trelawny, Jamaica. This is designed to produce predictive models of where Taino sites are likely to be found in the parish. The use of imagery poses significant limitations, as not only does Trelawny have thick canopy covers but also obviously no aerial photographic record of the parish existed during the time of the Tainos 500 years ago. However, this study proposes to mitigate this problem by conducting global positioning systems (GPS)-assisted field investigations.

Geoinformatics provides the wherewithal to efficiently and comprehensively study archaeological sites as well as reveal considerable information on past cultures in the Caribbean region. With reference to Trelawny, a parish in north-central Jamaica, this chapter will demonstrate how an integrated use of geographic information systems (GIS) technologies, global positioning systems (GPS) imagery, and digital maps enables researchers to conduct site reconnaissance, detailed on-site mapping, and post-fieldwork analysis of an area of interest in the Caribbean. The study not only pulls together different and diverse data sets but also takes advantage of recent advancements in digital image collection, which have led to rapid land-use classification by means of infrared imagery and three-dimensional surface models created from stereo-imagery. The ultimate objective of this study is to provide models for efficiently isolating likely Taino sites in Trelawny. These models are based, to a considerable extent, on existing knowledge of Taino cultural practices. Given their centrality to this study, a brief discussion of the Tainos and the parish of Falmouth is presented below.

THE TAINOS

The Tainos, formerly referred to as the Arawaks, constituted a distinct cultural group in the Greater Antilles around A.D. 600 to A.D. 1500. They were the primary inhabitants of Jamaica prior to the arrival of Columbus in 1494. The Tainos had an ordered social structure and lived a largely agrarian lifestyle. They lived in houses made from wood and thatch, with the chief or *cacique* occupying a rectangular building, a *bohio,* while ordinary Tainos lived in circular *caneys* (Rouse 1992:10; Wilson 1990:57). Their way of life was largely centered around the natural environment on which they subsisted. They grew their root crop, cassava, on mounds of earth or *conucos.* They used cotton trees for making boats and used gourds from calabash trees for dishes and utensils. Pots were fashioned from clay. Taino sites are usually identifiable by the presence of pottery sherds, bones, seashells, and terrestrial gastropods in large quantities inland and beads as well as petroglyphs (rock carvings) in caves or in rockshelters.[1] Since the Tainos used cotton and calabash and thatch palms either to make artifacts or to build their *caneys* and *bohios,* the presence of such flora also serves to identify potential Taino sites. Additionally, the Tainos in Jamaica preferred to settle on hilltops and near rivers or ponds (Allsworth-Jones et al. 1999; Howard 1965).

TRELAWNY

The principal area of interest for this research is the parish of Trelawny, where early research by Dr. James Lee and ongoing research on the pre-Columbian peoples by the University of the West Indies have uncovered 23 Taino sites. These discoveries were either accidental or were based on information provided by locals. The parish of Trelawny (Figure 7.1), located in north-central Jamaica, is largely a karst landscape (Day 1978; Lyew-Ayee 2004; Sweeting 1957), with many notable features such as caves and karstic springs that may have been associated with the Taino way of life. The Cockpit Country, located in southern Trelawny, is an extremely rugged karst landscape that has been largely undisturbed and, as a result of its inaccessibility to both Tainos and modern archaeologists, has yielded few Taino artifacts. The bulk of this chapter focuses on the basin of the Martha Brae, whose origins are within the Cockpit Country but which rises from multiple springs along the northern edge of the Cockpit Country (UNDP/FAO 1972).

The Martha Brae itself flows north from Windsor to Falmouth and is a

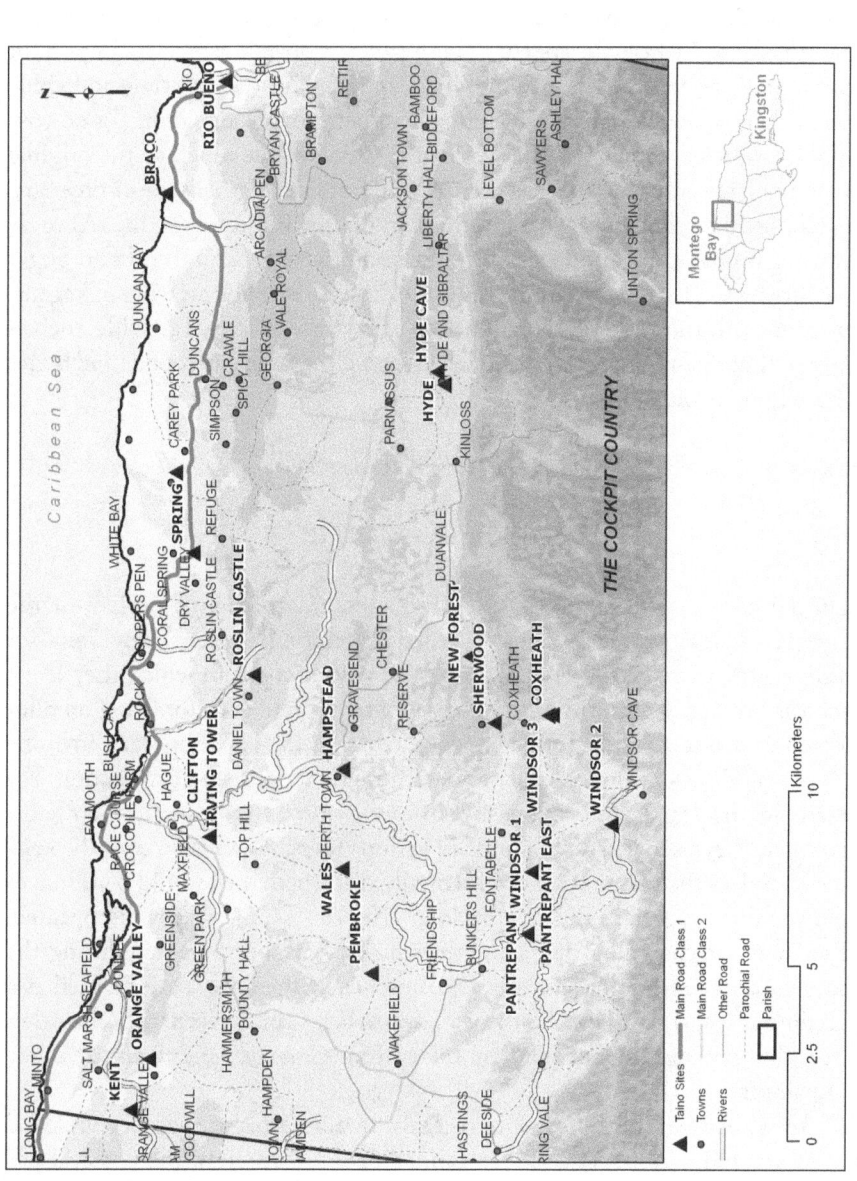

Figure 7.1. Map of the parish of Trelawny located in north-central Jamaica.

major perennial river allowing transport of people and products by rafts and canoes, as well as providing readily available freshwater for domestic purposes. The floodplain of this river might have allowed extensive crop cultivation by Taino settlers. The caves that dot the region are also products of the wider Martha Brae hydrologic system. These caves probably served as important ceremonial centers for the Tainos, where the remains of important individuals in their societies were buried and where petroglyphs depicting Taino cosmology were carved on the surfaces of the walls. While much of the original vegetation cover for the area has been altered from its original state of pre-1494, patches still remain and reveal information on the Taino way of life. At present, sugar cane cultivation exists in the region, serving the Long Pond Sugar Factory near Clark's Town in the middle of the parish. The clearing of vegetation for cultivation and settlement has revealed traces of past Taino life, such as pottery fragments, stone tools, and beads, as well as large gastropods and bones (both human and animal).

METHODS

Aerial Imagery and GPS

On the basis of site surveys of 23 Taino sites, environmental profiles of the area of interest were generated in order to determine other likely areas for Taino settlements. Aspects of the physical environment in which they lived, such as proximity to freshwater sources and their preference for living on hills, were taken into consideration. The land cover of the contemporary environment was also evaluated in order to determine other areas for exploration. For example, the Tainos grew calabash (*Crescentia cujete*) trees close to their habitation as they used calabash gourds in various ways. As a result, over the centuries, unless the plants were detrimentally disturbed, they would continue to grow and propagate in the vicinity long after the Taino villages disappeared. Even while recognizing that some trees might have been planted during the colonial and postcolonial periods, the presence of these trees can be used as a preliminary and tentative indicator of an earlier Taino presence. Some other trees that fall into this category are silk cotton (*Ceiba pentandra*) and a variety of palm trees.

Aerial photography and, more recently, satellite imagery can be employed to locate and investigate possible Taino sites. In this study, the physical parameters determining the locations of these sites will be identified. Photogrammetry, coupled with GPS-assisted field investigations, will be used to investigate the topographic characteristics of the area of interest to narrow down a potential field area and to generate a three-dimensional surface, while multispectral satellite imagery will be used to investigate vegetation characteristics.

Thick canopy covers in Trelawny, as well as the lack of aerial photographic records of the terrain 500 years ago, limited the usefulness of utilizing imagery in the area of interest. However, these limitations can be somewhat minimized by GPS-assisted field investigations. Known sites can be mapped using GPS, and areas physically matching these sites may be identified and investigated, reducing the element of chance site discoveries.

Aerial imagery provides the means by which large expanses of land can be evaluated remotely, looking at characteristics of land use, and can be used as well for planning field excursions. As earlier indicated, the use of GPS also allows users to place themselves at a location on the photograph, which greatly improves mapping accuracy in the field. However, advances in digital image processing mean that much more information can be extracted from images. For example, multispectral images provide information from the invisible spectrum, particularly infrared radiation, which yields considerable information on land-cover characteristics. A series of aerial photographs can also be processed to create three-dimensional surfaces through photogrammetric processing, which in turn can now be used for environmental modeling of the area.

The GPS survey of the study region provided information for different components of this research. These included ground control points for use in georeferencing photographs and the creation of the digital surface model; elevation readings to both augment and verify digital surface model information; and map locations of known Taino sites in the study region. These pieces of information were used to build an environmental profile for each site location. A Trimble ProXR differential GPS unit was used to collect ground control points as well as elevation data, while a Wide Area Augmentation System (WAAS)-enabled handheld GPS unit was used to map known Taino locations.

Photogrammetry

Photogrammetry refers to the "science and technology of obtaining spatial measurements" from photographs (Lillesand and Kiefer 2000) and is widely used in remote sensing to reliably map large areas and provide much information on these places. Successive aerial photographs taken along a flight line contain some degree of overlap. Stereoscopic pairs of these photographs provide different perspectives in the region of the overlap, which, when viewed with a stereoscope (or three-dimensional glasses in the case of some digital photogrammetric software), provide a three-dimensional view of the landscape, as each eye sees objects at different angles. The quantification of this to create three-dimensional surface models is described in the following section.

GIS

In order to begin exploring possible Taino locations in Jamaica, data had to be assembled in a GIS. ESRI's suite of GIS software, including ArcView GIS 3.3 and ArcGIS 9, the Spatial 3D and Image Analyst extensions, and Leica Geosystems' ERDAS software and Stereo Analyst extension were used for this study. True-color and multispectral IKONOS imagery and aerial photographs of north-central Jamaica were acquired from Spatial Innovision, Ltd., the Forestry Department, and the Jamaica Bauxite Institute. Infrared Landsat imagery was also used. Three-dimensional surfaces were created using digital photogrammetric techniques, available contour data, and a systematic GPS survey of the areas. The identification of possible Taino sites was then carried out based on satisfying a predetermined environmental site profile.

Generation of Three-Dimensional Surfaces from Imagery

Aerial photographs of the study areas were assembled and correctly oriented and scaled according to ground control points provided by the GPS survey. Camera information (such as focal length, principal points, fiducial marks) was inputted into the software before digital photogrammetry proceeded. A stereo effect is achieved when two overlapping photographs (a stereopair) are aligned. This allows depth in the landscape to be perceived, measured, and captured. The parallax in the image reflects changes in elevation and provides measurable three-dimensional information. Changes in perspective generated over successive images allow the perception (and subsequent creation) of three-dimensional surfaces. The X-parallax is influenced by the relative elevations of a ground point over successive images. Figure 7.2 provides an example of how the X-parallax is observed.

Feature A has a higher elevation than Feature B. When viewed in three dimensions, Feature A has more depth than Feature B. This is a function of the X-parallax, where the parallax for Feature A is greater than that for Feature B. This measurement of depth throughout the image is used to generate the three-dimensional surface. The Y-parallax is caused by several factors, such as unequal fly-by heights (which cause differences in scale between stereo pairs) and flight-line alignment. These produce blurs when the 3D surface is viewed and need to be corrected before generating the digital three-dimensional surface. This is achieved by scaling each image correctly (using ground control

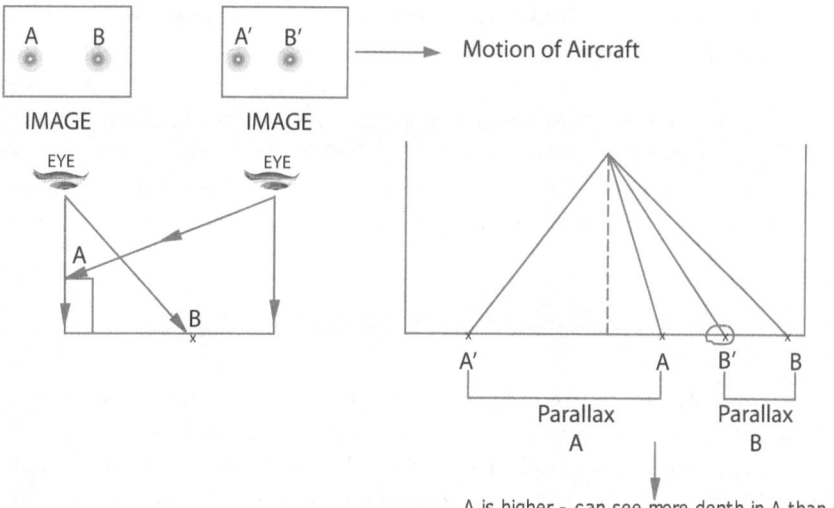

Figure 7.2. An example of how the X-parallax is observed.

points) and translating and rotating the images as needed. Once the X- and Y-parallax information is known, three-dimensional surface creation may proceed using a three-dimensional floating cursor on the computer. Using information provided by the X-parallax, the floating cursor rests on the surface model and maintains all areas with the same elevation. Different elevations are measured by adjusting the cursor to follow a different X-parallax.

Digital Terrain Modeling

The digital surface model created enabled analysis and evaluation of the study area. Topographic features (hills, plains, and so on) were identified from the landscape and a virtual terrain showing the distribution of the sites in a three-dimensional environment was created. Landforms were identified using the compound topographic index (Lyew-Ayee 2004; Moore et al. 1991), where slope-runoff relationships in the terrain were analyzed in order to extract individual hills and depressions from the overall landscape model. The index is defined by the following equation: *Compound Topographic Index* = $ln\,[a/tan\,\beta]$, where a represents the catchment area per pixel and β refers to the slope, in degrees. Areas with low compound topographic index values represent places with small catchments and steep slopes or hills, while areas with large catchments and gentle slopes are depressions or plains.

Positive relief features (ridges, hill slopes, hilltops, and so on) were identified as significant to the study, given that Taino artifacts and settlements in Jamaica have been associated with these types of landforms. Also of importance is the fact that many caves where Taino burials and petroglyphs have been found are located on these positive relief features. Caves are common in the karst landscape of the study region, and with the significant exception of vertical shafts, most are found along the sides of hills (Fincham 1997). Perennial rivers were identified from true-color imagery and 1:12,500 topographic maps of the region.

Land Cover Classification

Land cover was categorized according to the Rapid Ecological Assessment of Jamaica using multispectral imagery (The Nature Conservancy 1994). This categorization considers both manmade and natural land cover and includes both undisturbed areas and areas affected by human activities (construction, agriculture, industry, and so on). Understanding contemporary land cover is considered essential in determining likely areas for Taino site exploration. By clearly categorizing land cover, researchers are able to determine where to concentrate their reconnaissance efforts, particularly in places that have not been significantly altered by contemporary human activities. It is conceivable that Taino sites located in an area where a sugar factory or market once stood would have been either destroyed or irretrievably lost.

Vegetation characteristics are primarily observed from multispectral imagery. However, vegetation is influenced by the physical environment, such as geology, soil, climate, and topography, and these factors must also be taken into consideration. The level of disturbance is also considered in classifying land cover. Evergreen forests are always leafy, semievergreen trees lose their foliage at the end of the vegetation season, and deciduous trees lose their leaves at the end of the dry season. Jamaican forests, unlike their temperate-region counterparts, are heterogeneous. Forests, however, may be classified as a single type, where one species occupies more than 50 percent of the area. In this study, supervised image classification was carried out in order to generally categorize land cover on the basis of multispectral imaging. Figure 7.3 shows an infrared image of the study region.

RESULTS

Twenty-three sites were identified for this study and represented control points for the identification of potential Taino sites. Pre-Columbian artifacts such as pottery and beads were found at each site, confirming that these places were in fact once inhabited by Tainos. The sites were all marked using GPS and were

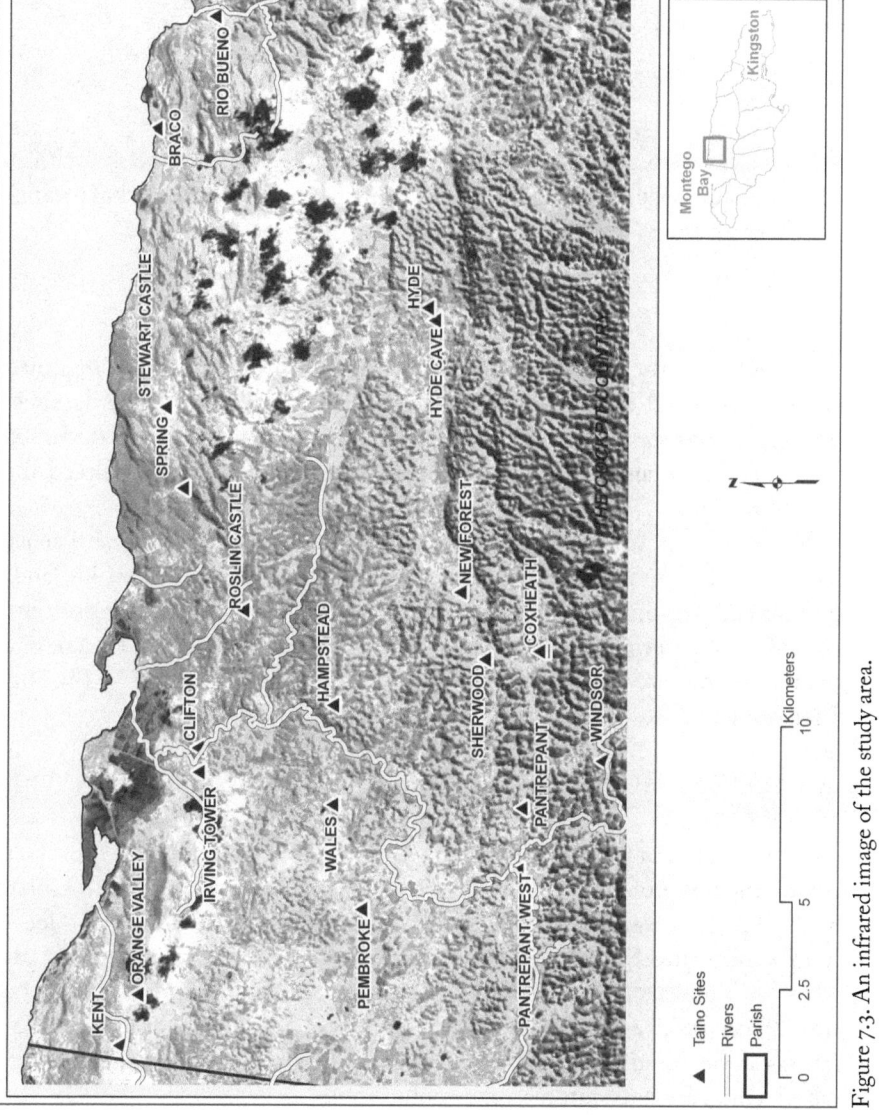

Figure 7.3. An infrared image of the study area.

all located in the parish of Trelawny (see Figure 7.1). As earlier indicated, environmental profiles were subsequently created for each of these sites. These profiles were designed to determine the physical environments usually associated with Taino settlements in Trelawny as well as other potential areas for future exploration. The following are environmental profiles of the sites that were investigated.

Terrain and Hydrological Properties

Twenty sites were situated on hills. Most sites were situated inland, with 18 sites situated over 50 m above sea level. Thirteen sites were within 1 km of a perennial river, and 21 were within 5 km.

Land Cover Characteristics

With respect to the study region, 13 different land-cover types were identified (see Figure 7.4 and Table 7.1). Two major land-cover types—mixed herbaceous/shrubland, subsistence plantation, and grasslands (23.8 percent) and disturbed lowland/submontane seasonal evergreen forest (35.3 percent)—occupied the bulk of the area.

Fourteen sites were located on mixed herbaceous/shrubland, subsistence plantation, and grasslands, while four were situated in disturbed lowland/submontane seasonal evergreen forest—three of these (two at Windsor and one at Coxheath) within the Cockpit Country proper. Two sites (at Hyde) were situated within areas of sugar cane cultivation, while another three (Spring, Sherwood, and Roslin Castle) were within relatively developed areas.

LOCATING POTENTIAL AREAS FOR EXPLORATION

Using information gathered from the terrain, hydrology, and land-cover data, environmental profiles for the known sites were created, and other areas that fit these profiles were identified. The four land-cover types where Taino locations were positively identified were used, excluding the other land-cover types where no Taino artifacts were found. Similarly, areas within 5 km of a river and situated on positive relief features were identified. Potential regions for exploration can be found where these criteria overlapped. Figure 7.5 is a map showing potential areas for future exploration.

The area that satisfies the criteria for identifying potential Taino locations covers 117.6 km^2, or roughly 26.5 percent of the study region. This considerably narrows down our search area, and field sampling strategies can now be em-

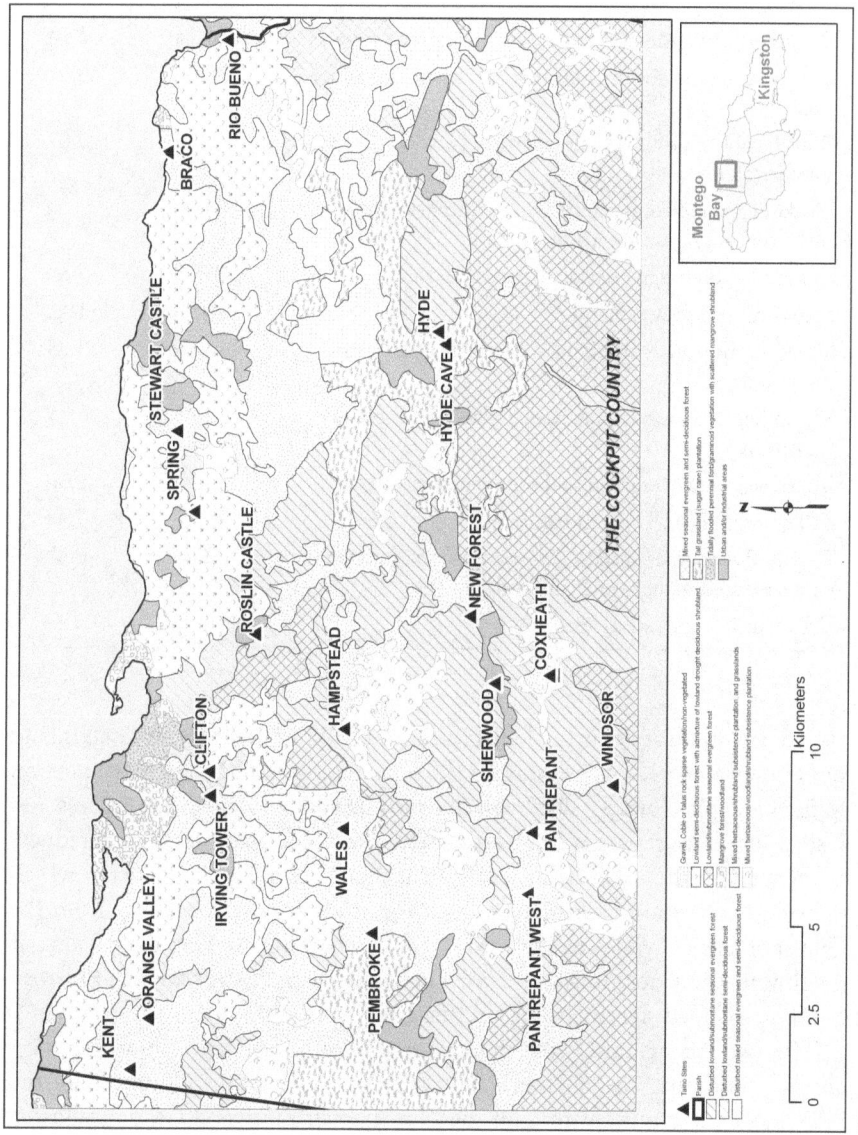

Figure 7.4. Land-cover classifications of the study area.

Table 7.1. Land-cover characteristics of the study region

Characteristics	Area (km^2)	% Cover
Disturbed lowland/submontane seasonal evergreen forest	83.76	17.65
Disturbed lowland/submontane semideciduous forest	10.14	2.14
Disturbed mixed seasonal evergreen and semideciduous forest	16.64	3.51
Gravel, cobble, or talus rock; sparse vegetation/nonvegetated	0.33	0.07
Lowland semideciduous forest with admixture of lowland drought deciduous shrubland	64.04	13.49
Lowland/submontane seasonal evergreen forest	83.73	17.64
Mangrove forest/woodland	6.73	1.42
Mixed herbaceous/shrubland, subsistence plantation, and grasslands	113.19	23.85
Mixed herbaceous/woodland/shrubland subsistence plantation	32.15	6.77
Mixed seasonal evergreen and semideciduous forest	5.04	1.06
Tall grassland (sugar cane) plantation	35.57	7.49
Tidally flooded perennial forb/graminoid vegetation with scattered mangrove shrubland	2.23	0.47
Urban and/or industrial areas	21.06	4.44

ployed within these areas to identify Taino sites. Most areas are situated inland along the watershed of the Martha Brae, stretching into the northern portion of the Cockpit Country, although not into its sparser areas where access and availability of water are more restricted as a result of the extreme ruggedness of the area of interest. The broadest area, and therefore a likely area in which to begin exploration, is in the south of the study region, stretching from the Queen of Spain's Valley in the west to Duanvale in the east, an overall area of roughly 70 km^2 (including those portions that do not fit the criteria). Thirteen of the 23 mapped sites are found in this area.

The two major Taino site clusters in southern Trelawny (shown in Figure 7.5), bordering the northern boundary of the Cockpit Country, are the Windsor/Pantrepant cluster and the New Forest/Sherwood Content cluster. Notwithstanding these clusters, there might have been Taino habitation on the outer margins of the cluster (see Coxheath, south of Sherwood Content, in Figure 7.5). Areas of interest, such as Coxheath, show up outside the cluster

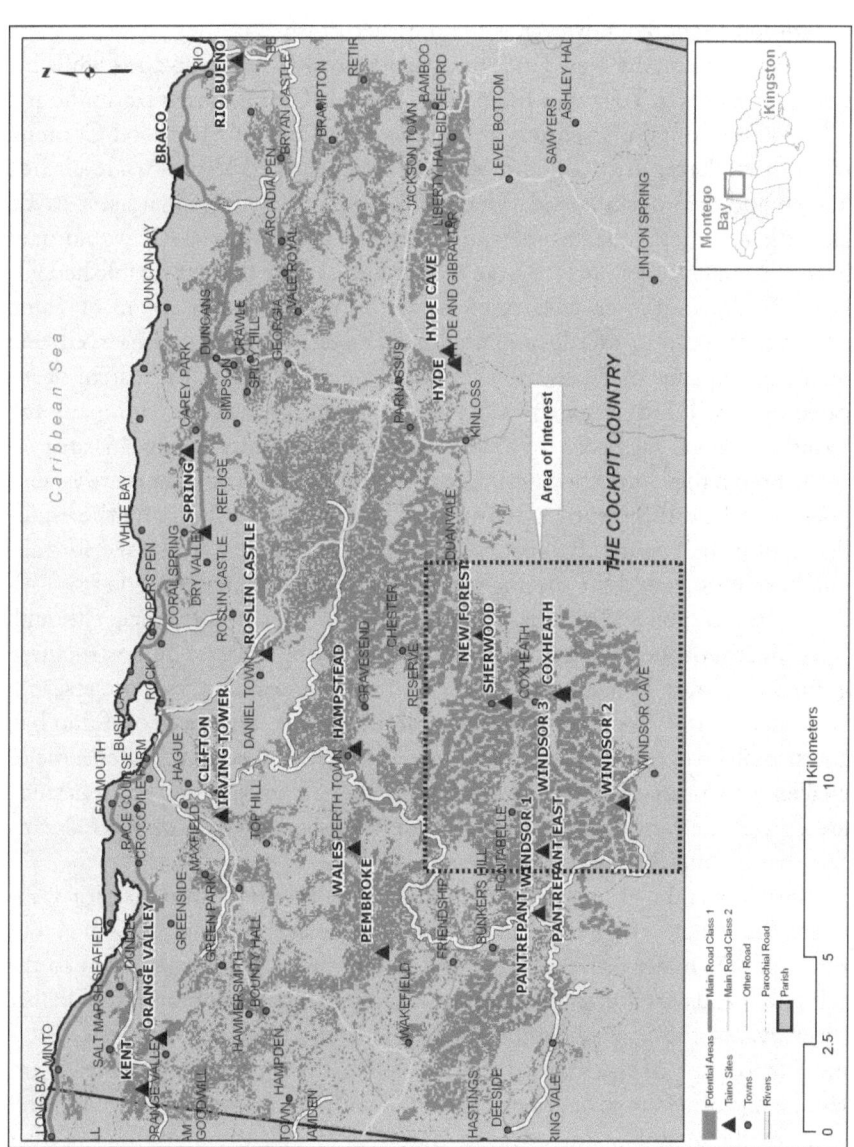

Figure 7.5. Map showing potential areas for future Taino site exploration.

and may contain Taino settlement sites that have not yet been identified. The Martha Brae supplied freshwater to the Windsor/Pantrepant cluster. The New Forest/Sherwood Content cluster received its freshwater supply from ponds in the area.

Not to be ignored, however, is the presence of caves in these areas. A small cave was found on the New Forest property by Ivor Conolley in 2004 while investigating sites in Trelawny. In 2005 the Jamaica Caving Organization found a Taino cave containing pottery in the Piedmont area of Sherwood Content, within the cluster area. Taino caves in Pantrepant and Windsor are already known and well documented. The Tainos, while they did not inhabit caves, used them for religious purposes, including secondary burials. It would have been convenient, therefore, to have such facilities close to their established villages. To date, seven caves have been found that are within 100 m of Taino sites. Of these, four are documented burial sites. It has been observed that many known sites in Trelawny have caves either associated with them or located nearby. Taino petroglyphs have been found in caves in Pantrepant and Windsor. This is suggestive of a vibrant Taino community within this area.

Although these interior clusters are in mountainous terrain, there are various pockets of land sufficiently extensive and level enough to facilitate the establishment of ball courts. Ball courts were large rectangular areas used for religious ceremonies and the playing of a ball game called *batey* (Alegría 1983). To date, however, no ball court has been definitively located in Jamaica, although Spanish ethnohistorians have referred to the playing of *batey* on unstructured ground in eastern Jamaica (see Rouse 1992). It is hoped that, as more research is conducted in these environmentally profiled areas, evidences of Taino ball courts may be found on these level plots of land.[2] However, it may be a major challenge to locate undisturbed, relatively intact Taino ball courts in this study area, given the considerable degree of site disturbance that took place during the Spanish and British colonization of Jamaica.

Notwithstanding the possibility of missing ball courts within the area of interest, the evidence suggests that the Tainos extensively occupied this area. Future research, by way of excavations and radiocarbon dates, may point to the full extent and chronology of these sites. Taino occupation of these sites before the arrival of the Spanish would confirm a natural tendency for these Amerindians to settle in the interior regions. Some Taino groups were already inland, while others may have been forced inland into relatively inaccessible regions by the marginalizing effect of European colonization. During the early Spanish colonial period, the Tainos might have been operating out of temporary villages or camps. In any event, the research on the Tainos in Trelawny indicates "hills" as their preferred location.

CONCLUSION

The methodology described here provides a means by which the currently random manner in which Taino sites are found can be improved. Using digital tools, the study has clearly demonstrated that field exploration of potential sites of archaeological interest can be carried out by identifying the physical parameters that govern the location of Taino sites in Trelawny, Jamaica. Field exploration, as such, can be guided by the use of these digital tools.

It is important to point out that as the sites in this study were accidentally discovered, they form a nonsystematic, biased sample. Therefore, the GIS predictive models generated, though useful, should be considered as preliminary at this stage. In order for them to be ground truthed, future site surveys should be carried out in those high- and low-probability areas in Trelawny, as predicted by the models.

The actual discovery of Taino sites on the ground may be a challenge, but certainly not an insurmountable one. Without the massive architecture of Central and South America (for example, Mayan pyramids and Aztec temples) that is distinguishable from the surrounding environment in remotely sensed images, Taino sites in Jamaica can only be positively identified through traces of past settlement on the ground, such as pottery, gastropods, beads, and burials. Some Taino sites might have been either destroyed permanently or disturbed extensively by both colonial and postcolonial settlements, as well as by quarrying or agriculture. Where such areas are identified as potential exploration zones, site disturbances could make their survey and excavation very problematic.

Additionally, the use of imagery is restricted by the fact that there is no photographic record of the pre-Columbian terrain on which Taino settlements were actually situated, so there are no true controls when using imagery to identify potential areas for exploration. While the hydrological and topographic environment for the Trelawny region is roughly similar to what it was 500 years ago, over the centuries its vegetation cover has been, in some cases, dramatically altered by colonial and postcolonial activities. Despite this, the contemporary environment can serve, albeit tentatively, as a basis for creating environmental profiles of Taino sites as well as making assessments about possible Taino settlement locations.

ACKNOWLEDGMENTS

We wish to thank the following: the Graduate Studies at the University of the West Indies, Mona, for their financial contribution, which made the archaeology input in the chapter possible; Mrs. Anne Lyew-Ayee, Sub-Dean Faculty of Pure and Applied Sciences, for agreeing to review this chapter prior to sending it to the editor; the staff of the Mona GeoInformatics Institute, particularly Ms. Valerie Hoo Fatt, for providing logistical support; and Mr. Alexander Grennell, for providing technical support for this research and for helping with the preparation of the final document.

NOTES

1. A petroglyph in Windsor is much worn and in poor condition and may thereby be open to debate as to its authenticity.

2. This refers to mountainous regions. It is worthwhile to note, however, that sites have been found on elevated areas within a plain (for example, the Negril Spots Taino site, Westmoreland).

IV
Archaeology and Geophysics

8
Geophysics and the Search for Raleigh's Outpost on Trinidad

Eric Klingelhofer

Fieldwork searching for evidence of Sir Walter Raleigh's briefly occupied Caribbean outpost on Trinidad is part of a long-term study of English protocolonial expansion. Documentary and cartographic sources pointed to a location on Trinidad as the site of earthwork fortifications erected for forces to engage in exploration and colonization. Among the earliest English sites in the New World, it stemmed from Sir Walter Raleigh's efforts to confront Philip of Spain and to found a rival, Elizabethan empire. The project, funded by Mercer University, began in 1996 and since then one-week seasons of fieldwork have usually taken place in alternate years. A site at Los Gallos Point, Trinidad, was studied by geophysical surveys using a magnetometer and a resistivity meter, as well as soil sampling and the experimental use of soil thermography. Anomalies were tested by excavation, with positive, though not definitive, results. Because the scope of the project has been limited and the fort had been occupied for only a matter of weeks, the site has not yet yielded identifiably sixteenth-century artifacts, but soil changes do corroborate the geophysics. Future excavation will supply additional stratigraphy, and more intensive geophysical surveys will be used to expand the existing data.

In 1997, 1998, 2002, and 2004, I undertook on behalf of Mercer University and the National Archaeological Committee, Trinidad and Tobago, archaeological explorations for the site of a fort built by Sir Walter Raleigh in 1595. One of the earliest English sites overseas, the fort is known to have stood at the southwest corner of Trinidad, close to Venezuela's Orinoco River, which Raleigh explored in his search for El Dorado, the mythical City of Gold. Sir Walter was famous for his explorations and his interest in English colonization but also for having introduced tobacco from Trinidad to Queen Elizabeth's court and for making smoking a symbol of the fashionable gentleman. In 1595 Raleigh constructed a fortified base camp for his expedition to El Dorado, which he undertook after having expelled the Spanish from Trinidad and claiming it in the name of Queen Elizabeth. The locale of Raleigh's fort was determined by me to be at Los Gallos Point, Trinidad (Figure 8.1), based upon documentary study (British Library n.d.; Camba 1842; Lopez 1791; Map of Ponce Province 1898) and a review of secondary sources. Protecting Raleigh's fleet in Columbus Bay with mounted cannon, the fort may be expected to have similarities with the other two Elizabethan planned defenses in the New World: Sir Richard Grenville's 1585 fortified encampment on Puerto Rico and the 1586/1587 fort on Roanoke Island, North Carolina (Klingelhofer 2000). Like the other two sites, Los Gallos was occupied only briefly, because Raleigh quickly abandoned Trinidad when he failed to find quantities of gold.

METHODS

Magnetometry

The potential of the locality was corroborated by field inspection in May 1997, when a team of Mercer University students and I examined the topography of the area of Columbus Bay and Los Gallos Point, at 10° 05' N, 65° 54' W in southwestern Trinidad (Figure 8.2). The next stage of research was to locate the fort site more precisely. Attempts to acquire infrared photographs at a high resolution were met with disappointment (Nelson [SPOT Image Corporation], personal communication 1997; Strande [USGS EROS Data Center], personal communication 1997). The most promising plan, and one that would need to be undertaken irregardless of the availability of aerial infrared photographs, was a geophysical survey of the location. A review of the various approaches (Tite 1972) ruled out some techniques as inappropriate (metal detectors) or beyond the available budget (ground-penetrating radar) as the best geophysical means of obtaining evidence of Raleigh's site. In May 1998 Mercer students carried out archaeological prospecting by remote sensing, using equipment and an operator from the University of Georgia geoarchaeology program, directed by Ervan Garrison (Littman 1998). This survey took place on the St. Quentin Estate coconut plantation at Columbus Bay using a single-coil proton precession magnetometer, with data processed by Windsurf 6.04 surface mapping system (Figure 8.3). The survey covered two adjacent areas of the plantation: a 70-×-60-m North Survey Area bordering the mangrove swamp at Los Gallos Point and, separated by a modern road, a southern 90-×-150-m Main Survey Area along Columbus Bay beach (Figure 8.4).

The results of the magnetometer survey proved that although the equipment was effective in identifying both metal objects and subsurface features as magnetic anomalies, conditions specific to the site made its application problematic. Early twentieth-century maps show that the modern road separating the two survey areas was then lined by several small houses. Extreme readings in the North Survey Area and the north end of the Main Survey Area reflected

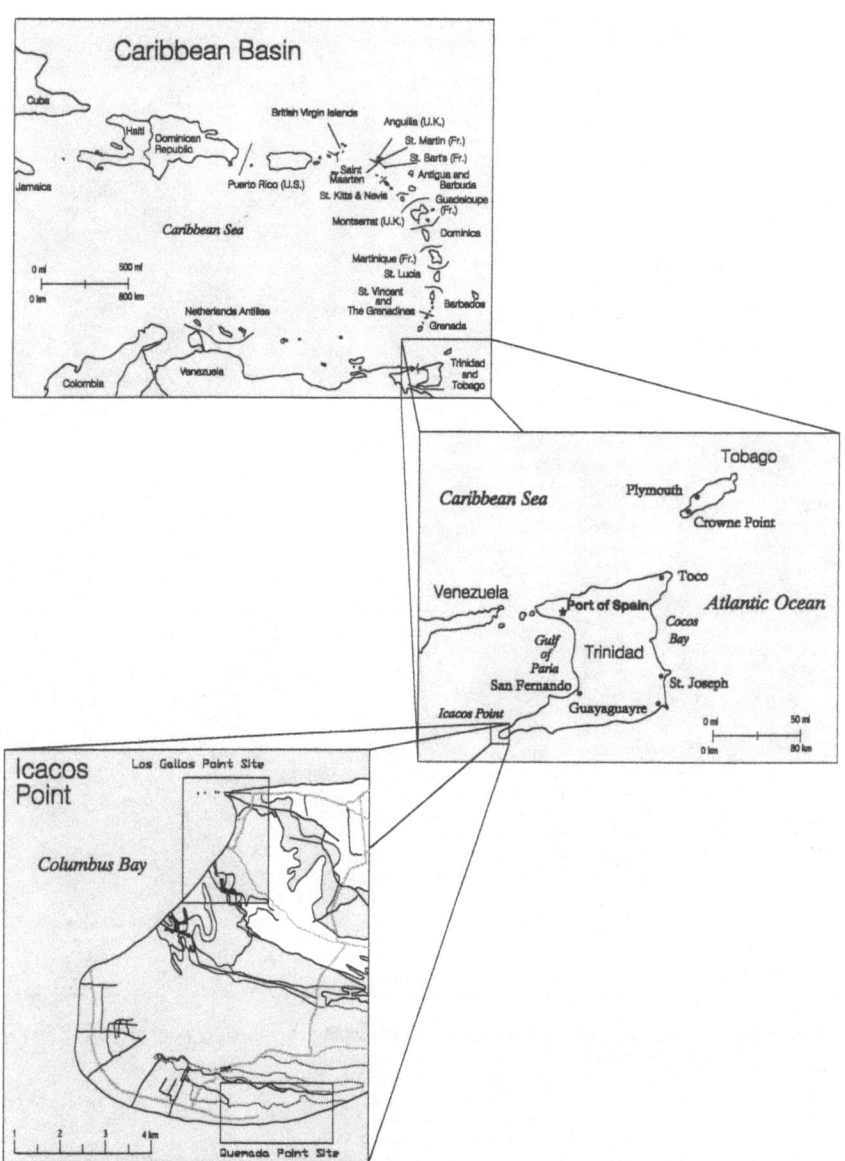

Figure 8.1. Locational map of Los Gallos Point, Trinidad.

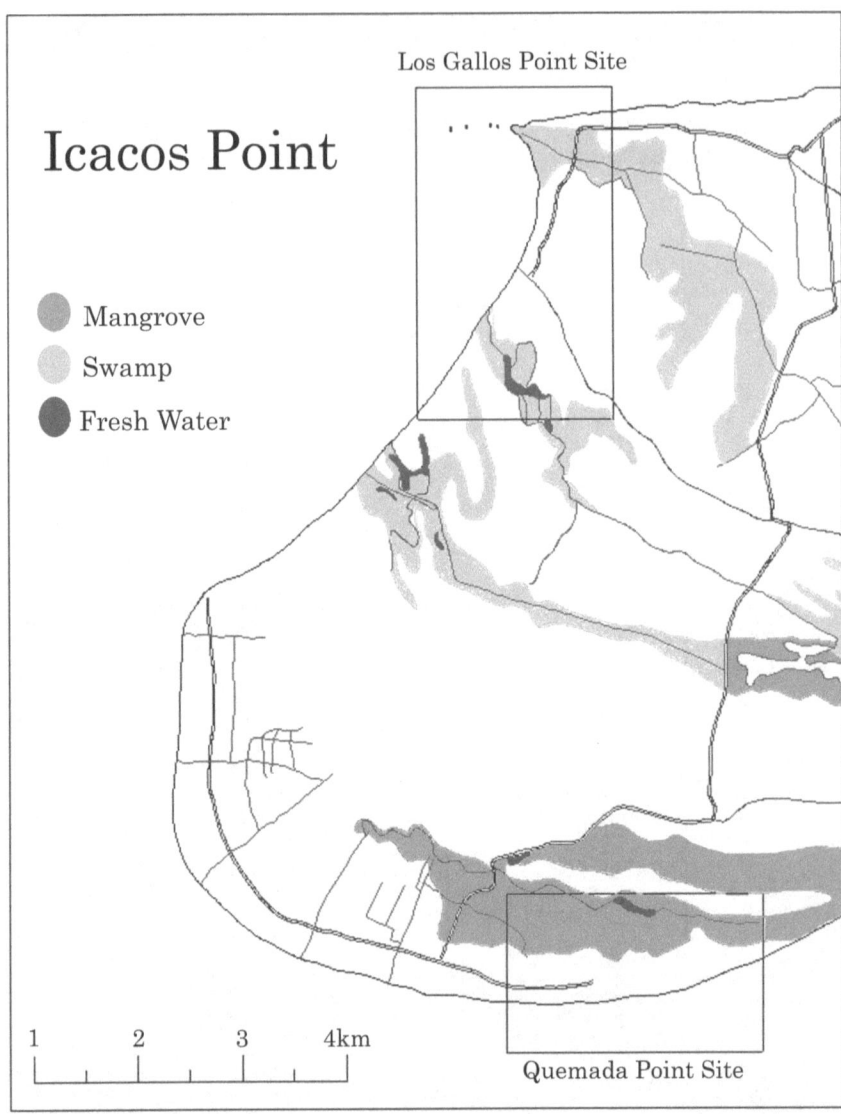

Figure 8.2. Site map of Los Gallos Point, also depicting the possibly contemporary aboriginal Quemada Point site.

this activity. More recently, oil-industry operations have dug bore holes in the site, and a small "donkey" well presently operates about 300 m to the northeast. Metal debris from both the domestic occupation and the industrial operations created numerous extraneous anomalies, reducing the effectiveness of the magnetometer.

Geophysics and Raleigh's Outpost on Trinidad / 159

Figure 8.3. Mercer team employing magnetometer at Los Gallos Point in 1998.

Soil Sampling and Test Pits

Fieldwork in May 1999 tested the readings from the 1998 magnetometer survey by soil sampling and selective test pits. Examining the 90-×-150-m Main Survey Area along Columbus Bay, the team first laid out a permanent site grid, based on the survey grid of 1998. As many as 690 test holes by auger or shovel examined soil types at 2-m intervals along 15 90-m east–west lengths spaced 10 m apart. These holes were supplemented by six 1-m test pits, placed to study stratigraphy at points where the 1998 magnetometer survey yielded anomaly readings.

The soil testing proved immediately successful, not by locating Raleigh's fort but by establishing the pre-twentieth-century shoreline, an important step in removing from consideration areas where the fort could not be. The shore had previously angled eastward, away from the north–south Columbus Bay, to form a broad opening for a freshwater stream. This watercourse now passes through a mangrove swamp to end near the tip of Los Gallos Point in a narrow channel, reputedly constructed by the U.S. Army in World War II. The shoreline recorded in eighteenth- and nineteenth-century maps was observed in auger holes as a deposit of shell fragments on a northeast–southwest orientation, lying 30–40 m from the edge of the present beach. This pattern was corroborated by the test pits, two of which also exposed deeper stratigraphies that sug-

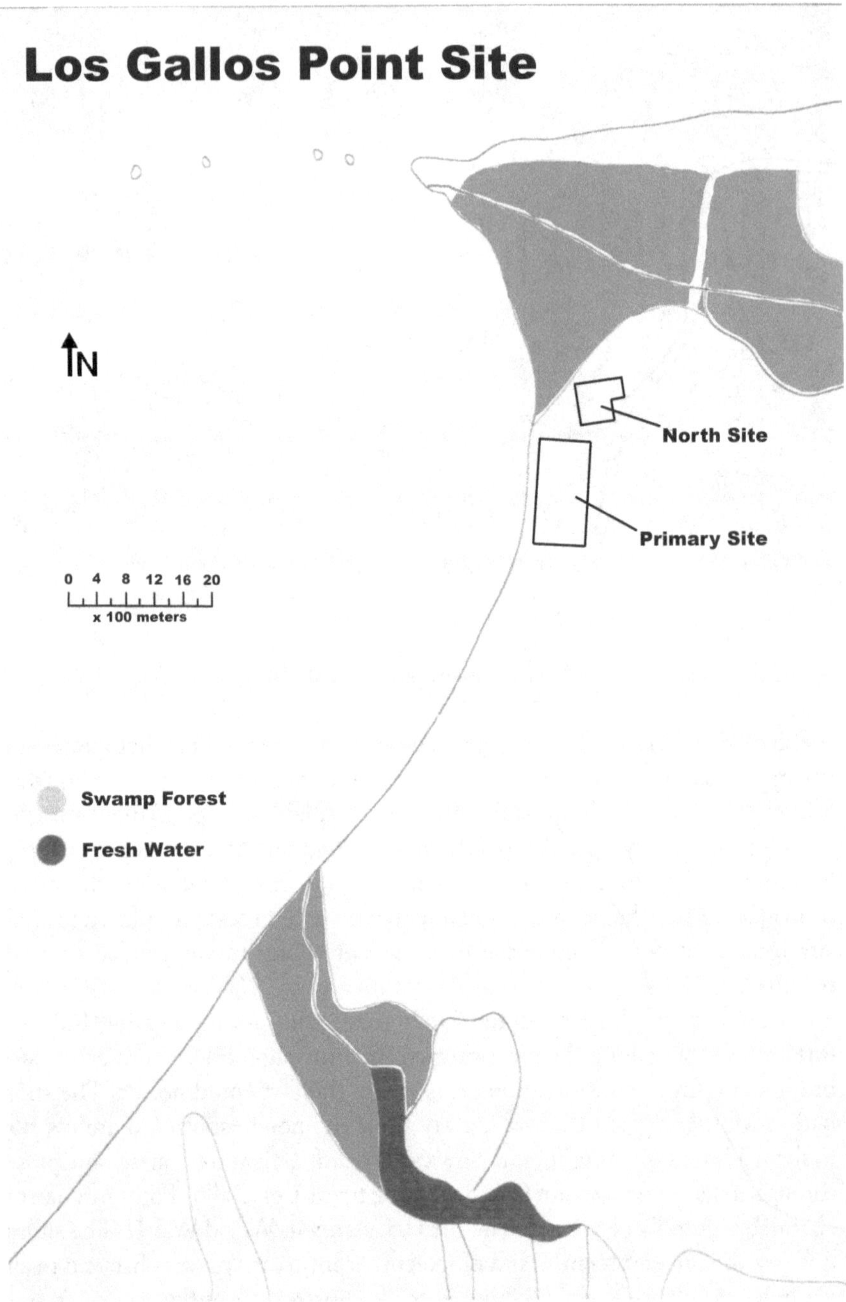

Los Gallos Point Site

Figure 8.4. Plan of the 1998 magnetometer surveys.

gested earlier, manmade activities. Unfortunately, no artifactual evidence was located to date these strata.

The geophysicist Bruce Bevin of GeoSight was apprised of the situation at Los Gallos Point. He noted that the geography of the Los Gallos site was sandy with a high (salt)water table, similar to sites he studied in Tidewater Virginia (e.g., Jamestown). Because of the similar environments, and the later industrial activity at Los Gallos, he advised against further prospecting with a magnetometer and advised use of a resistivity meter to search for Raleigh's fort (Bevin, personal communication 1999).

Resistivity Surveys

In March 2002, another team of Mercer students and I returned to Los Gallos Point to employ the Mercer Mark 1 prototype resistivity meter, with two attached probes and two distant probes, each on a 20-m wire (Figure 8.5). It was constructed for this project under the supervision of Matthew Marone of Mercer's physics department and based on fundamentals published by Mark Williams of the Lamar Institute at the University of Georgia (Williams 1984). The survey comprised a series of east–west transects, 5 m apart and 40 m long, to examine a 30-×-40-m portion of the Main Survey Area covered in 1998 (Figure 8.6). This section was chosen because of its pattern of strong readings and because a previous excavation unit (Test Unit 6, 1 × 1 m) had located promising soil differentiation. Despite some largely mechanical problems with the new equipment, the 2002 resistivity readings formed a distribution pattern that in part resembled, and in part supplemented, the previous magnetometer survey (Figure 8.7). Two test trenches, Test Unit 7 (1 × 4 m) and Test Unit 8 (1 × 3 m), were excavated to examine the stratigraphy at loci of strong comparative readings. The eastern 1.5 m of Test Unit 8 revealed a decided stratigraphic change: 0.43 m below modern grade, the removal of the general grey sandy loam exposed a 0.10-m-thick brown silt sealing a light brown silty sand, which was found to descend at least 0.75 m below modern grade. These soils indicate a subsurface feature with a well-defined linear western edge, but the lack of artifacts meant that its date was unknown.

The Mark 1 prototype resistivity meter was found to be susceptible to tropical heat, and the Mark 2 model was later developed to correct this problem (Bowen et al. 2004). It has been employed successfully in the Caribbean, but not on Trinidad. The wiring is internal, within a metal body that is compact and collapsible: it has a central column that pulls out for use and two arms that fold down and telescope out for probe attachment. At the same time, the distant array was changed to a four-probe fixed array, which makes the unit more functional in the field, especially where cables prove to be a problem in coco-

Figure 8.5. Mercer team using Mark 1 prototype resistivity meter in 2002.

nut groves. The soils where the unit would be employed are typically alluvial formations and beach sand, so the advantage that a distant array offers in providing a background for a broad area of differing geologies is not as important as mobility and a more localized comparison of soil resistivity.

Geothermography

At the same time, the Mercer team experimented with another application of geophysics to archaeology: geothermography. On the basis of the principle that infrared photography reveals heat differences on the ground, I proposed that a survey employing standard soil thermometers should yield comparable

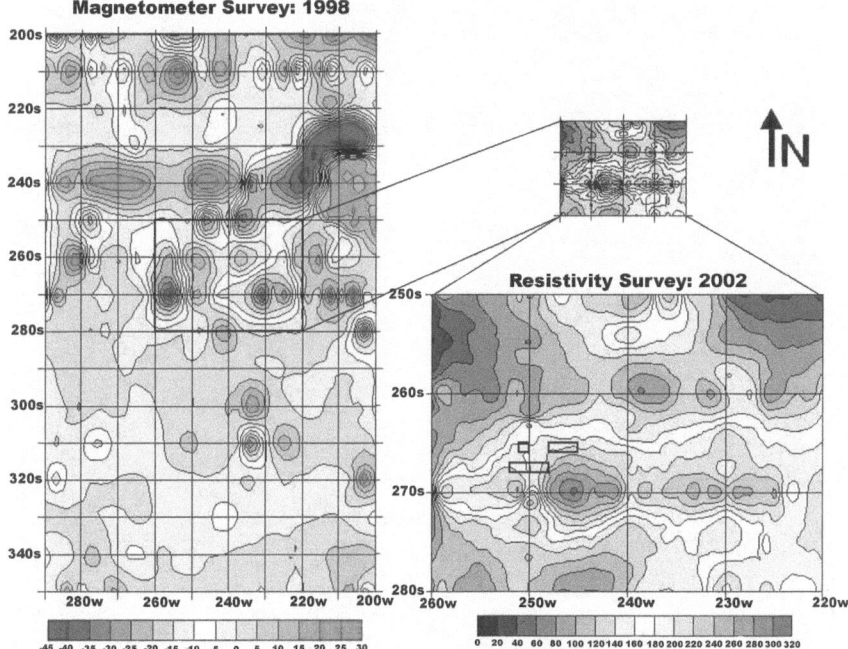

Figure 8.6. Magnetometer survey (1998) of the Main Survey Area (90 × 150 m), with the smaller 2002 resistivity survey area (30 × 40 m) imposed.

distribution plans. It could be employed in areas where aerial photography was not possible and carried out by students or volunteers at little expense (Figure 8.8). Experimentation revealed that the most accurate temperatures were taken during the morning hours before 11:00 AM and that probes must be inserted 0.20 m to avoid the effects of the tropical sun and air. Soil temperature readings were taken over a portion of the 2002 survey area; the resulting distribution map suggested that this procedure is promising, in that the two readings taken on different days by different teams showed, first, strong patterns of spatial distribution and, second, strong replications of those patterns. But the experimental survey also determined that subsurface temperatures can be affected by several factors. The on-site microclimate may be influenced not only by recent precipitation but also by particular local factors, for example, tree shadows and root systems. Subsurface temperatures could be affected by such surface "interference," and though tree shadows can be eliminated by taking measurements early in the day, the precise locations of root systems must be noted to establish "clean" geothermal patterns similar to the infrared photographs used to locate archaeological features.

Archaeological investigations were resumed in March 2004 when Mercer

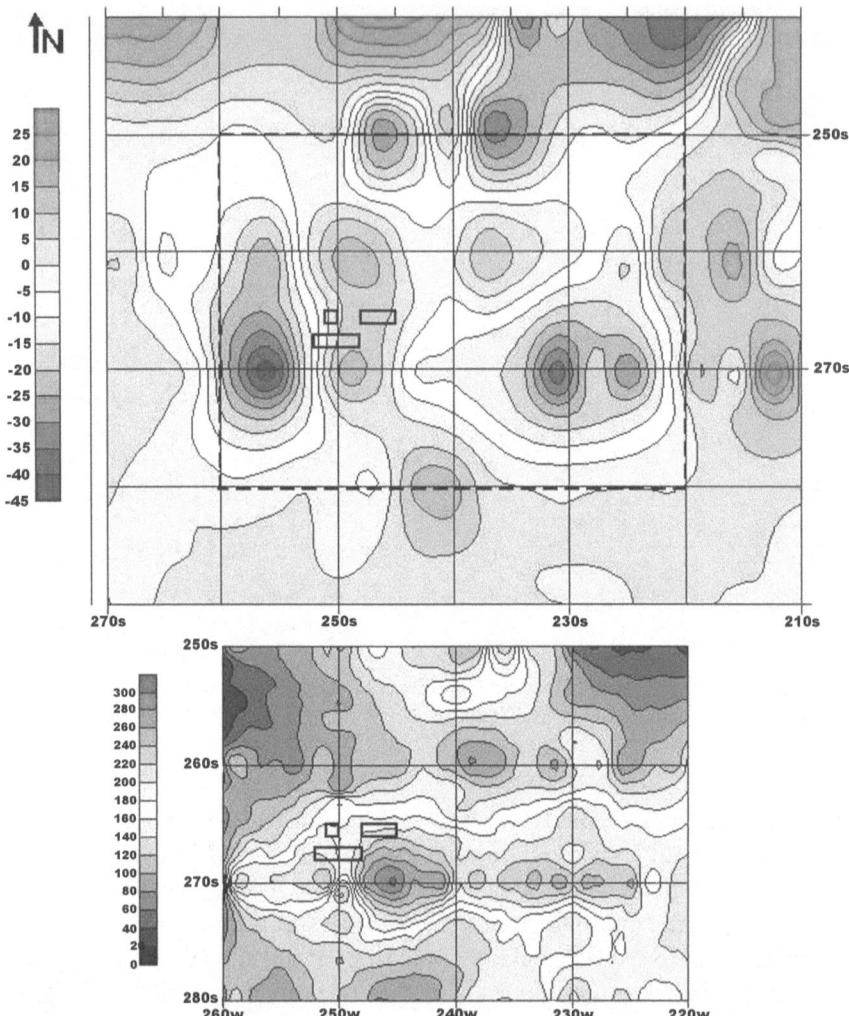

Figure 8.7. Detail of the 1998 magnetometer survey with the same area of the 2002 resistivity survey.

students and I returned to dig by shovel and trowel two additional excavation units. Test Unit 9 (2 × 3 m) was set southeast of Test Unit 8, to pick up the line of the presumed large, linear feature there. Excavation revealed the same north–south soil change, but it extended less than 1 m southward into the unit, and its eastern edge was a slope curving to the northeast. Other soils appeared at the same stratigraphic level, suggesting a general activity here (perhaps relating to the fort) before the formation of the generic grey sandy loam (Figure 8.9). Test Unit 10 (1 × 11 m) lay to the east, where the soil temperature

Figure 8.8. Mercer team taking soil temperature readings in 2002.

readings had indicated anomalies. Although some soil differentiations were noted along the length of the trench, all seemed natural in origin except at the western end, where careful troweling revealed soil stains that appear to be manmade features, possible slots and a small posthole (Figure 8.10). No artifacts were associated with these features, and their further examination must wait for a future season of excavation.

PLAYA DE GUAYANILLA, PUERTO RICO

Details of the design and use of an Elizabethan shoreline fortification in the Caribbean have survived in a unique illustration, which offers a direct com-

Figure 8.9. Test Unit 9, 2004. Excavated test unit, from the south (scale increments = 10 cm).

parison to the Los Gallos site. Another of Sir Walter Raleigh's outposts was erected at "Mosquito Bay" in Puerto Rico. This site is the earliest of the three known Elizabethan planned fortifications in the New World and was an essential element in the expedition to establish Sir Walter Raleigh's "Virginia" colony (Roanoke Island, North Carolina). Sir Richard Grenville challenged the Spanish government of Puerto Rico by constructing there a defended staging point on his 1585 expedition to North America. With two ships, he fortified a base camp for several weeks of operations: resting the crews, refitting the ships, constructing a pinnace, and seizing Spanish ships. Quinn (1955) assembled the relevant documents and compiled a thorough narrative of Grenville's expedition.

The fortification is well known to historians of Elizabethan voyages, but there has been no consensus about its location. A review of the evidence, however, indicates that Grenville's fort was erected at the former mouth of the Guayanilla River, at what is now Playa de Guayanilla, west of Ponce on the south coast. English and Spanish documentary references to the events taking place there are supplemented by an original picture map in the British Museum (Lorant 1946:185; White ca. 1585). The map was drawn by John White, one of Raleigh's associates and later governor at Roanoke. Its scale (assuming an English geometric pace of 5 feet) suggests a 200-foot-wide (65 m) band of earthworks and tent encampments along three 660-foot (230 m) sides of a quad-

Figure 8.10. Test Unit 10, 2004. East–west soil stain of possible slot, from the east (scale increments = 10 cm).

rangle against the Guayanilla River. Identification of the site was made during a 1998 examination of the southwest coast of Puerto Rico, as part of a long-term study of protocolonial English activities in Ireland and the Americas. Comparison of the U.S. National Geodetic Survey topographic map (National Geodetic Survey n.d.), nautical charts (*The West Indies Pilot* 1931), and aerial photography (Morison 1971:633–637) with on-site landscape features proved that, of all the coastal sites of southwestern Puerto Rico, Guayanilla Bay matched most accurately the sixteenth-century documentary and cartographic details. These observations support the identification earlier proposed by Samuel Eliot Morison (1971:633–637) and challenge that first published by David Quinn (1955:160–161, 175–176, 180–183, 403–405, 733–735, 746–747, and 1985:57–60, 430–431n2).

White captioned his map "The XIth of Maye the general in the Tiger arrived at St. John's Island where he fortified in this manner, toke in fresh water and buylt a Pynnes, And then departed from thence the XXIIIth of the same month. 1585." In the 1500s, San Juan was the name of the island and Puerto Rico its main port. The map depicts earthworks as bank-and-ditch defenses, typical of the fortified camps illustrated in Renaissance military handbooks (Ive 1972 [1589]). The ditch was probably V-shaped and perhaps 1 m deep and 2 m wide. The soil from the ditch was banked up to form a defensive wall at least 1.5 m high, behind which the soldiers could shoot their harquebuses.

The colors chosen by White suggest that the ditches here were water-filled, which would be appropriate to low-lying terrain. The water table at Playa de Guayanilla is now less than 1 m below the ground surface. The earthworks were designed to thwart a Spanish attack by land or sea. The bank would absorb both musket and cannon shot, in contrast to the wooden palisades that were effective against Amerindian weapons. Unlike the accounts of some other English protocolonial forts, such as those on Roanoke and Trinidad, the accounts of Grenville's fort make no mention of cannons being brought ashore, and the map correspondingly shows none. Otherwise, it seems likely that many of the details of Grenville's fort could be found at Raleigh's fort at Los Gallos Point, which was also located on a sandy beach beside a freshwater stream.

In addition to the campgrounds and entrenchments, White places in the camp a small corral for captured horses, the fire of a forge for the expedition's smithy, and the construction of a small ship, a pinnace. Outside, soldiers are bringing logs back to be sawn into planks, and a ship's boat conveys water barrels on the "fresh ryver." Other soldiers accompany Grenville from a meeting with the Spanish. According to the report of Grenville's voyage, when the Spanish later failed to arrive at a rendezvous for trading, he anticipated an attack. The pinnace was by then complete, so the expedition could depart for Roanoke. Grenville fired the woods to forestall an attack and destroyed the fort rather than have it fall into Spanish hands. On Trinidad, the Spanish did not report their reuse of the Los Gallos fortification, so it is likely that it was similarly destroyed when Raleigh headed back for England.

CONCLUSION

The search for Elizabethan forts in the Caribbean is a work in progress, and such progress has been slow. Difficulties in site access and using various kinds of geophysical survey have limited the fieldwork, while funding, logistics, and other research commitments have restricted most on-site activities to alternate years. Certain geophysical techniques have been employed and proven unsatisfactory, while others have come to be recognized as more suited to site conditions. Experimentation with thermographic surveying suggests a promising new technique for the tropics. It has been the project's good fortune to have received institutional support from Mercer University, which undertook the design, assembly, and employment of geophysical instruments specifically for use by small, nonprofessional teams in the Caribbean. Just as the Mercer resistivity meter is being transformed into a functional and inexpensive research tool, so too the sites on Trinidad and elsewhere will slowly yield their secrets—the clues to Raleigh's outposts and the earliest English sites in the Caribbean.

ACKNOWLEDGMENTS

I wish to thank the following: the Dean of the College of Liberal Arts at Mercer University for funding the research on Trinidad; Will Robinson and Jerome Gratigny of Mercer University for helping with the illustrations in this chapter; the landowner, Mr. Cavallo Sebastien, for granting me permission to conduct the fieldwork; and Mr. Rupert Boodram and Mrs. Mary Lalgee at St. Quinton Estate for their cooperation and assistance.

9
Geophysics and Volcanic Islands
Resistivity and Gradiometry on St. Eustatius

R. Grant Gilmore III

St. Eustatius, once known as the "Golden Rock," is now called the "Historical Gem" due to its unequaled concentration of colonial period archaeological sites. Geophysical instruments, including a resistivity meter and a fluxgate gradiometer, have guided recent excavations at two sugar plantations on the island. English Quarter Plantation is located in a flat open agricultural plain called the Cultuurvlakte while the Pleasures Estate Plantation is located on the slopes of the Quill volcano. Although some archaeologists have suggested that geophysical instruments are not able to provide accurate data in the highly variable magnetic environments found on volcanic Caribbean islands, the data presented in this chapter prove otherwise. The resulting information is essential in interpreting the history of slave quarters and sugar/rum-processing buildings identified with the aid of geophysical instruments.

Historical archaeological research began on St. Eustatius with visits by Ivor Noël Hume in the late 1960s and early 1970s (Noël Hume 2001). The College of William and Mary in Virginia began a two-decade research program in 1979 (Dethlefsen et al. 1982). However, during this period no geophysical surveys were conducted on the island. In 2000, when the present research was undertaken, very few geophysical surveys had been attempted on colonial period sites in the Caribbean. This chapter examines the efficacy of using a resistivity meter and a fluxgate gradiometer to locate archaeological remains in a volcanic environment. The instruments were used on two sites on St. Eustatius—the Pleasures Estate Plantation and English Quarter Plantation—in an attempt to identify the location of slave villages and additional industrial buildings. The results indicate that each instrument was suitable in a volcanic environment with certain parameters. Both instruments were successfully used to identify previously unknown archaeological remains.

ST. EUSTATIUS AS A TRADING CENTER

Given its present relative tranquillity, it is difficult to conceive of the place that St. Eustatius once held in the world's trade economy. An illustration of this point can be found in the negotiations between Britain and France at the end of the Seven Years War, or the French and Indian War to Americans (1756–1763). In the Treaty of Paris, France gave to Britain large parts of Canada in exchange for the sugar-producing island of Guadeloupe. Likewise, St. Eustatius was once known as an important trading center in the New World. During the colonial period, there was no other trading place on earth that could be said to be its equal (Jameson 1903; O'Shaughnessy 1987, 2002).

Called variously the "Golden Rock," "Diamond Rock," and the "New Tyre," St. Eustatius was *the* entrepôt for raw materials and finished products in the Americas. Almost any product manufactured in the Old or New World could be acquired on the island. On St. Eustatius, as with the Internet, millions of products were bought and sold each year in auctions held in the more than 600 warehouses built along Oranje Bay. During the last half of the eighteenth century, up to 3,400 ships landed on Statia per year (Goslinga 1985). In comparison, other ports such as Bristol, Liverpool, New York, Charleston, Bordeaux, Nantes, Marseilles, and Amsterdam processed far fewer ships during the same time period (Table 9.1). One must bear in mind that St. Eustatius was an island only 8 km in length and 4 km in width. The population during this time may have exceeded 25,000 persons at its peak.

There were three primary reasons for the success of St. Eustatius as a trading center. First, nature had endowed the island with an ideally situated harbor on the leeward side and geological conditions inhibited the condensation of rain clouds on the Quill volcano. This severely reduced the quantity of rain that fell and therefore restricted the quantity and quality of sugar cane, tobacco, and other farm products that could be produced on the island. Left with no natural agricultural promise, trade was the only option for residents. The second reason for Statian success was the ideal location of the island on the busy sea-lanes centrally placed between the northwestern Caribbean islands (including Cuba, Jamaica, Puerto Rico, and the Bahamas) and those of the southwest (Barbados, Guadeloupe, St. Kitts/Nevis, and Martinique) (Figure 9.1 depicts the geographical location of St. Eustatius). Being located downwind from the latter islands and upwind from the former helped to make Statia into a successful trading port. Third, and probably most important, Holland made St. Eustatius into a free port. As such, the government did not tax or regulate products entering or leaving the island. As with today's online auctions, the trade occurring on the island was uninhibited by governmental inter-

Table 9.1. Relative shipping activity in colonial ports

Country/Colony	Port	Year of Max. Ships	Entering	Clearing	Total
Britain	Bristol[a]	1768	178	—	356[b]
British North America	New York[c]	1772	710	709	1,419
France	Bordeaux[d]	1786	—	281	562[e]
	Nantes[d]	1704	—	151	302[e]
	Marseilles[d]	1787	—	146	292[e]
St. Eustatius	Oranjesta[d][f]	1778	—	—	3,182

[a]Morgan 1993.
[b]Total is estimated based on *Entering* ships.
[c]Matson 1998.
[d]Clark 1981.
[e]Total is estimated based on ships *Clearing*.
[f]Goslinga 1985.

action and commenced at a breakneck pace. For example, although there were over 80 plantations on St. Eustatius in 1775 (Ottens 1775), ostensibly producing sugar, the output was only 600,000 pounds around this time. However, St. Eustatius exported 20 million pounds of sugar in 1770. The extra 19.4 million pounds were brought over illegally from St. Kitts and other islands to be sold tax free on Statia to maximize profit (Goslinga 1985). A review of plantation inventories indicates that a large percentage also had distilleries. This suggests that plantations on St. Eustatius were processing raw sugar and molasses from other islands into rum to be sold tax free as well.

Therefore, the foregoing factors combined to make the Golden Rock a corner post in the Atlantic trade. Lumber, wood, rum, cotton, and iron were brought from the North American colonies. In exchange, ships from the Carolinas, Virginia, New York, and Rhode Island received manufactured items from England, Holland, France, and sometimes Italy and Spain, including such things as ceramics, wine, books, and finished cloth and clothing. Ships outbound from Africa would bring ivory, ebony, and—most important—slaves.

ST. EUSTATIUS PLANTATIONS

As on other islands, slaves provided the labor to run plantations, where they would plant, harvest, and process sugar, tobacco, and cotton. On Statia, they may have played a significantly different role in that they would have aided and abetted the processing of illegally imported raw sugar into refined products, including rum. The physical space that slaves occupied on some plantations

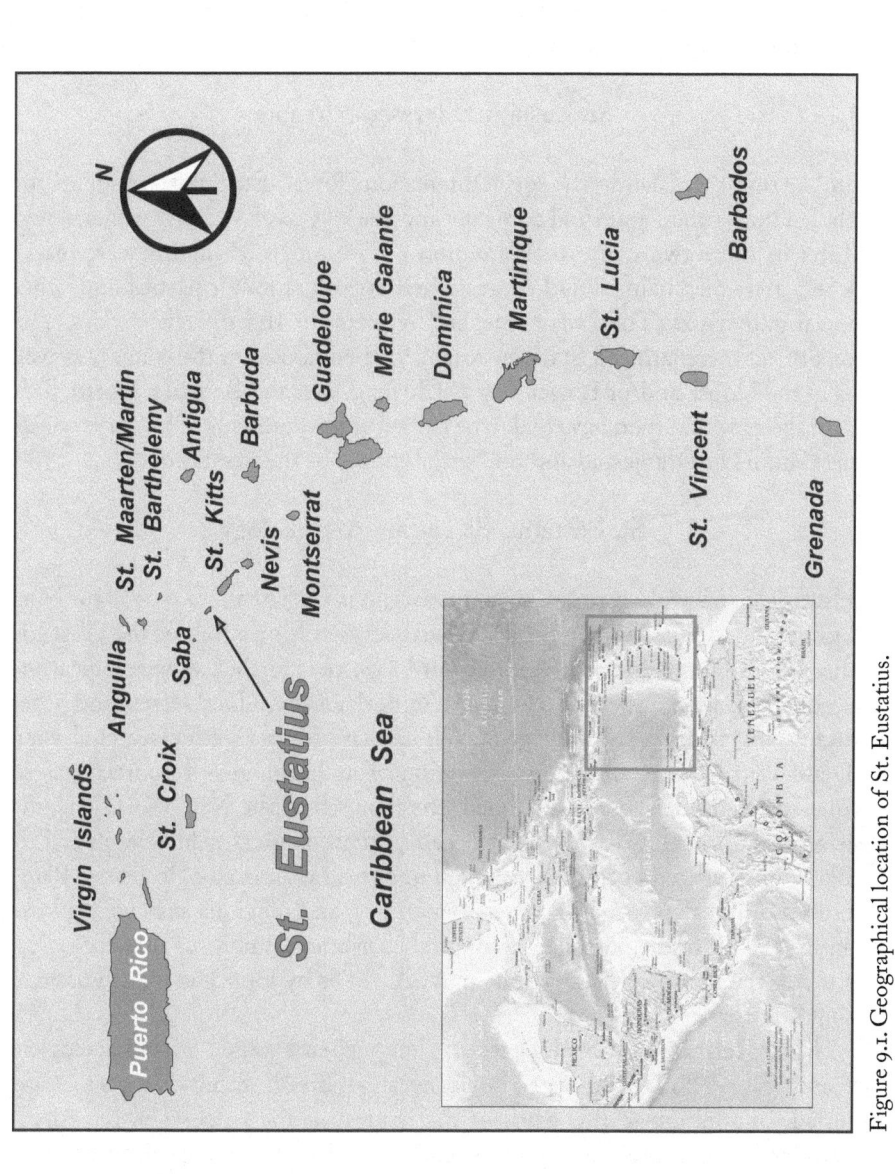

Figure 9.1. Geographical location of St. Eustatius.

was different from that found on other Caribbean islands (Gilmore 2004). On other islands, slaves' work and resting places were separated. They were housed in buildings set apart from the sugar-processing facilities. The social and economic roles that these slaves occupied may have been significantly different from those on plantations on other islands.

St. Eustatius Slaves as Servants

Unlike on other islands, the social dimensions for St. Eustatius's residents included both urban and rural contexts, and the role of slaves as servants would differ in these two contexts. Plantation homes on St. Eustatius were places where rich merchants could express their wealth through parties and other social gatherings. They were weekend retreats for the merchant class. The wealthiest merchants on Statia invariably owned houses in the country as well as in the Upper and/or Lower Towns (Boven Dorp and Beneden Dorp). Servant slaves would then have had to be skilled at the demands of both the "business" home in Oranjestad and the "social" home of the plantation.

St. Eustatius Plantation Archaeology

Historical archaeology on St. Eustatius began in the late 1960s when Ivor Noël Hume visited the island and collected artifacts while on a tour of the West Indies (Noël Hume 2001). It was not until 1979 that further archaeological investigations were undertaken by Norman Barka, Edwin Dethlefsen, and other archaeologists from the College of William and Mary (Dethlefsen et al. 1981; Dethlefsen et al. 1979). The preservation of archaeological resources was so amazing that the island was dubbed "the Pompeii of the New World" (Dethlefsen et al. 1982). Over the next decade, archaeological field schools led by Barka investigated both terrestrial and underwater archaeological sites. Plantations, military posts, urban sites, cemeteries, and religious sites were all examined. The result has been a comprehensive assessment of archaeological sites on the island summarized in an M.A. thesis by John Eastman (Eastman 1996).

I first excavated on St. Eustatius in 1997 when I joined an archaeological team from William and Mary in an investigation of an urban site in Oranjestad. In addition to this work, at the request of the landowner, Dr. Albert van der Waag, a preliminary investigation of the archaeological potential at the Pleasures Estate Plantation was conducted (Gilmore and Goodrich 1998, 1999). Supported by the Institute of Archaeology at the University College London, I led an expedition back to the island in order to survey the Pleasures

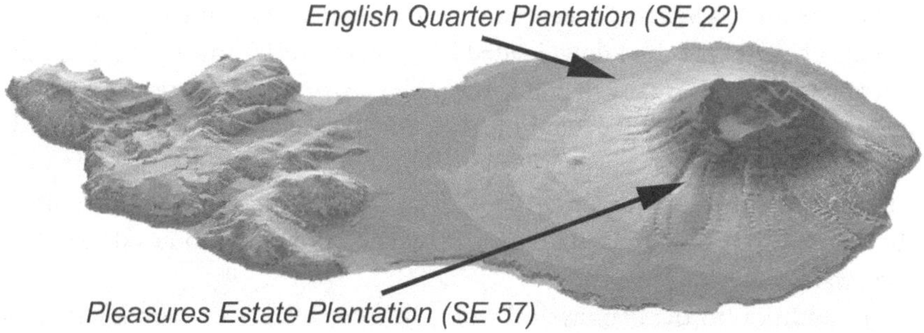

English Quarter Plantation (SE 22)

Pleasures Estate Plantation (SE 57)

Figure 9.2. Location of Pleasures Estate Plantation and English Quarter Plantation on St. Eustatius.

Estate and English Quarter plantations using geophysical instruments in the spring of 2000 (Figure 9.2 shows plantation locations on St. Eustatius).

GEOPHYSICAL SURVEYS

Geophysical instruments have rarely been used on Caribbean historic sites (Armstrong and Reitz 1990; Deagan 1989). This is primarily because of the difficulties involved in transporting bulky instruments to remote areas on the islands and their relatively high cost. Their efficacy in locating buried archaeological remains is well proven (Clarke 1990). Such features include buried trash pits, hearths, burials, stone walls, and foundations. Typically these remains are identified by chance or through exhaustive and time-consuming test excavations. By using geophysical instruments it was hoped that these areas could be more expeditiously and systematically identified at the plantation sites. The geophysical surveys conducted on St. Eustatius represent the first time such instruments were used on the island.

On both Pleasures Estate and English Quarter plantations, a grid was set up using a total station that was then tied to an island-wide grid system. A fluxgate gradiometer was used at Pleasures Estate Plantation while a resistivity meter survey was completed at English Quarter. Although an attempt was made to use the resistivity meter at Pleasures Estate the soil did not contain enough moisture for electrical current to pass through successfully. As soil moisture was greater at English Quarter, the resistivity meter was used successfully on this site. Geoscan Research Ltd. manufactured both instruments, which were provided by the Institute of Archaeology at the University College London. The fluxgate gradiometer detects variations in magnetic field intensity across a site caused by magnetic anomalies that disturb the natural magnetic field.

Readings are taken every meter and are automatically recorded by the instrument. The data are then downloaded into a computer using a program, called Geoplot, provided by the manufacturer. The resistivity meter readings are also taken in every meter square and the data downloaded into Geoplot. With this instrument an electric current is run between a pair of probes and the variations in resistance are then recorded. The resulting data sets were then plotted both in Geoplot and in Surfer, a data-processing program produced by Golden Software, Inc.

In addition to the geophysical work, surface collections were made over a 1-ha area on both sites. Artifacts were placed in bags and labeled according to specific recovery locations in the 1-m grids. At English Quarter, a 1-×-1-m test unit was excavated in the target area to determine stratigraphic sequences and to obtain additional artifactual evidence. Artifacts were recovered in order to establish preliminary dates for the occupation period of this area and also to supply information on the economic and social status of this area's occupants.

Each site was excavated using the standard archaeological excavation methods described below. Soil was excavated stratigraphically and was screened through 0.65-cm mesh (1/4 inch). All recovered artifacts were placed in polyethylene bags appropriately labeled for each context. Detailed plan and profile drawings were made of all structures and excavation areas. Both digital and film photographs were used to document the excavation process. Standard St. Eustatius Center for Archaeological Research Context Record Forms were completed for each context. Finally, soil chemical and micromorphology samples were taken from most layers (Bakare 2002). Upon making intersite and intrasite comparisons, Bakare determined that some aspects of site function were reflected in the geomorphological and geochemical record of St. Eustatius.

RESULTS OF GEOPHYSICAL SURVEYS

The geophysical research phase was undertaken in March and April 2000 utilizing a fluxgate gradiometer and a resistivity meter. The objective of this survey was to locate potential slave sites for excavation during the coming summer. As a result of this effort, two possible slave residence areas were located, one at English Quarter Plantation and the other on the Pleasures Estate.

No previous geophysical instruments had been used on St. Eustatius so this was also a methodological experiment to determine which geophysical instruments would produce the optimal results under various conditions. Geologically speaking, the two sites are very different. English Quarter is on a relatively level plain while the Pleasures Estate lies on a 15-degree slope. The soil at

English Quarter is also better hydrated than that of the Pleasures Estate. Finally, vegetation was denser at Pleasures Estate than at English Quarter. As a result of these three factors, the resistivity meter was more effective at English Quarter as the adequate soil moisture content and the fewer shrubs permitted the use of this more-accurate geophysical instrument on this site. The fluxgate gradiometer proved more useful at Pleasures Estate as it did not have cables (making it easier to get around vegetation) and the moisture content of the soil did not affect the results.

Possible slave residences were found on English Quarter Plantation through the identification of seven discrete foundation platforms and associated artifacts approximately 100 m west of the central plantation area (Figure 9.3). These possible foundations were constructed of volcanic rock. Artifacts recovered during surface collections included Afro-Caribbean ware, iron kettle fragments, cattle bone, and a small amount of European ceramics. European ceramic types included North Staffordshire slip, creamware, and pearlware. The foundations were likely parts of impermanent structures used to house slaves during the eighteenth century. A 1781 map, located after the fieldwork was completed, depicts slave quarters in precisely the same area (Figure 9.4) (Martin 1781). Thus far, no archaeological evidence for separate slave quarters has been found at the Pleasures Estate Plantation. The same 1781 map mentioned above does show the location of the slave quarters at Pleasures Estate (Gilmore 2004). It is hoped that in the near future, testing in these locations for the presence of slave dwellings may prove the accuracy of this map. It is important to note, however, that though discrete foundation areas were not identified, a fire pit was identified in addition to Afro-Caribbean wares within one of the structures, which is indicative of past domestic activities. One can therefore surmise that slaves moved into the industrial facilities once the plantation became a cattle farm in the 1820s.

The gradiometer work did add to the overall picture of ruins on the plantation by defining areas that required investigation through excavation. Additional ruins associated with the industrial complex are clearly evident in Figure 9.5. The darker grey areas indicate where magnetic readings were highest. Several of these highly magnetic areas correspond with walls uncovered during the later excavation periods. North of the "Large Cistern Structure" is located a wall that runs from the southeastern edge of the cistern into the hillside. According to the geophysical evidence, this wall continues further underground in a northerly direction. A similar pattern can be seen for buried walls associated with the distillery complex. Finally, a somewhat circular, highly magnetic area can be seen a few meters west of the warehouse structure. This particular area was not excavated but it may represent the location of the animal mill, or sugar mill, depicted by P. F. Martin in Figure 9.4.

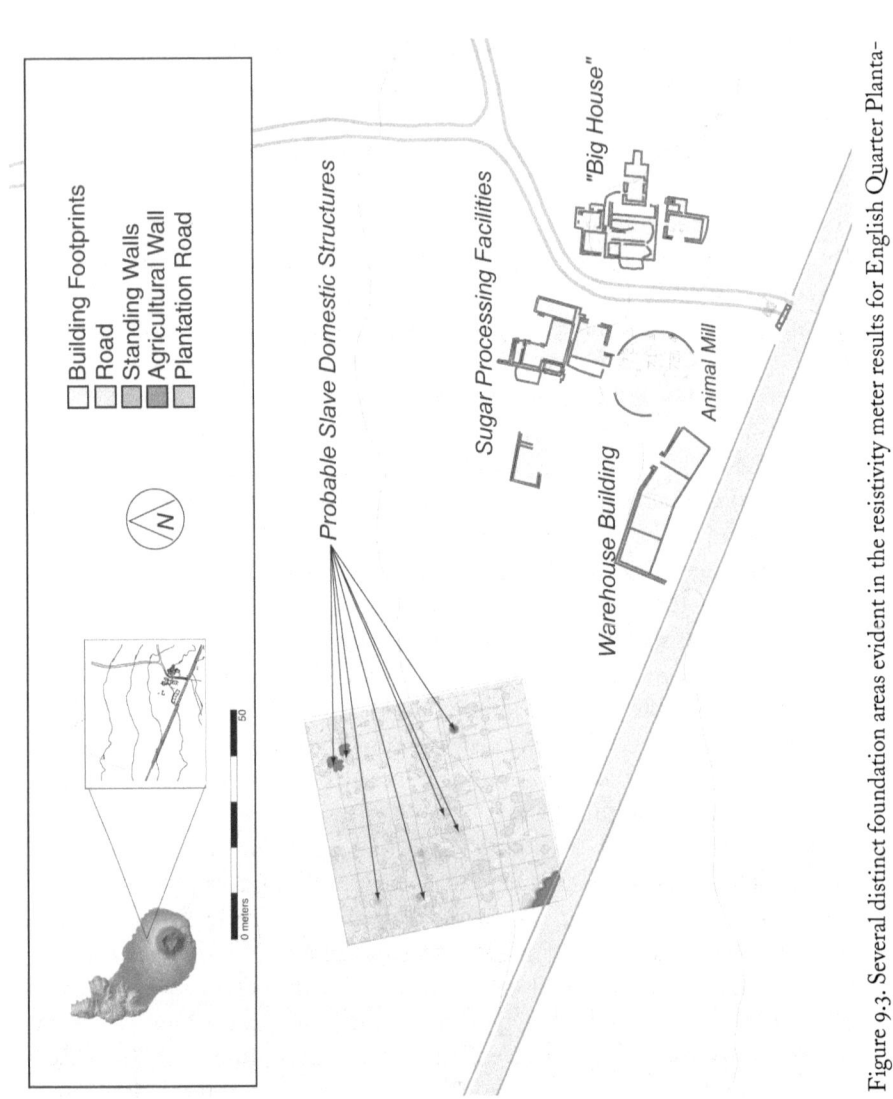

Figure 9.3. Several distinct foundation areas evident in the resistivity meter results for English Quarter Plantation. They were located northeast of the main industrial area on the plantation.

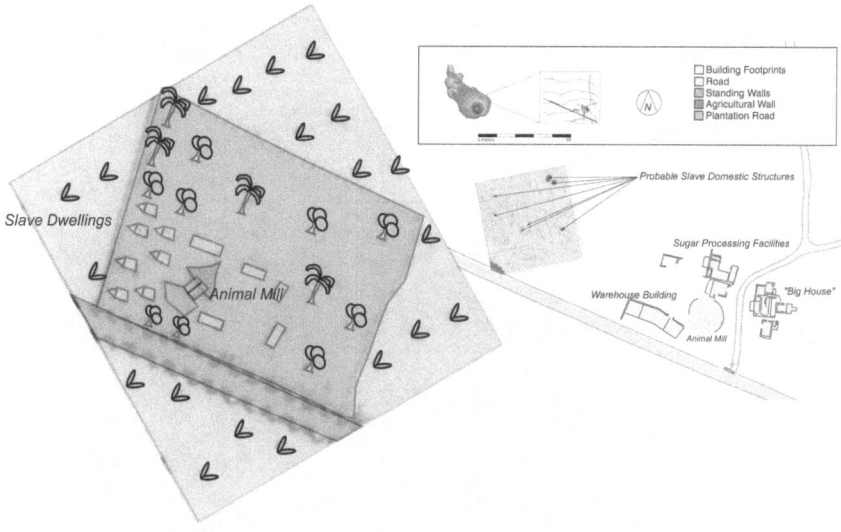

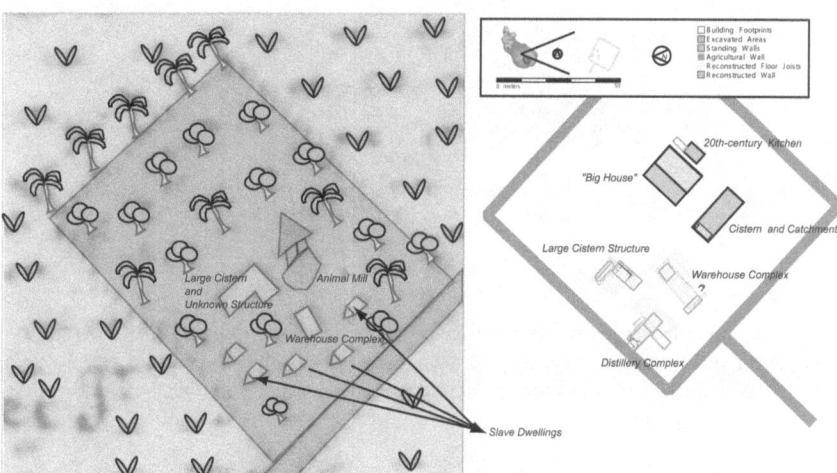

Figure 9.4. Top, English Quarter Plantation as depicted on the 1781 P. F. Martin map from the University of Michigan, Clements Library. Bottom, the Pleasures Estate Plantation as depicted on the same map. In both cases, the location of slave dwellings, the animal mill, and additional plantation structures are clearly shown.

OVERVIEW OF PLEASURES ESTATE PLANTATION ARCHAEOLOGY

On the basis of both cartographic and archaeological evidence, Pleasures Estate was in use as a sugar plantation from the mid-1700s until the 1820s. Four main building areas have to date been identified for the Pleasures Estate. In

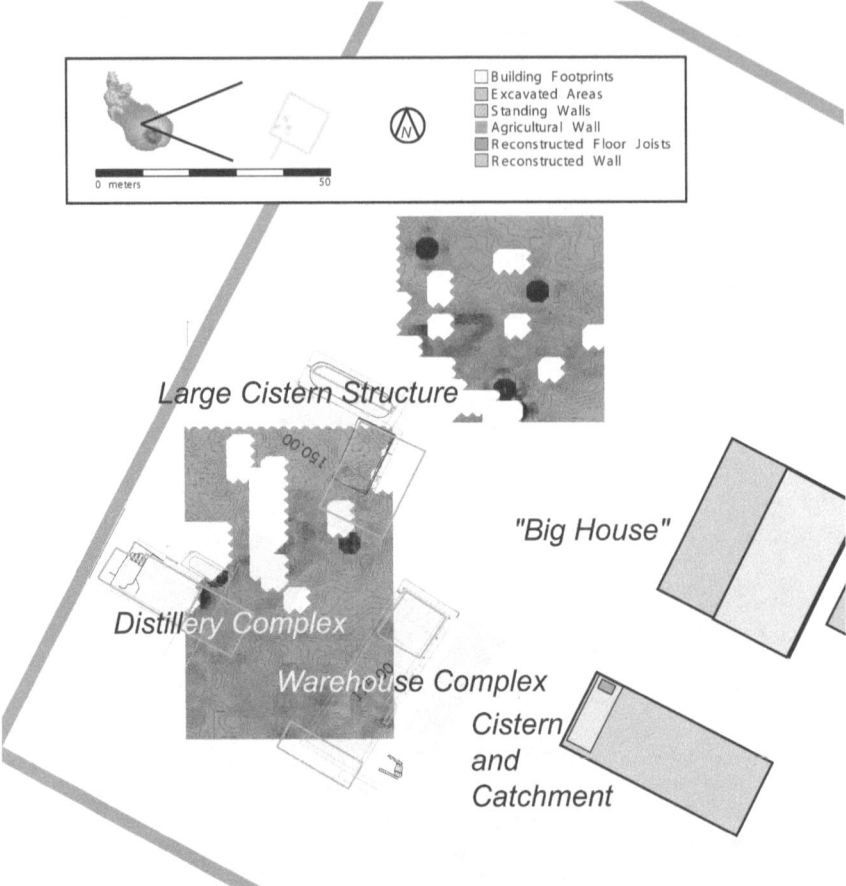

Figure 9.5. Geophysics identified additional structural remains at the Pleasures Estate Plantation, indicated by the darker grey areas. Many match the footprints of buildings uncovered during the excavation season. White areas within the geophysical data are either large trees or large stones.

what is currently called the "Big House," more recent construction dating entirely to the twentieth century utilizes building materials taken from the rest of the property. However, the foundations are clearly stylistically related to other plantation "Big House" foundations dotted around the island and likely date to the mid-eighteenth century. The warehouse complex consists of a two-floor stone building that was likely used to store processed sugar and other goods. The "Large Cistern Structure" is associated with a large cistern. The concentration of domestic artifacts and red painted plaster suggests that this building may have at one time hosted some domestic activities of enslaved Africans.

Additional excavations will provide further insight into its function. Finally, a set of structures known as the "distillery complex" performed the distillation of rum, which was the primary eighteenth-century function of the plantation. In all likelihood, molasses and perhaps raw cane juice were imported from adjacent islands to supplement the sugar cane grown on the Pleasures Estate. Its peak occupation and sugar-production period probably occurred during the 1790s. This was within the context of the island-wide economic boom associated with a great increase in West Indian interisland trade and trade with the newly established United States (Goslinga 1985).

With the decline in this trade, plantations suffered and the Pleasures Estate was converted to a cattle farm by 1834 (Teenstra 1836). It was during this period that the "Large Cistern Structure" might have become a domestic residence for slaves. The relatively lower quantity of ceramic and glass artifactual evidence dating to this period (such as whiteware [1820–1900], porcellaneous [post-1800], and mold-blown glass bottles [post-1840]) corresponds with the historical evidence. Its use as a cattle farm continued until 1905 when the Pleasures Estate was again revived to become a home for the manager of the sisal factory on the island (Attema 1976; Veenenbos 1955). By 1928 the enterprise failed as a result of workers moving to Aruba to work in the oil refinery located there (Hartog 1976). After this, the plantation again reverted to grazing land used by shepherds and their goats.

The main structures at the Pleasures Estate continued to be used in less-formal capacities until the Blaire family left the property in 1977. The home occupied by the Blaire family was constructed in the 1950s and was built from breezeblocks (also known as C.B.S. blocks). This home burned in 1981 and no one has lived on the property since that time. Although privately owned, the property has since been used for grazing by goat farmers.

SUMMARY AND CONCLUSION

Geophysical surveys at both plantations were instrumental in guiding research design and confirming cartographic evidence in relation to both the Pleasures Estate and English Quarter plantations. Cartographic evidence included a number of maps depicting the plantations and their owners on St. Eustatius. One detailed map, drawn by British conquerors in 1781, shows in minute detail 90 plantations and their slave quarters (Martin 1781). My fieldwork (Gilmore 2000) and that of Jay Haviser (Haviser 1981) have provided information attesting to the accuracy of this map. On the two plantations studied here, artifact assemblages provided evidence for the location of slave quarters in the precise location indicated on the 1781 P. F. Martin map. In addition, Haviser's mapping of foundations replicated precisely what is shown on this map.

The 1781 map depicts a total of 290 quarters for the plantations on the island. According to Goslinga (1985:152), the slave population for 1779 was 1,631 and in 1784 stood at 2,962. Given the rate of increase from 1779 to 1784, it is possible that the slave population in 1781 might have been 2,163. If about half of these slaves worked in Oranjestad as skilled tradesmen and along the harbor in warehouses (as is indicated by the documentary evidence), then around 1,080 slaves lived on the plantations at the time the map was drawn. This would provide an estimated 3.7 slaves per quarter. In order to verify this figure, slave-to-quarter ratios were calculated for a few plantations for which the exact numbers for dates near 1781 were known. On Jacob Seys's Peace and Rest Plantation, the ratio was 3.5; on M. D. Godet Senior's plantations Casjoe Bovemen, Don, and Rotteniem, the ratio was 3.7; on Judith Stewart's Fair Play the ratio was 3.8; and finally on Michael Cuvellier's Gilboa the ratio was 3.8. Taken together, these ratios average out to 3.7 slaves per quarter. Regarding the location of plantation quarters on Statia, the majority (82 percent) were located near sugar-processing facilities and almost 50 percent were organized in rows. The rest were located in small clusters of two or three spread across the various plantation fields.

The social and economic implications for slave life on St. Eustatius can be inferred from all of this information. In contrast to Curaçao and other Dutch colonies, because of its status as a trading center, the resident population on St. Eustatius was a cosmopolitan mix of English, French, Spanish, Portuguese, Danish, Italian, African, and Dutch. The resulting community probably varied greatly in perspectives on slavery. However, the archaeological and documentary evidence does provide some specific ideas on where and in what accommodations slaves lived on the island.

Unlike many other places in the eighteenth-century Caribbean, slaves were provided with homes built from wood and cedar shingles (Gilmore 2004). On Curaçao, a cosmopolitan population and a merchant economy were present but slave houses were not built in the same way as on St. Eustatius, which also had these two conditions. Therefore, slave housing on Statia, St. Eustatius, was arguably a reflection of slave-owner wealth and an ostentatious display of power, not necessarily for the slaves but primarily for both foreign and local visitors to the plantations. Other evidence indicates that the plantations on St. Eustatius were geared toward promoting social status. Charles Kingsley (1874) and Schaw (Schaw et al. 1934 [1778]) both related their experiences regarding the lively social activities at the Statia plantations. Also, Teenstra (1836) described one of the plantations that I have studied, the Pleasures Estate, as having a ballroom with silk wallpaper and two chandeliers in it. In this sort of social climate, well-built slave quarters organized adjacent to main houses and sugar-processing facilities (as was found at both Pleasures Estate and English

Quarter) would have been ideal expressions of social status. As a result, slaves might have lived in better conditions than their cohorts on other islands and indeed elsewhere in the New World.

Geophysical surveys were instrumental in guiding research design and confirming cartographic evidence in relation to both the Pleasures Estate and English Quarter plantations. The volcanic nature of St. Eustatius did not affect the results of either instrument in any significant way. Instead, dry soil and vegetation were the primary detriments to using the resistivity meter at the Pleasures Estate. However, the information derived from the fluxgate gradiometer has provided guidance for potential future excavation locations. Most significantly, the resistivity meter helped to identify the location of the slave village at the English Quarter Plantation. Future work at this plantation will undoubtedly contribute significantly to the understanding of slave life on St. Eustatius and the contributions made by slaves to the colonial Atlantic world. The geophysical instruments performed as designed and significantly improved the researcher's ability to focus limited resources on specific areas of each site. The continued use of geophysical instruments on St. Eustatius and elsewhere in the Caribbean will surely contribute to improving site identification and interpretation.

ACKNOWLEDGMENTS

I would like to thank the following: the Institute of Archaeology, University College London, for the use of their geophysical equipment; Anna Bakare and Oliver Pryce for assisting in the initial surveys; and my wife, Joanna Gilmore, for her patience and encouraging words during the completion of my research and writing.

Conclusion

Postscript: Archaeology and Geoinformatics from a Caribbeanist Perspective

Basil A. Reid

This volume brings to the fore the use of geoinformatics within the context of Caribbean archaeology, an approach that originates from the question of how we can most effectively identify, assess, survey, document, and manage diminishing archaeological resources. By providing working hypotheses and occasional field-tested demonstrations of the analytical rewards of geoinformatics, most of the chapters address these important issues of cultural resource management (CRM). Looming large in the Caribbean, the need for CRM emanates from persistent hurricanes, soil erosion, agriculture, industrialization, and urbanization, which have negatively impacted myriad archaeological sites. Given the limited local archaeological expertise and funding constraints in the region, the noninvasive techniques of geoinformatics should resonate well with archaeologists, many of whom desire to achieve optimal field results at minimal costs. CRM aside, this volume seeks to actively promote a research agenda designed to ask searching and penetrating questions about the role of environmental and symbolic factors in Caribbean archaeology. This approach clearly necessitates the incorporation of a wide spectrum of geoinformatics techniques, which can shed much-needed light on prehistoric and historic sites archaeology in the West Indies.

VISIBILITY MODELS AND CARIBBEAN ARCHAEOLOGY

Torres and Rodríguez Ramos's essay in Chapter 1 exemplifies this research agenda as it concentrates on issues of pre-Columbian migration, based on phenomenology and landscape approaches. Their chapter also stands out for being the only one that focuses on the Caribbean region rather than on sites or areas specific to Caribbean islands. Essentially, it articulates the powerful technique of visibility modeling, which although well established in North America and Europe (Gaffney and van Leusen 1995; Harris and Lock 1995; Kvamme 2006; Wheatley 1993) is not as extensively used in Caribbean archaeology. Over the years, discourses on pre-Columbian Caribbean migrations have invariably been dominated by archaeological and linguistic data (Noble 1965; Rouse 1992) coupled with computer simulations relating to ocean currents and trade winds (Callaghan 1990). Against this background, Torres and Rodríguez Ramos not only provide refreshingly new perspectives on an important topic but their essay could also be seen as a harbinger of future archaeological trends in the West Indies.

Constituting an important part of Chapter 1 are digital elevation models (DEMs), which are a type of raster GIS (geographic information systems) layer. In a DEM, each cell has a value corresponding to its elevation. The fact that locations are arranged regularly permits the raster GIS to infer many interesting associations among locations and hence the location of visibility models. As a significant number of Taino sites in Jamaica are located on hilltops (Allsworth-Jones et al. 1999), a fact alluded to by Lyew-Ayee and Conolley in Chapter 7, visibility models may be incorporated in settlement studies in Jamaica to determine the slopes and aspects of pre-Columbian sites as well as their intervisibility. Such an approach will enable us to gain rich insights into a host of thought-provoking issues such as landscape perception, spatial allocation, territoriality, and site access.

Significantly, visibility models may also examine possible relationships between site locations and defense—quite a popular approach in both North America and Europe since the 1990s (e.g., Harris and Lock 1995; Lock and Stancic 1995; Maschner 1996). Harris and Lock (1995) used the concept of field-of-view to examine the defensibility of sites in southern England. Sites that had a larger field-of-view were considered more easily defended. They used this relationship to determine that defense was a declining factor in settlement location in southern England. From the Neolithic through the Iron Age, they noticed that the viewsheds of hillforts decreased in size and became more localized on economic holdings. In a similar study, Maschner (1996) examined the factors behind settlement patterns along the Northwest Coast of North America, with viewshed analysis again being used as a measure of defensibility. The results of Maschner's analysis prompted him to argue that there was an enormous amount of variability in settlement locations in this area and that people did not always choose the location of their settlement on the basis of resource availability and their mode of subsistence. He concluded that while certain environmental variables such as beach quality, climatic exposure, and island size affected the distribution of archaeological sites, defensibility (i.e., total area of surface water visible from a village) became an increasingly important factor in the placement of sites (Maschner 1996:186–188). The question of visibility models and defense may be applied to the Saladoid site of Gandhi Village in south Trinidad. Perched on the top of a hill approximately 26 m above sea level, Gandhi Village, with its commanding view of the surrounding countryside of southwestern Trinidad, was apparently an important defensive hilltop settlement (Reid 2006).

The visibility of monuments or features can also be a social statement or means of control (Kvamme 1999), an issue that bears much relevance to the study of the cultural dynamics of many sugar plantations throughout the Caribbean, where the overseers' great houses were on higher elevations, overlooking slave villages nearby (e.g., Armstrong 1990; Hall 1996; Knight 1997). James Delle (1998), by using a mix of archival and archaeological data, critically examined landscapes and spaces on Jamaica's Blue Mountains coffee plantations dating from 1790 to 1865. It would also be interesting to see whether visibility models would provide fresh insights into the issue of spatiality, as articulated by Delle.

GIS, CRM, AND CARIBBEAN ARCHAEOLOGY

Chapter 2 (Reid), Chapter 3 (Farmer), and Chapter 4 (Ramlal and Reid) furnish the most explicit examples of the significance of GIS in the management of archaeological resources in the Caribbean. Besides their value as a heuristic device for exploring data associations and testing hypotheses, weights-of-evidence models, as articulated by Reid in Chapter 2, may be effectively employed in CRM. Even if the reasoning behind these models appears circular, as they invariably predict site favorability in areas near previously known sites (represented by training points), the fact is that this approach is very much in line with spatial autocorrelation.[1] Spatial autocorrelation is further bolstered by Tobler's Law of Geography, which states that everything is related to everything else, but nearer things are more related to each other than are distant things. Despite this, it is imperative that models be truly representative of the data on the ground, and this can only be achieved through systematic surveys in search of sites in both favorable and unfavorable site locations (as predicted by the models). In this regard, models generated by Reid (Chapter 2) and Lyew-Ayee and Conolley (Chapter 7) will require systematic field verification, although this does not negate their value as working hypotheses, useful for guiding future archaeological research in the Caribbean and elsewhere.

Because of increasing availability of digital environmental data, it is now possible to produce weights-of-evidence predictive models of almost any Caribbean territory. The growing need to mitigate the effects of natural disasters such as hurricanes, storm surges, landslides, and earthquakes and the need to make informed environmental management decisions both have fueled the demand for digital environmental data. Since the launch of Landsat 1 in 1972 (Hester et al. 1997), there has been a steady increase in the availability of remotely sensed data. Both Landsat and SPOT remotely sensed images provide data on the entire planet, which can be easily accessed by agencies within Caribbean territories. For instance, in their study of Falmouth, Jamaica, Lyew-Ayee and Conolley obtained all their true-color and multispectral IKONOS imagery and aerial photographs from local organizations in Jamaica such as Spatial Innovision, Ltd., the Forestry Department, and the Jamaica Bauxite Institute. The presence of the Environmental Management Agency and the Institute of Marine Affairs in Trinidad and Tobago; the National Environment and Planning Agency and the Jamaica Environmental Trust in Jamaica; the Ministry of Planning, Development and Environment in Lucia; the Ministry of Culture, Tourism and Environment in St. Kitts and Nevis; the Coastal Zone Unit and the Barbados Marine Trust in Barbados; and the Ministry of Tourism and Environment in Antigua clearly suggests that environmental issues are being given greater prominence in the region. Greater environmental emphasis has, in turn, led to a concomitant increase in the acquisition of digital data by private- and public-sector companies. Several Land Survey Departments in the Latin American, French, and Anglophone Caribbean islands have in their custody a growing assortment of paper-based and digital materials that are available to researchers. The Lands and Surveys Division in Port of Spain, Trinidad and Tobago, for example, is actively developing a comprehensive array of digital aerial photographs of the twin island republic, which can be dexterously used for a range of automated functions. Aiding and abetting this process is the proliferation of GIS and other computer-based training programs throughout the region. For example, the University of the West Indies, St. Augustine, Trinidad and Tobago, and the University of Technology, Jamaica, both offer a range of geoinformatics courses to Caribbean nationals.

This rising environmentalism in the Caribbean (partly reflective of worldwide trends) and the increased access and use of digital data, as well as the need to keep both urban growth and agriculture in check, have had a knock-on effect on heritage management in Barbados, for example. According to Farmer (Chapter 3), competing demands on the scarce land resources from the agricultural and construction sectors have raised serious concerns about the long-term management of archaeological sites in Barbados. This is cited by Farmer as the rationale for the UNESCO-funded Sites and Monuments Inventory System at the Barbados Museum and Historical Society. Farmer's proposal concerning Bridgetown, the capital of Barbados and one of the largest urban centers in the eastern Caribbean, is deserving of mention. What is important is Farmer's advocacy of an eclectic GIS approach, based on the digital manipulation of land allotment and land-ownership data and soil profiles taken together with contemporary and historic maps (all of which can be used to create buffer zones). Farmer has, in essence, provided a blueprint for the simultaneous management of development, disaster mitigation, and historic sites preservation, a proposal that can be emulated by other Caribbean states. In light of the tentative listing of Bridgetown and its Garrison as a World Heritage site, these are very critical and relevant issues for Barbados.

World Heritage status has certainly placed a number of Caribbean territories into the international spotlight, from Haiti's Citadelle Laferrière and Sans-Souci Palace ruins, to the Dominican Republic's colonial city of Santo Domingo, Curaçao's historic city of Willemstad, Puerto Rico's La Fortaleza and San Juan National Historic Site, St. Kitts and Nevis's Brimstone Hill Fortress National Park, and St. Lucia's Pitons Management Area. Given the sensitivity of these cultural and natural features, GIS approaches are always highly recommended for creating and updating data sets in the comprehensive management of these sites—which leads me to Ramlal and Reid's Archaeological Information System (AIS) for Trinidad and Tobago in Chapter 4.

In 2005, the twin island republic became signatory to the UNESCO Convention prohibiting the illegal import, export, and transfer of ownership of cultural property, signaling the country's seriousness about CRM. Since the signing of this Convention, the National Trust of Trinidad and Tobago has been lobbying UNESCO to consider the 7,000-year-old site of Banwari Trace for World Heritage site status.[2] Ramlal and Reid's contribution (Chapter 4) provides an AIS for sites such as Banwari Trace, as well as all known sites in Trinidad and Tobago, based on attributes such as name, size, location, series, subseries, complex, characteristics, and age. If implemented, this AIS, like Farmer's Sites and Monuments Inventory System, will signal to UNESCO and other regional and international heritage bodies that Trinidad and Tobago is making important strides in heritage management. While the start-up costs for this AIS may be significant, given the considerable capital outlay required for GIS expertise and computer hardware and software, the long-term benefits of more effective CRM that this system would provide will certainly outweigh these initial costs.

Despite the greater availability of digital data sets, a number of Caribbean islands still heavily depend on paper-based methods for the documentation and management of archaeological sites. Using paper-based maps, site records, and inventories—especially materials that are easily torn and difficult to decipher—can be both time consuming and cumbersome. The GIS AIS, proposed by Ramlal and Reid and Farmer, should therefore be considered as a viable "parallel system" to paper-based methods, as it will allow for easy retrieval and mapping of spatial data. And I hasten to use the term *parallel system*, because it would be both precipitous and unwise to digitize materials with the intention of eventually discarding paper-based records, given that digital data can sometimes be lost by unexpected computer glitches and problems with software programs, floppy disks, and CD-ROMs.

GIS, CARTOGRAPHY, GPS, SATELLITE IMAGERY, AERIAL PHOTOGRAPHY, AND PHOTOGRAMMETRY WITHIN THE CONTEXT OF CARIBBEAN ARCHAEOLOGY

GIS, cartography, global positioning systems (GPS), satellite imagery, aerial photography, and photogrammetry may be used in a variety of combinations to aid in the interpretation of Caribbean archaeological landscapes. Clearly demonstrated in the contributions of Armstrong, Hauser, Knight, and Lenik (Chapter 5), Leech (Chapter 6), and Lyew-Ayee and Conolley (Chapter 7) is the usefulness of a multipronged approach. Using an archaeological and historical GIS of St. John's cultural landscape for the years 1780 and 1800, based on Peter Oxholm's maps (1780–1800) in combination with satellite imagery, *matricals* (tax records), and archaeological survey data, Armstrong and colleagues successfully reconstructed the social context of ownership and control in eighteenth-century St. John, Danish West Indies. Their study revealed that in the late eighteenth century, free persons of color on St. John took advantage of the relative flexibility in the Danish land tenure system to establish informal and formal landholdings for themselves and their families in the less-contested lands of St. John.

Issues of land topography, estate consolidation, land ownership, and land tenure have always been central to historical debates on plantation societies in Caribbean historiography and Caribbean archaeology. Indeed, examples of studies that may be amenable to this type of GIS analysis are Verne Shepherd's *Liberation Struggles of Jamaican Livestock Farms during and after Slavery* (2001) and Veronica Dujon's *Land Ownership and Economic Freedom among Post-Slavery Plantation Societies in the Caribbean* (2001), both of which are located in Kofi Agorsah's *Freedom in Black History and Culture* (2001). Satellite remotely sensed imagery, GIS visibility models, aerial photographs, and photogrammetry may be incorporated in these studies to compare and analyze land sizes, land topography, ease of access, and the manner in which buildings, other human structures, and natural features are disposed across the landscape, as well as the economic, political, and symbolic associations of these dispositions. In this regard, Armstrong and colleagues' chapter can be an important frame of reference for similar studies throughout the Caribbean.

Maps and historical data in libraries and archives throughout the Caribbean may be used in a GIS environment, similar to what was undertaken in Chapter 5 by Armstrong, Hauser, Knight, and Lenik. For example, *Jamaica*

Surveyed, by B. W. Higman (1988), contains hundreds of plantation maps and plans of eighteenth- and nineteenth-century Jamaica, with matching contemporary prints, aerial photographs, diagrams, and topographic plans, many of which were obtained from the National Archives and the National Library of Jamaica. Historical maps often mark features that are no longer distinguishable (such as dirt roads or paths) and may be helpful in determining the use of a particular site or part of the site at a given time. At the time the map was drawn, patterns of erosion or weathering may have been different from present ones, owing to climatic changes. A river may have changed its course; waves may have undermined shore cliffs. Despite this, historical maps can become vital data sources in understanding and interpreting the past (Joukowsky 1980). Provided that they are scanned at a very high resolution and properly georeferenced, historical maps can be effectively used within a GIS environment. They therefore hold much promise for scholarship in Caribbean archaeology.

But what if the maps of the period being studied do not exist or are woefully inadequate, as was the case with Leech's study of seventeenth-century St. Kitts? According to Roger Leech (Chapter 6), seventeenth-century maps of the island were destroyed by the French in 1706. This has made it difficult for archaeologists to study the colonial landscapes of Nevis. In order to circumvent this problem, Leech used mid-twentieth-century maps of Nevis and aerial photographs together with GPS surveys of the island to reconstruct Nevis's colonial landscape, particularly as regards the abandonment of plantations and estate consolidation. Though not specifically framed within GIS, this case study is very useful and, in fact, can be emulated by archaeologists working in other Caribbean territories, where maps pertaining to certain periods are either nonexistent or lacking.

Realizing that the use of total stations and/or baselines and offsets would have been inappropriate for surveying many of the widely spaced features in Nevis within dense woodland, notably roads, tracks, and field boundaries, Leech successfully used navigation-grade GPS, which worked well in forest when supplemented by a handheld aerial. Leech's experience in Nevis is important, as it is demonstrative of how relatively inexpensive GPS technology can be effectively used in the field. A similar success story comes from St. Lucia, where an island-wide GPS survey was carried out in 2002 by a team of 11 archaeologists, student assistants, and volunteers from Leiden University and the Florida Museum of Natural History. The project was highly successful, as several new sites were identified and mapped using GPS. Recent developments in GPS technology now enable archaeologists to survey landscapes quickly and efficiently and to make detailed plan maps of archaeological sites and features. What should be particularly encouraging for GPS users in the Caribbean is the excellent satellite coverage that is generally available in the region. According to Leech, the Wide Area Augmentation System (WAAS) differential satellite is easily accessible to the Caribbean and generally the satellite coverage seems much better than in Europe, possibly because of the United States's defense interests in the Caribbean or because of the proximity of the equator. Further, the recent establishment of a Reference Station Network web site (http://201.238.69.22/) by the Lands and Surveys Division of Trinidad and Tobago will undoubtedly provide qualitatively better postprocessed data for the southern Caribbean.

The principal advantage of satellite remotely sensed imagery in archaeology is that it furnishes general information on a very large area, revealing widespread patterns of vegetation and landforms (Avery and Berlin 1992). The spectrum of sunlight reflected by the earth's surface contains information about the composition of the surface, and it may reveal traces of past human activities such as agriculture or settlement patterns. Since sand, cultivated soil, vegetation, and all kinds of rocks each have distinctive temperatures and emit heat at different rates, sensors can "see" things beyond ordinary vision or cameras (Hester et al. 1997). As a prelude to predictive modeling, Lyew-Ayee and Conolley (Chapter 7) used multispectral satellite imagery of contemporary Trelawny in order to create several manmade and natural land covers of the parish. While accepting that secondary, not primary, forests characterize much of the Caribbean landscape, satellite imagery is still a useful tool as it may detect archaeological remains not easily identifiable on the ground such as irrigation ditches, buried stone walls, and pre-Columbian plazas. Although pre-Columbian plazas, similar to Caguana (Puerto Rico), are yet to be found in Jamaica, Rouse (1992) argues that they might have existed on the island but on "unstructured grounds." Through careful analysis, it may be possible for satellite imagery to identify likely plaza locations in Jamaica. The Pitons in St. Lucia were recently declared a World Heritage site. The ability of satellite imagery, with its ability to penetrate darkness, cloud cover, thick canopies, and even the ground, may provide significant clues on past human activities associated with this important environmental landmark.

While GPS, satellite remotely sensed data, and aerial photography are all essential to the work of Armstrong and colleagues (Chapter 5), Leech (Chapter 6), and Lyew-Ayee and Conolley (Chapter 7), the inclusion of photogrammetry in Lyew-Ayee and Conolley's contribution adds considerably to the breadth of knowledge and techniques available to Caribbean archaeologists. Defined as the science of measurement by photography (Slama 1980), photogrammetry may be used to record cultural resources such as plan views of features, vertical aspects (elevations), aerial views of structures in the built environment and roads (e.g., at Chaco Canyon, New Mexico [Hayes et al. 1981]), entire historical districts, and many other types of cultural and natural features. Typical Saladoid village patterns in Puerto Rico and adjacent islands consist of a semicircular series of mounded middens, frequently serving as the village cemetery, facing a central plaza. Considering the utility of photogrammetry, the technique may be used to identify many of these mounded middens in the Caribbean, in landscapes often covered by dense, lush vegetation. The Maroon trail over the Blue Mountains between Portland and St. Thomas parishes of Jamaica is the historic trail once used by freed slaves and Maroons. The trail provided passage, by foot and donkey, for produce grown in the upper Rio Grande Valley to markets on the southern plains (National Geographic Traveler 2007). Photogrammetric images may reveal other historic trails in Jamaica and elsewhere in the Caribbean, providing data that may be used to putatively reconstruct patterns of intraisland travel networks in the Caribbean. Finally, Samuel Wilson (1990) posits that regional Taino chiefdoms in Hispañiola were delimited by geographical boundaries such as mountains, coastal plains, and rivers. Stereoscopic images, depicting spatial relationships among mountains, rivers, and valleys of various Caribbean islands (such as eastern and central Cuba, Puerto Rico, and Jamaica), may, therefore, help us to better demarcate regional Taino chiefdom societies and, by extension, develop better understandings of patterns of social complexity in the northern Caribbean.

CARIBBEAN ARCHAEOLOGY AND GEOPHYSICS

Resistivity survey methods need not be restricted to detecting and delimiting individual archaeological features. They also may be used to locate, characterize, and distinguish different kinds of use areas or activity areas as whole geographic units within sites (Carr 1982), such as buried walls, ditches, burial mounds, graves, ancient water courses, and field boundaries. Survey results can be used to guide excavation and to give archaeologists insight into the patterning of nonexcavated parts of the site. Geophysical surveys are not invasive or destructive. For this reason, they are often used where preservation (rather than excavation) is the goal. Both Klingelhofer (Chapter 8) and Gilmore (Chapter 9) should be lauded for their seminal essays on archaeological geophysics, as their work signals important CRM trends in Caribbean archaeology. While Klingelhofer has yet to unequivocally identify Raleigh's outpost in Trinidad, documentary and cartographic data, as presented by Klingelhofer, clearly suggest that the outpost might have existed at Los Gallos Point. Comprising his repertoire of techniques are magnetometry, resistivity surveys, soil sampling, and geothermography. Gilmore's contribution demonstrates the value of geophysical surveys in guiding research design and confirming cartographic data in relation to both the Pleasures Estate and English Quarter plantations in St. Eustatius. His chapter is therefore a good example of the value of geophysical survey as it goes beyond results to interpretation.

The work of both Klingelhofer and Gilmore has implications for future research in the Caribbean. A case in point is the historical archaeology of the Bahamas, as described by Farnsworth (2001:255–256). According to Farnsworth, a relatively small number of plantations have, to date, been excavated in the Bahamas. He made reference to 30 "wattled and plastered" slave houses in Bellefield, described in an 1805 newspaper report. However, archaeological surveys by Farnsworth and his associates, based on a visual inspection and surface collection, found no trace of these slave houses on the surface. Maps of the area reveal two other clusters of ruins in the vicinity of the main house that would have been part of the original estate, one approximately 200 m northwest of the main house and the other 250 m southwest. Dense brush prevented Farnsworth and his team from visiting them, but it is possible that they represent the wattle-and-plaster houses described in the newspaper or, more likely, stone-built replacements. On the face of it, this example from the Bahamas seems tailor-made for geophysical surveys. After clearing the brush, archaeologists could set up grids and subject the landscape to geophysical surveys for the purposes of delineating archaeologically significant areas for "targeted" excavations. Geophysical surveys may also be applied to the historical archaeology of Guadeloupe, where there is insufficient knowledge of the archaeology of the tobacco, indigo, and coffee colonial industries (Delpuech 2001:44). Applying geophysical surveys to prehistoric archaeology in the Caribbean is also a viable option, considering that the region has a motley collection of pre-Columbian sites bearing features amenable to geophysical detection, such as postholes, pits, hearths, middens, and burials.

However, like any other technique, geophysical surveys cannot be used arbitrarily. The archaeologist, or the archaeologist working in conjunction with the geophysicist, should decide on the best time to conduct a survey. The soil condition is a limiting factor when using a resistivity meter, as skewed readings may be generated if sites are too dry or too wet. In Trinidad and Tobago, there are basically two seasons: wet and dry. The dry season, which extends from late December to late May, is characterized by reduced frequency and intensity in rainfall. During the rainy season, which extends from June to early December, rainfall is both higher in frequency and longer in duration. Most archaeological projects conducted in the twin island republic, including Klingelhofer's geophysical surveys of Los Gallos Point (Chapter 8), are conducted during the "fairly wet" dry season, when both climatic and soil conditions better facilitate fieldwork. Essentially, knowledge of the microclimatic and microenvironmental conditions specific to Caribbean territories should always be factored into our fieldwork scheduling decisions, including those relating to geophysical surveys.

The local geology is also an important consideration in archaeological geophysics, although this may, on occasion, be overstated. Gilmore's geophysical surveys (Chapter 9) disproved the commonly held view that geophysical surveys do not produce optimal results on volcanic islands. Considering that the Lesser Antilles is made up of volcanic islands, with a rich array of archaeological sites, this information should serve to actively encourage future geophysical surveys in this part of the Caribbean. Finally, while geophysical surveys are useful, they may be preceded by aerial photography, photogrammetry, and satellite imagery in order to obtain an initial idea of the "structure of the archaeological record" (Carr 1982:1–2). The area covered by a given Landsat image is 115 × 106 miles (about 185 km east–west by 170 km north–south), with a ground resolution of objects and features of about 30 m^2 (Hester et al. 1997). Before subjecting archaeologically significant areas to geophysical surveys, it is recommended that Landsat satellite imagery, aerial photography, and photogrammetry be used to delimit areas of interest, thereby facilitating more targeted surveys and excavations. Even if we accept that time and funding constraints as well as a lack of technical personnel may render this approach impractical in some Caribbean territories, a multiscalar methodology (based on a healthy mix of geoinformatics techniques) should always be the ideal for archaeologists working in the region.

CONCLUSION

Academic publications may be generated wherever in the world geoinformatics is practiced within an archaeological framework. However, what makes this volume a significant milestone is that it presents a collage of scholarly essays that focus on issues specific, but not necessarily unique, to the Caribbean such as pre-Columbian migration, cultural histories, European colonization, African slavery, plantation economies, and colonial patterns of land tenure. Implicitly or explicitly, most of the contributions underscore the value of geoinformatics to CRM. This volume not only is useful for developing well-integrated research designs but it also, in many ways, helps to legitimize the application of geoinformatics within the context of Caribbean archaeology.

NOTES

1. Please read *Geographical Information Systems in Archaeology*, by James Conolly and Mark Lake (2006), for a fuller discussion of spatial autocorrelation.

2. Located in south Trinidad, Banwari Trace is considered the oldest site in the West Indies.

Glossary of Terms

Aerial photography
Photographic coverage of the land surface obtained from the air. Aerial photographs are useful in locating and recording site positions.

Anthropomorphic
Pertaining to the elements of human motivation, characteristics, or behavior in relation to inanimate objects, animals, or natural phenomena.

Arauquinoid
Arauquinoid pottery is a prehistoric style that originated from the Barrancoid cultures in northeastern South America, the Orinoco Valley, and Trinidad. Arauquinoid ceramics replaced those of the preceding Barrancoid tradition around A.D. 500. There was apparently extensive trading in Arauquinoid times between Trinidad and the middle Orinoco (Saunders 2005).

AutoCAD DXF
A CAD data file format, developed by Autodesk as their solution for enabling data interoperability between AutoCAD and other programs.

Barrancoid
A ceramic tradition possibly originating on the Caribbean coast of Colombia and established in the Orinoco Delta by circa 1,000 B.C. It spread down the coast and (at the turn of the millennium) east and west to Guyana and Colombia. The pottery is skillfully modeled with biomorphic ornamentation and broad-lined incised patterns. The type site is Barrancas in Venezuela.

Bayesian logic
Named after Thomas Bayes, an English clergyman and mathematician, Bayesian logic is a branch of logic applied to decision making and inferential statistics that deals with probability inference.

Buffer
A polygon enclosing an area within a specified distance from a point, line, or polygon. In ArcView Weights-of-Evidence, buffering is performed using Spatial Analyst so that the output is always a grid (raster). The buffering function generates one or more buffers of equal distance from the input features. Input can be either vector or raster data.

Cartography
Cartography is the study and making of maps.

Categorical weights calculation (analysis)
Refers to weights calculated for each class in an evidential theme. In ArcView Weights-of-Evidence, categorical analysis describes one of the tables of weights that can be created using the Calculate Theme Weights function, distinguishing it from Cumulative Weights.

Conditional independence
Conditional independence of evidential themes with respect to the training points is assumed for the weights-of-evidence. The product of area and posterior probability summed over each unique condition is the number of points predicted by the model. A ratio is calculated by dividing the actual number of training points input to the model by this predicted number of points. The ratio will be between 1 and 0. A value of 1 (never occurs in practice) indicates conditional independence among the evidential themes used in the model. Values <1 indicate a conditional independence problem although values >.05 may produce reasonable results.

Continentality
The quality or state of being a continent.

Contrast
The difference between weights, W+ and W–. Difference between the natural logs of conditional odds that A and B occur together and the natural log of the conditional odds that A and B do not occur together. $C = ln(Odds\{B\,|\,A\text{-}\})$, where A = evidence layer and B = training set.

The relationships with respect to probability, odds, and weight (natural logarithm of odds) are shown in the table below.

Probability	Odds	Weight²
0.1	1/9	−2.2
0.5	1/1 (even)	0.0
0.75	3/1	1.1
0.88	88/12	2.0
0.99	99/1	4.6

Cultural resource management
The management and preservation of cultural resources such as cultural landscapes, archaeological sites, historical records, historic buildings, industrial heritage, and artifacts.

Cumulative weights (analysis)
Refers to weights calculated for a cumulative number of points for classes for ordered data. Cumulative weights calculated from either the highest to lowest (descending) or lowest to highest (ascending) class can be calculated from a single evidential theme in the Calculate Theme Weights function of ArcView. Calculating cumulative weights can be useful in reducing noise from variation that occurs in categorical weights, making it easier to determine the optimum cutoff points for generalization of data.

Digital elevation models
Digital elevation models are data files that contain the elevation of the terrain over a specified area, usually at a fixed grid interval over the surface of the earth. The interval between each of the grid points will always be referenced to some geographical coordinate system. This is usually either latitude-longitude or the Universal Transverse Mercator (UTM) coordinate system. The closer together the grid points are located, the more detailed the information will be in the file. The details of the peaks and valleys in the terrain will be better modeled with a small grid spacing than when the grid intervals are very large.

Evidence (predictor) theme
A map or area layer (in either vector or raster format; shape or grid file) used for prediction of point objects (such as archaeological sites). The polygons or grid cells of the evidential themes have two or more values (class values). For example, a soil map may have three or more values representing the classes

(map units) present (e.g., land capability, soil texture, and soil relief). Although weights-of-evidence was originally defined for binary evidential themes (also named binary patterns in several publications), it can also be applied to themes with more than two classes. Frequently, multiclass evidential themes will be generalized (simplified) by combining classes into a small number of values, facilitating interpretation.

Fluxgate gradiometer
A magnetic surveying instrument used in subsurface detection that records changes in the intensity of a magnetic field. Readings can be obtained continually rather than as individual spot measurements of a proton magnetometer.

Geodesy
The science of measuring the size and shape of the earth and its gravitational and magnetic fields.

Geographic information systems (GIS)
These are tools used to gather, transform, manipulate, analyze, and produce information related to the surface of the earth. These data may exist as maps, three-dimensional virtual models, tables, and/or lists.

Geoinformatics
An interdisciplinary field that develops and uses information science and science infrastructure to address the problems of geosciences. Several disciplines fall within the general purview of geoinformatics, for example, geographic information systems (GIS), global positioning systems (GPS), satellite imagery, aerial photography, photogrammetry, cartography, and geophysical surveys.

Geophysics
The branch of geology that studies the physics of the earth, using the physical principles underlying such phenomena as seismic waves, heat flow, gravity, and magnetism to study the various physical properties of the earth and the composition and movement of its component layers of rock. The use of geophysical surveys in archaeology provides an invaluable technique for noninvasively mapping the subsurface and features.

Global positioning system (GPS)
GPS was developed and is operated by the U.S. Department of Defense. It is a satellite navigational system formed by 24 satellites orbiting the earth at approximately 12,000 miles above the surface and making two complete or-

bits every 24 hours. This is used for navigation all over the world. The satellites are equipped with atomic clocks that are precise to within a billionth of a second.

Ground resolution
A measure of the resolving power of a sensor when expressed as cycles per unit length on the ground from a given altitude.

Harquebuses
Muzzle-loaded firearms, lighter in weight than muskets.

Herbaceous
Of or pertaining to herbs: having the nature, texture, or characteristics of an herb, as herbaceous plants; an herbaceous stem.

Hydrology
The study of the movement, distribution, and quality of water throughout the earth.

Insularism
The state of being isolated or detached.

Magnetometer
A magnetometer is a scientific instrument used to measure the strength of magnetic fields. Magnetometers are used in geophysical surveys to find deposits of iron because they can measure the magnetic pull of iron. Magnetometers are also used to detect archaeological sites, shipwrecks, and other buried or submerged objects.

Mapping-grade GPS
Mapping-grade GPS units are used in general land inventories and often in research projects where higher accuracy is important. Mapping-grade units can be further subdivided into those that have the capability of about 1-m accuracy and those capable of sub-meter accuracy due to differences in receiver and antennae instruments. Mapping-grade GPS units use differential correction for high accuracy.

Mayoid
Mayoid pottery was a late development, arriving in Trinidad in the years immediately preceding European arrival, brought by Amerindians from the mainland. A distinctive feature of Mayoid ceramics is that their fabric always in-

cludes a temper called *caraipé*, made from the ash of burned bark of the tree *Licania apetala* (Boomert 1985).

Missing data integer
An integer required to define areas of missing data for each evidential theme. The missing data integer is required even if missing data are defined by "No Data" or the evidential theme does not contain any missing data within the study area.

Negative weight, W-: natural logarithm of the quantity
Odds that the evidence layer and training set do not occur together divided by the odds of the training set occurring within the study area. $W- = In(Odds\{B|A-\}/Odds\{B\})$, where A = evidence layer, B = training set.

Normalized contrast
Contrast divided by the standard deviation of contrast.

Ortoiroid
Sometime between 5000 and 2000 B.C., Ortoiroid (Archaic) groups began migrating from Trinidad or mainland South America into the Lesser Antilles. The oldest Ortoiroid site in the West Indies is the 7,000-year-old site of Banwari Trace in south Trinidad. Traditional Archaic sites are characterized by an abundance of marine mollusks, the absence of pottery, and the use of ground stone and shell tools (Keegan 1994).

Ostionoid
The Ostionoid culture is the name given to the pottery-making horticulturalists of the Caribbean Sea between about A.D. 500 and A.D. 1000.

Panchromatic
Describes a type of black-and-white photographic film that is sensitive to all wavelengths of visible light. A panchromatic film therefore produces a realistic image of a scene.

Pattern generalization
In weights-of-evidence, this is the result of the reclassification of the thematic information of an evidential theme generated by classifying (or grouping) existing classes in the theme attribute table to fewer classes in a new field.

Phenomenology
An approach to philosophy that begins with an exploration of phenomena (what presents itself to us in conscious experience) as a means to finally grasp

the absolute, logical, ontological, and metaphysical spirit that is behind phenomena.

Photogrammetry
The art, science, and technology of obtaining reliable information about physical objects and the environment through the processes of recording, measuring, and interpreting photographic images and patterns of electromagnetic radiant energy and other phenomena.

Physiography
The characteristic(s) of a site's physical geography.

Polychromatic
Light or other electromagnetic radiation composed of more than one wavelength.

Positive weight, W+: natural logarithm of the quantity
Odds that the evidence layer and training set occur together divided by the odds of the training set occurring within the study area. Difference between the unconditional or prior logit of A and the posterior logit of A. A logit equals the In odds. $W+ = In(Odds\{B|A^*\}/Odds\{B\})$, where A = evidence layer: B = training set.

Posterior probability
A redistribution of the prior probability based on the weights.

Predictive modeling
Predictive modeling is used to create a statistical model of future behavior. A predictive model is made up of a number of predictors, which are variable factors that are likely to influence future behavior or results.

Prior probability
Number of points in the training set divided by the study area, expressed by the same area unit (cell size).

Resistivity meter
A portable instrument that measures the conductivity of a magnetic field through various surface materials. It is used to determine the presence of material such as postholes, pits, ditches, underground walls, and burials.

Response theme
An output map that expresses the probability that a unit area contains a training point, estimated by combining the weights of the predictor variables. Each response theme is based on a unique conditions grid and its attribute table.

Saladoid
The Saladoid culture is the name given to immigrants from South America who moved into the Caribbean region about the fourth century B.C. The Saladoid people were horticulturalists living in the Orinoco Valley and along the northeast coast of South America, making a distinctive white-on-red pottery and tending manioc and fishing.

Satellite images
These are digital data obtained from sensors carried in satellites, which are collected both in the visible and nonvisible portions of the electromagnetic spectrum.

Soil aggradations
The increase in soil volume in a particular region due to either natural or artificial (manmade) means.

Soil thermography
The study of soil temperature rate in relation to conditions of an archaeological site and the presence and absence of artifacts.

Steward's Circum-Caribbean Theory
This theory was proposed in the late 1940s by the American anthropologist Julian Steward, editor of *Handbook of South American Indians*, who assigned the term *tropical forest culture* to the indigenous inhabitants of Guiana and the Amazon Basin. According to Steward these peoples originated in the circum-Caribbean area and over the millennia spread southeastward along the coast of South America and into the Amazon Basin.

Structured Query Language (SQL)
A popular computer language used to create, modify, retrieve, and manipulate data from relational database management systems. The language has evolved beyond its original purpose to support object-relational database management systems.

Study area theme
In Arc-SDM, this is the study area in an integer grid theme that defines the area of interest. It acts as a mask on areas of evidential themes and, if they are being used, training points outside the study are ignored during the calculation of weights and output maps.

Survey-grade GPS
Survey-grade GPS units are used for surveying tasks that require very high accuracy (within 1 cm), such as bridge construction. Survey-grade GPS units use differential correction for highest accuracy.

Training points
Training points are point features used in the calculation of weights and usually represent archaeological sites in weights-of-evidence archaeological modeling.

Unique conditions grid/table
In weights-of-evidence, the unique conditions table and map are produced by an overlay of the evidential themes selected for prediction.

Unit cell area
In weights-of-evidence and logistic regression, each training point is assumed to occupy a small unit area named the unit cell.

UTM (Universal Transverse Mercator) coordinates
A system of plane coordinates based upon 60 north–south trending zones (each 6 degrees of longitude wide) that circle the globe. The coordinates are in meters as opposed to degrees, minutes, and seconds.

Vector data sets
Digital data consisting of coordinate pairs (x,y) to represent locations on the earth. Features can take the form of single points, lines, arcs, or closed lines (polygons).

Weights-of-evidence
A Bayesian approach for combining data to predict occurrence of events. It is based on the presence and absence of a characteristic or pattern and the occurrence of an event. The method was originally developed for a nonspatial application in medical diagnosis, in which the evidence consisted of a set of symptoms and the hypothesis was of the type "this patient has disease x." For each symptom, a pair of weights was calculated, one for presence of the symptom, one for absence of the symptom. The magnitude of the weights depended on the measured association between the symptom and the pattern of disease in a large group of patients. The weights could then be used to estimate the probability that a new patient would get the disease, based on the presence or absence of symptoms. In spatial analysis, it has been used extensively in the mineral and mining fields but only recently has been applied to archaeological research.

X- and Y-parallax
The apparent displacement or difference of position of a grid, as seen from two different stations, or points of view.

Zoomorphic
Pertaining to the use of animal forms to represent the spiritual world or gods.

References Cited

Aarons, G. A.
1984 Archaeological Sites in the Hellshire Area. *Jamaica Journal* 16(1):76–88. Institute of Jamaica Publications.

Alegría, Ricardo E.
1983 *Ball Courts and Ceremonial Plazas in the West Indies*. Yale University Publications in Anthropology 79, Yale University, New Haven, Connecticut.

Allen, K. M. S., S. W. Green, and E. B. W. Zubrow (editors)
1990 *Interpreting Space: GIS and Archaeology*. Taylor & Francis, London.

Allsworth-Jones, P., G. Lalor, G. Lechler, S. Mitchell, E. Rodrigues, and M. Vutchkov
1999 *The Taino Settlement of the Kingston Area*. Department of History, International Centre for Environmental and Nuclear Sciences, and Department of Geography and Geology, University of the West Indies, Mona, Jamaica.

Anschuetz, Kurt F., R. H. Wilshusen, and C. Scheick
2001 An Archaeology of Landscapes: Perspectives and Directions. *Journal of Archaeological Research* 9:157–211.

Arjoon, S.
1999 *A Guide to Understanding Statistics*. Institute of Business, University of the West Indies, St. Augustine, Trinidad and Tobago. Litho Press, Trinidad.

Armstrong, Douglas V.
1990 *The Old Village and the Great House: An Archaeological and Historical Examination of Drax Hall Plantation, St. Ann's Bay, Jamaica*. University of Illinois Press, Champaign.

2003a *Creole Transformation from Slavery to Freedom: Historical Archaeology of the East End Community, St. John, Virgin Islands*. University Press of Florida, Gainesville.

2003b Social Relations in a Maritime Creole Community: Networked Multifocality in the East End Community of St. John, Danish West Indies. In *Proceedings of the XIX International Congress for Caribbean Archaeology*, edited by Luc Alofs and Raymundo A. C. F. Dijkhoff, pp. 195–210. Museo Arqueologico Aruba 9(2).

Armstrong, Douglas V., and Mark W. Hauser
2005 Reassessing the Cultural Landscape of St. John, USVI, Using GIS. In *Proceedings of the XX Congreso International de Arqueologia del Caribe*, pp. 515–520. Museo del Hombre 38(2). Santo Domingo, Dominican Republic.

Armstrong, Douglas V., Mark W. Hauser, Stephen Lenik, and Kenneth Wild
2007 Estate Consolidation, Land Use, and Ownership: A GIS Archaeological Landscape of St. John, Danish West Indies (1780–1800) with Particular Focus on Annaberg Plantation. In *Proceedings of the Twenty-First Congress of the International Association for Caribbean Archaeology (IACA)*, edited by Basil Reid, Henri Petitjean Roget, and Antonio Curet, pp. 69–80. The University of the West Indies, School of Continuing Studies, St. Augustine.

Armstrong, Douglas V., David W. Knight, and Mark W. Hauser
2006 *Historical Archaeology of the Cinnamon Bay Shoreline, St. John, United States Virgin Islands: Explorations of a Small Cotton Estate and Its Transformation in an Emerging Danish Sugar Economy.* Syracuse University Archaeological Research Center Report. Syracuse University, Syracuse, New York.

Armstrong, Douglas V., and E. J. Reitz
1990 *The Old Village and the Great House: An Archaeological and Historical Examination of Drax Hall Plantation, St. Ann's Bay, Jamaica.* University of Illinois Press, Champaign.

Attema, Y.
1976 *St. Eustatius: A Short History of the Island and Its Monuments.* Walburg Pers, Zutphen, The Netherlands.

Avery, T. E., and G. L. Berlin
1992 *Fundamentals of Remote Sensing and Airphoto Interpretation.* 5th ed. Macmillian, New York.

Ayubi, E., and J. B. Haviser (editors)
1991 *Proceedings of the Thirteenth International Congress for Caribbean Archaeology.* Reports of the Archaeological-Anthropological Institute of the Netherlands Antilles, No. 9. Curaçao.

Bakare, Anna
2002 Saint Eustatius from a New Perspective: Defining Historic Archaeology through Geoarchaeological and Chemical Analyses. Unpublished thesis, Institute of Archaeology, University College London.

Baksh, Michael
1991 Applications of a Hand-Held GPS Receiver in South America Rain Forests. In *Applications of Space Age Technology in Anthropology*, edited by C. A. Behrens and T. L. Sever, pp. 227–236. National Aeronautics and Space Administration, John C. Stennis Space Center, Mississippi.

Baldwin, J. A. D., P. F. Fisher, J. D. Wood, and M. Langford
1996 Modeling Environmental Cognition of the View with GIS. In *Proceedings of the Third International Conference/Workshop in Integrating Geographic Infor-*

mation Systems and Environmental Modeling [CD-ROM]. National Center for Geographic Information and Analysis, Santa Barbara, California.

Barker, Phillip
1982   *Techniques of Archaeological Investigation*. B. T. Batsford, London.

Barnett, Captain E., and assistants, HMS Thunder
1848   St Christopher and Nevis, 1:56,700, London: Admiralty (can be found at National Archives, Kew, England, Wo78/603).

Beck, Jens
1754   Jens Beck's Map of St. Croix. Library of Congress, Washington, D.C.

Bernhardsen, Tor
1999   *Geographic Information Systems: An Introduction*. John Wiley and Sons, New York.

Boleneus, D. E., G. L. Raines, J. D. Causey, A. A. Bookstrom, T. P. Frost, and P. C. Hyndman
2002   *Assessment Method for Epithermal Gold Deposits in Northeast Washington State Using Weights-of-Evidence GIS Modeling*. U.S. Geological Survey Open-File Report 01-501. Electronic document, http://pubs.usgs.gov/of/2001/of01-501/, accessed January 3, 2003.

Bolstad, P.
2001   *GIS Fundamentals: A First Text on Geographic Information Systems*. Eider Press, White Bear Lake, Minnesota.

Bonham-Carter, G. F.
1994   *Geographic Information Systems for Geoscientists—Modeling with GIS*. Permagon, Oxford.

Bonham-Carter, G. F., F. P. Agterberg, and D. F. Wright
1988   Integration of Geological Data Sets for Gold Exploration in Nova Scotia. *Photogrammetric Engineering and Remote Sensing* 54(11)1585–1592.

Boomert, Arie
1985   The Guayabitoid and Mayoid Series: Amerindian Culture History in Trinidad during Late Prehistoric and Protohistoric Times. In *Proceedings of the Tenth International Congress for the Study of Pre-Columbian Cultures of the Lesser Antilles*, pp. 93–148. Centre de Recherche Caraïbes, Université de Montreal, Montreal, Canada.
2000   *Trinidad, Tobago and the Lower Orinoco Sphere: An Archaeological and Ethnohistorical Study*. Cairi Publications, Alkmaar, The Netherlands.

Bourdieu, Pierre
1977   *Outline of a Theory of Practice*, translated by Richard Nice. Cambridge University Press, Cambridge.

Bowditch, N.
1995   *The American Practical Navigator*. U.S. Defense Mapping Agency. Hydrographic/Topographic Agency, Bethesda, Maryland.

Bowen, Brandon, Jody Eason, James Prolizo, and James Sipe
2004   *Preliminary Design Review for Improved Soil Resistivity Meter*. Mercer Ar-

chaeological Research Systems, School of Engineering, Mercer University, Macon, Georgia.

Bradley, Richard
2003 Seeing Things: Perception, Experience and the Constraints of Excavation. *Journal of Social Archaeology* 3(2):151–168.

British Library
n.d. Venezuela-Guiana border treaty papers. MSS Add. MS 36317.

Brophy, Kenneth, and Dave Cowley
2005 *From the Air: Understanding Aerial Archaeology*. Tempus Publishing, Stroud, Gloucestershire, U.K.

Bullen, R.
1974 Were There Pre-Columbian Cultural Contacts between Florida and the West Indies: The Archaeological Evidence. *The Florida Anthropologist* 27:149–160.

Burdon, Major J. A.
1920 *Nevis, Compiled and Brought up to Date from Existing Surveys by Major J. A. Burdon*. Geographical Section, General Staff War Office, London.

Burrough, P., and R. McDonnell
1998 *Principles of Geographical Information Systems*. Oxford University Press, Oxford.

Calkins, Hugh, C. J. Côté, C. Finneran, G. Hayes, T. Murdoch
1989 *GIS Development Guide*. Local Government Technology Services, State Archives and Records Administration, Albany, New York.

Callaghan, R. T.
1990 *Mainland Origins of the Preceramic Cultures of the Greater Antilles*. Ph.D. dissertation, Department of Archaeology, University of Calgary, Alberta, Canada. UMI, Ann Arbor.
1995 Antillean Cultural Contacts with Mainland Regions as a Navigation Problem. In *Proceedings of the Fifteenth International Congress for Caribbean Archaeology*, edited by R. E. Alegría and M. Rodríguez, pp. 181–190. Centro de Estudios Avanzados de Puerto Rico y el Caribe, San Juan, Puerto Rico.
2001 Ceramic Age Seafaring and Interaction Potential in the Antilles: A Computer Simulation. *Current Anthropology* 42:308–313.
2003 Comments on the Mainland Origins of the Preceramic Cultures of the Greater Antilles. *Latin American Antiquity* 14(3):323–338.

Camba, Garcia
1842 Map of Puerto Rico (ca. 1:570,000). Map Division. Library of Congress, Washington, D.C.

Carr, Christopher
1982 *Handbook on Soil Resistivity Surveying*. Center for American Archaeology Press, Kampsville, Illinois.

Certeau, Michel de
1984 *The Practice of Everyday Life*, translated by Steven Rendall. University of California Press, Berkeley.

Chagnon, Napoleon A.
1991 GIS, GPS, Political History and Geo-demography of the Aramamisi Yanomamo Expansion. In *Applications of Space Age Technology in Anthropology*, edited by C. A. Behrens and T. L. Sever, pp. 35–62. National Aeronautics and Space Administration, John C. Stennis Space Center, Mississippi.

Chanlatte, Luis
2003 Las sociedades agricolas en el Caribe: las Antillas Mayores y las Bahamas. In *General History of the Caribbean:* Vol. 1, *Autochtonous Societies (Sociedades Autoctonas)*, edited by J. Sued Badillo, pp. 228–258. Palgrave Macmillan, New York.

Clark, J. G.
1981 *La Rochelle and the Atlantic Economy during the Eighteenth Century.* Johns Hopkins University Press, Baltimore.

Clarke, A.
1990 *Seeing Beneath the Soil: Prospecting Methods in Archaeology.* Batsford, London.

Cleere, H. F. (editor)
1989 *Archaeological Heritage Management in the Modern World.* Unwin Hyman, London.

Conolly, James, and Mark Lake
2006 *Geographical Information Systems in Archaeology.* Manuals in Archaeology. Cambridge University Press, Cambridge.

Cooney, Gabriel
2003 Introduction: Seeing Land from Sea. *World Archaeology*, Special edition: *Seascapes* 35(3):323–328.

Cowen, David J.
1990 GIS versus CAD versus DBMSL: What Are the Differences. In *Introductory Readings in Geographic Information Systems*, edited by Donna J. Peuquet and Duane F. Marble, pp. 52–61. Taylor & Francis, London.

Crock, J. G.
2000 Inter-Island Interaction and the Development of Chiefdoms in the Eastern Caribbean. Unpublished Ph.D. dissertation, Department of Anthropology, University of Pittsburgh, Pittsburgh.
2005 Losing Ground at Rapid Rate: The Effects of Two Decades of Hotel Development. Paper presented at the 21st Congress of the International Association for Caribbean Archaeology (IACA), Trinidad and Tobago.

Curet, L. Antonio
1992 The Development of Chiefdoms in the Greater Antilles: A Regional Study of the Valley of Maunabo, Puerto Rico. Unpublished Ph.D. dissertation, Department of Anthropology, Arizona State University, Tempe.
2004 Island Archaeology and Units of Analysis in the Study of Ancient Caribbean Societies. In *Voyages of Discovery: The Archaeology of the Islands*, edited by S. M. Fitzpatrick, pp. 187–201. Praeger, Westport, Connecticut.
2005 *Caribbean Paleodemography: Population, Culture History, and Sociopolitical Processes in Ancient Puerto Rico.* University of Alabama Press, Tuscaloosa.

Curet, L. Antonio, J. Torres, and M. Rodríguez
2004   Political and Social History of Eastern Puerto Rico: The Ceramic Age. In *Late Ceramic Age Societies in the Eastern Caribbean,* edited by André Delpuech and Corinne L. Hofman, pp. 59–85. BAR International Series S1273, Paris Monographs in American Archaeology 14. Archaeopress, Oxford.

Davis, S. D., S. J. M. Droop, P. Gregerson, L. Henson, C. J. Leon, J. Villa-Lobos, H. Synge, and J. Zantovska
1986   *Plants in Danger: What Do We Know?* IUCN (The World Conservation Union), Gland, Switzerland, and Cambridge, U.K.

Day, M. J.
1978   The Morphology of Tropical Humid Karst with Particular Reference to the Caribbean and Central America. Unpublished D.Phil. thesis, University of Oxford, Oxford.

Deagan, Kathleen
1989   *Report on the 1989 Sub-surface Test Program at La Isabela, Dominican Republic.* Florida Museum of Natural History, Gainesville.
1990   Sixteenth-Century Spanish-American Colonization in the Southeastern United States and the Caribbean. In *Columbian Consequences,* Vol. 2, *Archaeological and Historical Perspectives on the Spanish Borderlands East,* edited by D. H. Thomas, pp. 225–250. Smithsonian Institution Press, Washington, D.C.

Delle, James
1998   *An Archaeology of Social Space: Analyzing Coffee Plantations in Jamaica's Blue Mountains.* Plenum, New York.

Delpuech, André
2001   Historical Archaeology in the French West Indies: Recent Research in Guadeloupe. In *Island Lives: Historical Archaeologies of the Caribbean,* edited by Paul Farnsworth, pp. 21–59. University of Alabama Press, Tuscaloosa.

Dethlefsen, Edwin, Norman F. Barka, Stephen J. Gluckman, and R. Duncan Mathewson
1981   Historical Archaeology and Documentary Silence: A Case for the Spade. In *Underwater Archaeology: The Challenge Before Us,* edited by G. P. Watts, Jr., pp. 107–133. Special Publication No. 2. Fathom Eight, San Marino, California.

Dethlefsen, Edwin, Stephen J. Gluckman, R. Duncan Mathewson, and Norman F. Barka
1979   *A Preliminary Report on the Historical Archaeology and Cultural Resources of St. Eustatius, Netherlands Antilles.* Anthropology Department, College of William and Mary, Williamsburg, Virginia.
1982   Archaeology on St. Eustatius: The Pompeii of the New World. *Archaeology* 35:8–15.

De Wolf, Marian
1952   Excavations in Jamaica. *American Antiquity* 18:230–238.

Diggs, M. David, and Robert H. Brunswig
2006   *Modeling Native American Sacred Sites in Rocky Mountain National Park.* Electronic document, http://gis.esri.com/library/userconf/proc06/papers/papers/pap_2243.pdf, accessed January 9, 2007.

Directorate of Overseas Surveys
1959   *Nevis, Lesser Antilles 1:25,000.* Directorate of Overseas Surveys, Tolworth, U.K.
1975   *Nevis 3193 [and other sheets for areas surveyed at 1:2500].* Directorate of Overseas Surveys, Tolworth, U.K. (Revised 1980s by the Directorate of Overseas Surveys, Ordnance Survey.)

Dorst, Marc
2001   Manzanilla 1 (SAN 1): Phase II Proposal (The Study of a Patch of Open Space at a Pre-Columbian Site in Trinidad. Unpublished research proposal. Leiden, The Netherlands.

Drewett, Peter
1991   *Prehistoric Barbados.* Institute of Archaeology, University College, London.
2001   *Field Archaeology: An Introduction.* UCL Press, Taylor & Francis, London.

Dujon, Veronica
2001   Land Ownership and Economic Freedom among Post-Slavery Plantation Societies in the Caribbean. In *Freedom in Black History and Culture*, edited by Kofi Agorsah, pp. 165–185. Arrow Point Press, Portland, Oregon.

Duncan, Richard, and Kristen A. Beckman
2000   The Application of GIS Predictive Site Location Models within Pennsylvania and West Virginia. In *Practical Applications of GIS for Archaeologists*, edited by Konnie Wescott and R. Joe Brandon, pp. 33–58. Taylor and Francis, London.

Dunn, Richard S.
1972   *Sugar and Slaves: The Rise of the Planter Class in the English West Indies, 1624–1713.* University of North Carolina Press, Chapel Hill.

DVFV-I (Dokumenter vedk, forsvarsvaesenet og fortifikationerne i Vestindian [samt Oxholms Rejse 1778] 1775–1832)
1777a   Chamber of Customs: March 13, 1777. Rigsarkivet (Danish National Archives), Copenhagen.
1777b   Chamber of Customs: August 20, 1777. Rigsarkivet (Danish National Archives), Copenhagen.
1777c   Chamber of Customs: No 299, Vestindiske-Guineiske Rente og General Told-Krammer's orders to Oxholm, December 12, 1777. Rigsarkivet (Danish National Archives), Copenhagen.
1780   Rapport: Oxholm's Vestindisk Reise Rapport (Oxholm's final report, f. 115), August 30, 1780. DVFV-I, Rigsarkivet (Danish National Archives), Copenhagen.

Eastman, John A.
1996   An Archaeological Assessment of St. Eustatius, Netherlands Antilles. Un-

published M.A. thesis, Anthropology Department, College of William and Mary, Williamsburg, Virginia.

Ebert, J.
2000 The State of the Art in "Inductive" Predictive Modeling: Seven Big Mistakes and Some Smaller Ones. In *Practical Applications of GIS for Archaeologists: A Predictive Modeling Toolkit*, edited by K. Wescott, pp. 129–134. Routledge, New York.

English Heritage
2002 *With Alidade and Tape. Graphical and Plane Table Survey of Archaeological Earthworks.* English Heritage, Swindon, U.K. (Also available for download on the English Heritage Internet site: http://www.english-heritage.org.uk/).
2003 *Where on Earth Are We? The Global Positioning System (GPS) in Archaeological Field Survey.* English Heritage, Swindon, U.K. (Also available for download on the English Heritage Internet site: http://www.english-heritage.org.uk/).

Farag, Madiha, and Bheshem Ramlal
2005 GIS Analysis on the Archaeological Sites on the Island of St. Kitts. Paper presented at the 21st Congress of the International Association for Caribbean Archaeology (IACA), Trinidad and Tobago.

Farley, J. A., W. F. Limp, and J. Lockhart
1990 The Archaeologist's Workbench: Integrating GIS, Remote Sensing, EDA and Database Management. In *Interpreting Space: GIS in Archaeology*, edited by K. M. S. Allen, S. W. Green, and E. B. W. Zubrow, pp. 141–164. Taylor & Francis, London.

Farmer's Bookshelf
2002 *An Information System of Crops in Hawaii.* Department of Horticulture, University of Hawaii at Manoa. Electronic document, http://www.ctahr.hawaii.edu/fb/cassava/cassava.htm, accessed February 20, 2003.

Farnsworth, Paul
2001 "Negro Houses Built of Stone Besides Others Wat'd + Plaistered": The Creation of a Bahamian Tradition. In *Island Lives: Historical Archaeologies of the Caribbean*, edited by Paul Farnsworth, pp. 234–271. University of Alabama Press, Tuscaloosa.

Febles, J., and G. Baena
1995 La industria de piedra tallada del sitio arqueológico Medialuna, El Guaso, Provincia de Guantánamo. In *Contribuciones al conocimiento de las industrias líticas en comunidades aborígenes de Cuba*, edited by J. Febles, pp. 4–6. Editorial Academia, Havana.

Fincham, A. G.
1997 *Jamaica Underground.* The Press, University of the West Indies, Kingston, Jamaica.

Fitzpatrick, S. M.
2004 Synthesizing Island Archaeology. In *Voyages of Discovery: The Archaeology of the Islands*, edited by S. M. Fitzpatrick, pp. 3–18. Praeger, Westport, Connecticut.

Ford, Anabel, and Clarke Wernecke
2000   *El Pilar—2000 Field Report. Assessing the Situation at El Pilar: Chronology, Survey, Conservation, and Management Planning for the 21st Century.* Electronic document, http://www.marc.ucsb.edu/elpilar/brass/chron/fieldr/fieldreport.htm, accessed January 10, 2007.

Freehill, Lynne
2006   Volunteer Stewards Will Guard Against Looters at National Park. *Virgin Islands Daily News,* February 22, 2006.

Gaffney, V., and P. M. van Leusen
1995   Postscript—GIS, Environmental Determinism and Archaeology. In *Archaeology and Geographical Information Systems: A European Perspective,* edited by Gary Lock and Zoran Stancic, pp. 368–382. Taylor & Francis, London.

Garcia, Osvaldo
1984   *Influencias Mayas y Aztecas en los Tainos de las Antillas Mayores.* Ediciones Xibalbay, San Juan.

Gartrip
2007   Gartrip: The Windows PC Shareware Program for Garmin and Magellan GPS Receivers by Heinrich Pfeifer. Electronic document, http://www.gartrip.de, accessed May 16, 2007.

Gilmore, R. G.
2000   *Geophysics at English Quarter and Pleasures Estate Plantations (SE 22 and SE 57).* St. Eustatius Center for Archaeological Research, Research Report No. 1. St. Eustatius Center for Archaeological Research, Oranjestad, St. Eustatius.
2004   The Archaeology of New World Slave Societies: A Comparative Analysis with Particular Reference to St. Eustatius, Netherlands Antilles. Unpublished Ph.D. dissertation, Institute of Archaeology, University College London.

Gilmore, R. G., and B. D. Goodrich
1998   *Archaeological Investigations of the Pleasures Estate St. Eustatius, Netherlands Antilles.* Anthropology Department, College of William and Mary, Williamsburg, Virginia.
1999   *Archaeological Investigations of the Pleasures Estate St. Eustatius, Netherlands Antilles* (revised). Anthropology Department, College of William and Mary, Williamsburg, Virginia.

Goslinga, C. C.
1985   *The Dutch in the Caribbean and the Guianas 1680–1791.* Uitg. in samenwerking met het Prins Bernhardfonds Nederlandse Antillen door Van Gorcum, Assen/Maastricht.

Goveia, Elsa
1965   *Slave Society in the British Leeward Islands at the End of the Eighteenth Century.* Yale University Press, New Haven, Connecticut.

Gray, John
1999   Open Spaces and Dwelling Places: Being at Home on Hill Farms in the

Scottish Borders. In *The Anthropology of Space and Place: Locating Culture*, edited by Setha M. Low and Denise Lawrence-Zúñiga, pp. 224–244. Blackwell, Malden, Massachusetts.

Hall, Gwendolyn Midlo
1996 *Social Control in Slave Plantation Societies*. Louisiana State University Press, Baton Rouge.

Hall, Neville
1985 *The Danish Virgin Islands: Empire Without Dominion, 1671–1848*. Occasional Paper No. 8. Division of Libraries, Museums and Archaeological Services, U.S. Virgin Islands.

Hansen, David T.
2002 *Describing GIS Applications: Spatial Statistics and Weights of Evidence Extension to ArcView in the Analysis and Distribution of Archaeology Sites on the Landscape*. Electronic document, http://gis2.esri.com/library/userconf/proco0/professional/papers/PAP174/p174.htm, accessed June 25, 2007.

Hardy, F.
1974 *Land Capability Survey of Trinidad and Tobago No. 6. Land Capability of Trinidad*, edited by W. E. Searl. Government Printery, Port of Spain, Trinidad and Tobago.
1981 Soils. In *The Natural Resources of Trinidad and Tobago*, edited by St. George C. Cooper and Peter R. Bacon, pp. 23–42. Arnold, London.

Harris, Peter O'Brien
1978 A Revised Chronological Framework for Ceramics in Trinidad and Tobago. In *Proceedings of VII International Congress for Caribbean Archaeology, Caracas 1977*, Jean Benoist and Francine M. Mayer, editors, with the assistance of Elisabeth Crosnier, pp. 47–63. Montreal, Canada.

Harris, T. M., and G. R. Lock
1995 Toward an Evaluation of GIS in European Archaeology: The Past, Present and Future of Theory and Applications. In *Archaeology and Geographical Information Systems: A European Perspective*, edited by Gary Lock and Zoran Stancic, pp. 349–365. Taylor & Francis, London.

Hartog, J.
1976 *History of St. Eustatius*. Aruba? Central U.S.A. Bicentennial Committee of the Netherlands Antilles: distributors De Witt Stores N.V.

Haviser, Jay
1981 *Fieldnotes from St. Eustatius, Netherlands Antilles Fieldwalking*. Unpublished fieldnotes on file at College of William and Mary, Department of Anthropology, Williamsburg, Virginia.
1991 Development of Prehistoric Interaction Sphere in the Northern Lesser Antilles. *Nieuwe West-Indische Gids* 65(3–4):29–151.

Hayes, A. W., D. M. Brugge, and W. J. Judge
1981 *Archaeological Surveys of Chaco Canyon, New Mexico*. Publications in Archaeology 18A, Chaco Canyon Studies. National Park Service, U.S. Department of the Interior, Washington, D.C.

Heidegger, Martin
1977   *Basic Writings.* Harper & Row, New York.
Hester, Thomas R., Harry J. Shafer, and Kenneth L. Feder
1997   *Field Methods in Archaeology.* McGraw-Hill, Mayfield, Boston.
Higman, Barry W.
1988   *Jamaica Surveyed.* Institute of Jamaica Publications Limited, Kingston.
1995   Small Islands, Large Questions: Post Emancipation Historiography of the Leeward Islands. In *Small Islands, Large Questions: Society, Culture and Resistance in the Post-Emancipation Caribbean,* edited by Karen Fog Olwig, pp. 8–30. Frank Cass, London.
1996   Danish West Indian Slavery in Comparative Perspective: An Appreciation of Neville Hall's Contribution to the Historiography. In *Bondmen and Freedmen in the Danish West Indies, Scholarly Perspectives,* edited by George F. Tyson, pp. 1–17. Virgin Islands Humanities Council, St. Thomas, Virgin Islands.
Hilton, Mr.
1678   Map of Nevis. John Rylands Library, Stapleton MSS, 2/1. University of Manchester, Manchester, U.K.
Hirsch, Eric
1995   Introduction. Landscape: Between Space and Place. In *The Anthropology of Landscape: Perspectives on Place and Space,* edited by E. Hirsch and M. O'Hanlon, pp. 1–30. Clarendon Press, Oxford.
Hodell, D. A., J. H. Curtis, G. A. Jones, A. Higuera-Gundy, M. Brenner, M. W. Binford, and K. T. Dorsey
1991   Reconstruction of Caribbean Climate Change over the Past 10,500 Years. *Nature* 352:790–793.
Hopkins, Daniel P.
1988   The Danish Cadastral Survey of St. Croix, 1733–1754. Unpublished Ph.D. dissertation, Geography Department, Louisiana State University, Baton Rouge.
1993   Peter Oxholm and Late-Eighteenth Century Danish West Indian Cartography. In *The Danish Presence and Legacy in the Virgin Islands,* edited by Svend E. Holsoe and John M. McCullum, pp. 29–56. St. Croix Landmarks Society, Frederiksted, St. Croix.
Howard, Robert
1965   New Perspectives on Jamaican Archaeology. *American Antiquity* 31(2):250–255.
Huxhold, W., and A. Levinsohn
1995   *Managing Geographic Information System Projects.* Oxford University Press, New York.
Iles, John Alexander Burke
1871   *An Account Descriptive of the Island of Nevis, West Indies.* Privately printed, Norwich, U.K.
Ingold, Tim
1993   The Temporality of the Landscape. *World Archaeology* 25(2):152–174.

2000 *The Perception of the Environment: Essays on Livelihood, Dwelling and Skill.* Routledge, London.

Irwin, Geoffrey
1992 *The Prehistoric Exploration and Colonization of the Pacific.* Cambridge University Press, Cambridge.

Ive, Paul
1972 *The Practice of Fortification,* edited by Martin Biddle. London.
[1589]

Jameson, J. F.
1903 St. Eustatius in the American Revolution. *American Historical Review* 8(4):683–708.

Joukowsky, Martha
1980 *A Complete Manual of Field Archaeology.* Prentice-Hall, Englewood Cliffs, New Jersey.

Kappers, Michiel
2004 *Grand Bay Project, July 2004.* IACA Newsletter August 8, 2004. Electronic document, http://museum.archanth.cam.ac.uk/IACA.WWW/Newslet6.htm, accessed August 2006.

Kappers, Michiel, Scott F. Fitzpatrick, and Quetta Kaye
2007 Automated Data Collection and 3D Modeling of Archaeological Sites: Examining the Prehistory and Destruction of Grand Bay in Carriacou. In *Proceedings of the Twenty-First Congress of the International Association for Caribbean Archaeology (IACA),* edited by Basil Reid, Henri Petitjean Roget, and Antonio Curet, pp. 81–90. The University of the West Indies, School of Continuing Studies, St. Augustine.

Keegan, W. F.
1992 *The People Who Discovered Columbus: The Prehistory of the Bahamas.* The Ripley Bullen Series. Florida Museum of Natural History, University of Florida, Gainesville.
1994 West Indian Archaeology. 2: Overview and Foragers. *Journal of Archaeological Research* 2(3).
2000 West Indian Archaeology. 3: Ceramic Age. *Journal of Archaeological Research* 8(2).

Keegan, W. F., and J. Diamond
1987 Colonization of Islands by Humans: A Biogeographic Perspective. *Advances in Archaeological Methods and Theory* 10:49–92.

Kingsley, C.
1874 *At Last: A Christmas in the West Indies.* 4th ed. Macmillan, London.

Kirch, P. V.
1984 *The Evolution of Polynesian Chiefdoms.* Cambridge University Press, Cambridge.

Klingelhofer, Eric
2000 *Outposts of Empire: The Archaeology of Sir Walter Raleigh's Colonial Sites.* Pa-

per presented at the Forum for European Expansion and Gobal Interaction, Flagler University, St. Augustine, Florida.

Knapp, A. Bernard, and Wendy Ashmore
1999   Archaeological Landscapes: Constructed, Conceptualized, Ideational. In *Archaeologies of Landscape: Contemporary Perspectives,* edited by Wendy Ashmore and A. Bernard Knapp, pp. 1–30. Blackwell, Malden, Massachusetts.

Knight, Franklin W. (editor)
1997   *General History of the Caribbean:* Vol. 3, *The Slave Societies of the Caribbean.* UNESCO Publishing, Macmillan Caribbean, Oxford, U.K.

Knippenberg, S.
1999a   Lithic Procurement during the Saladoid Period within the Northern Lesser Antilles. Paper presented at the 18th International Congress for Caribbean Archaeology, Grenada.
1999b   Lithics of Sorce, Vieques. Manuscript on file, Centro de Investigaciones Arqueológicas, Universidad de Puerto Rico, San Juan.

Knowles, Anne Kelly (editor)
2002   *Past Time, Past Place: GIS for History.* ESRI Press, Redlands, California.

Kofi Agorsah (editor)
2001   *Freedom in Black History and Culture.* Arrow Point Press, Portland, Oregon.

Kvamme, K.
1995   A View from Across the Water: The North American Experience in GIS. In *Archaeology and Geographical Information Systems: A European Perspective,* edited by Gary Lock and Zoran Stancic, pp. 1–15. Taylor & Francis, London.
1999   Recent Directions and Developments in Geographical Information Systems. *Journal of Archaeological Research* 7(2):153–201.
2006   Archaeological Modeling with GIS at Scales Large and Small. In *Reading Historical Spatial Information from Around the World: Studies of Culture and Civilization Based on Geographic Information Systems Data,* Uno Takao, editor, pp. 75–92. International Research Center for Japanese Studies, Kyoto, Japan.

Landell Mills Limited
1992   *Oropouche Area Development Project.* Middle Catchment Feasibility Study. Engineering Planning and Surveying Service Limited, Port of Spain, Trinidad.

Landon, George V., and W. Brent Seales
2005   Bulking and Visualizing 3D Textured Models of Caribbean Petroglyphs. Paper presented at the 21st Congress of the International Association for Caribbean Archaeology (IACA), Trinidad and Tobago.

Lape, P. V.
2004   The Isolation Metaphor in Island Archaeology. In *Voyages of Discovery: The Archaeology of the Islands,* edited by S. M. Fitzpatrick, pp. 223–232. Praeger, Westport, Connecticut.

Lathrap, Donald
1970   *The Upper Amazon.* Thames and Hudson, London.

Leech, Roger

n.d. Understanding Nevis: Archaeological Field Survey in a Post-Colonial Landscape. In *The Colonial Landscape of the Caribbean,* edited by Roger Leech and Bruce Williams. Papers from the Society for Post-Medieval Archaeology Conference, Nevis, 2005. Forthcoming.

Lillesand, T., and R. Kiefer

2000 *Remote Sensing and Image Interpretation.* Wiley, New York.

Littman, Sherri B.

1998 *Magnetometer Survey at Los Gallos Point, Trinidad, 1998.* Field report on file, History Department, Mercer University, Macon, Georgia.

Lock, Gary, and Zoran Stancic (editors)

1995 *Archaeology and Geographical Information Systems: A European Perspective.* Taylor & Francis, London.

Longley, P. A., M. F. Goodchild, D. J. Maguire, and D. W. Rhind

2001 *Geographic Information Systems and Science.* Wiley, West Sussex, U.K.

Lopez, Thomas

1791 Map of Puerto Rico (1:570,000). Map Division. Library of Congress, Washington, D.C.

Lorant, Stefan

1946 *The New World.* Duell, Sloan & Pearce, New York.

Lyew-Ayee, Parris

2004 Digital Topographic Analysis of Cockpit Karst: A Morpho-Geological Study of the Cockpit Country Region, Jamaica. Unpublished D.Phil. thesis, School of Geography and the Environment, University of Oxford, Oxford.

McGinnis, S. A.

1997 Ideographic Expression in the Precolumbian Caribbean. Unpublished Ph.D. dissertation, Department of Anthropology, University of Texas at Austin.

McMahon, William

1828 *A New Topographical Map of the Island of St Christopher in the West Indies . . . by William McMahon Surveyor of the Island.* N.p.

MacManamon, Francis P.

1984 Discovering Sites Unseen. In *Advances in Archaeological Method and Theory,* Vol. 2, edited by M. B. Schiffer, pp. 223–292. Academic Press, New York.

Madry, Scott L. H., and L. Rakos

1996 Line-of-Sight and Cost-Surface Techniques for Regional Research in the Arroux River Valley. In *New Methods, Old Problems: Geographic Information Systems in Modern Archaeological Research,* edited by Herbert D. G. Maschner, pp. 104–126. Occasional Paper No. 23. Center for Archaeological Investigations, Carbondale, Illinois.

Map of Coral Harbor, St. John

1720 RAM 1720. Rigsarkivet (Danish National Archives), Copenhagen.

Map of Ponce Province
1898 Map of Ponce Province (Puerto Rico) (1:160,000). Map Division. Library of Congress, Washington, D.C.

Martin, P. F.
1781 *St. Eustatia. Topographically drawn & humbly dedicated to His Excellency General Vaughan commander in chief of His Majestys Forces in the West Indies.* Vaughan Papers/Germain Papers. William Clements Library, University of Michigan, Ann Arbor.

Maschner, Herbert D. G.
1996 *New Methods, Old Problems: Geographic Information Systems in Modern Archaeological Research.* Occasional Paper No. 23. Center for Archaeological Investigations, Carbondale, Illinois.

Matson, C.
1998 *Merchants and Empire: Trading in Colonial New York.* Johns Hopkins University Press, Baltimore.

Meggers, B. J.
1996 Possible Impact of the Mega-Niño Events on Pre-Columbian Populations in the Caribbean Area. In *Ponencias del Primer Seminario de Arqueológico del Caribe,* edited by M. Veloz Maggiolo and Caba Fuentes, pp. 156–176. Museo Arqueológico Regional Altos de Chavón, Dominican Republic.

Merleau-Ponty, Maurice
1962 *Phenomenology of Perception,* translated by Colin Smith. Routledge and Kegan Paul, London.

Moore, I. D., P. E. Gessler, G. A. Nielson, and G. A. Peterson
1991 Digital Terrain Modelling: A Review of Hydrological, Geomorphological and Biological Applications. *Hydrological Processes* 5:3–30.

Morgan, K.
1993 *Bristol and the Atlantic Trade in the Eighteenth Century.* Cambridge University Press, Cambridge.

Morison, S. E.
1971 *The European Discovery of America:* Vol. 1, *The Northern Voyages, AD 500–1600.* Oxford University Press, New York.

National Geodetic Survey (U.S.)
n.d. Topographic Map, 7.5-Minute Series, Yauco Quadrangle, Puerto Rico, N1800-W6645.

National Geographic Traveler
2007 Insider's Jamaica: 6. Walk the Maroon Trail over the Blue Mountains between Portland and St. Thomas parishes. Electronic document, http://www.nationalgeographic.com/traveler/features/insidersjamaica0503/, accessed January 14, 2007.

Nature Conservancy, The
1994 *Rapid Ecological Assessment of Jamaica.* The Nature Conservancy, Arlington, Virginia.

Nevis Heritage Project
2007   Interim Reports, 1999 to 2003. Electronic documents, http://www.arch.soton. ac.uk/Projects/default.asp?ProjectID=12, accessed May 16, 2007.

Newson, L. A.
1993   Native American Plant Use. Unpublished Ph.D. dissertation, Department of Anthropology, University of Florida, Gainesville.

Noble, G. Kingsley
1965   *Proto-Arawakan and Its Descendants*. Indiana University Publications in Anthropology and Linguistics, No. 38. Indiana University, Bloomington.

Noël Hume, Ivor
2001   *If These Pots Could Talk: Collecting 2,000 Years of British Household Pottery*. Chipstone Foundation; distributed by University Press of New England, Hanover, New Hampshire.

Olwig, Karen
1994   *The Land Is the Heritage: Land and Community on St. John*. Monograph 1, St. John Oral History Association. Reproduction Center of the Division of Social Sciences, University of Copenhagen.

Ordnance Survey
1984   *Nevis, Lesser Antilles 1:25,000*. Ordnance Survey, Southampton, U.K.

O'Shaughnessy, A. J.
1987   *The Politics of the Leeward Islands, 1763–1783 (British West Indies)*. University of Oxford, Oxford.
2002   The Other Road to Yorktown: The St. Eustatius Affair and the American Revolution. *Maryland Historical Magazine* 97(1):33–60.

Ottens, R.
1775   *Nieuwe kaart van het eyland St. Eustatius in derzelver ligging & plantagien met de naamen der bezitteren, op order van de generaale geoctroojeeroe West-Indische Compagnie gemeeten en getekeno*. Konst. Kaart en Boekverkoper, Amsterdam.

Oxholm, Peter L.
1777   Oxholm Draft Map of St. John, A18/46. Rigsarkivet (Danish National Archives), Copenhagen.
1780a   Oxholm Map of St. John 1780. Rigsarkivet (Danish National Archives), Copenhagen.
1780b   Fortification of Cruz Bay, Oxholm Plan XXIX, No. 3. Maps and Drawings Collection, Group 25, entry no. 337-343. Rigsarkivet (Danish National Archives), Copenhagen.
1780c   Fort at Coral Bay, Oxholm Plate XXX: Old Fort. Maps and Drawings Collection, Group 25, entry no. 337-343. Rigsarkivet (Danish National Archives), Copenhagen.
1800   Oxholm Map of St. John 1800. Rigsarkivet (Danish National Archives), Copenhagen.

Petersen, James, and David Watters
1997   Taino, Island Carib, and Prehistoric Amerindian Economics in the West Indies: Tropical Forest Adaptations to Island Environments. In *The Indigenous*

People of the Caribbean, edited by S. M. Wilson, pp. 118–130. University Press of Florida, Gainesville.

Quinn, D. B.
1985 *Set Fair for Roanoke: Voyages and Colonies, 1584–1606.* University of North Carolina, Chapel Hill.

Quinn, D. B. (editor)
1955 *The Roanoke Voyages.* Publications of the Hakluyt Society, 2nd series, pt. II, CIV. Hakluyt Society, London.

Reid, Basil A.
2006 Returning to Gandhi Village, 2006. In *Bulletin Humanitas,* vol. 8, no. 7. The Humanities Division of the University of the West Indies, St. Augustine. Electronic document, http://www.mainlib.uwi.tt/divisions/humanities/bulletins/2006/bulletinmar2006.doc, accessed January 14, 2007.

Robinson, L. S. (editor)
1991 *Proceedings of the Twelfth Congress of the International Association for Caribbean Archaeology.* IACA, Martinique.

Rodríguez, Reniel
2001 Lithic Reduction Trajectories at La Hueca and Punta Candelero Sites, Puerto Rico. Unpublished M.A. thesis, Department of Anthropology, Texas A&M University, College Station.
2002 Dinámicas de intercambio en el Puerto Rico prehispánico. *Caribe Arqueológico* 6:16–22.

Roosevelt, Anna
1980 *Parmana: Prehistoric Maize and Manioc Subsistence along the Amazon and Orinoco.* Academic Press, New York.
1997 *The Excavations at Corozal, Venezuela: Stratigraphy and Ceramic Seriation.* Yale University Publications in Anthropology 83. Yale University, New Haven, Connecticut.

Rouse, Irving B.
1953 The Circum-Caribbean Theory: An Archaeological Test. *American Anthropologist* 55(2):188–200.
1992 *The Tainos: Rise and Decline of the People Who Greeted Columbus.* Yale University Press, New Haven.

Rumsey, David, and Meredith Williams
2002 Historical Maps in GIS. In *Past Time, Past Place: GIS for History,* edited by Anne Kelly Knowles, pp. 1–18. ESRI Press, Redlands, California.

Saunders, Nicholas
2005 *The Peoples of the Caribbean: An Encyclopedia of Archaeology and Traditional Culture.* ABC-CLIO, Oxford, U.K.

Scarre, Chris
2002 Coast and Cosmos: The Neolithic Monuments of Northern Brittany. In *Monuments and Landscape in Atlantic Europe: Perception and Society during the Neolithic and Early Bronze Age,* edited by Chris Scarre, pp. 84–102. Routledge, London.

Schaw, J., E. W. Andrews, C. M. Andrews, and British Museum
- 1934 *Journal of a lady of quality; being the narrative of a journey from Scotland to the*
- [1778] *West Indies, North Carolina, and Portugal, in the years 1774 to 1776.* Yale University Press, New Haven, and H. Milford, Oxford University Press, London.

Schwemm, Cathy, and Mike Kaberline
- 2004 *Weights of Evidence Analysis of Cultural Resource Site Prediction and Risk Assessment.* National Park Service, U.S. Department of the Interior. Electronic document, http://www.nps.gov/gis/mapbook/tech/36.html, accessed January 8, 2007.

Shepherd, Verne
- 2001 Liberation Struggles of Jamaican Livestock Farms during and after Slavery. In *Freedom in Black History and Culture,* edited by Kofi Agorsah, pp. 62–92. Arrow Point Press, Portland, Oregon.

Siegel, Peter
- 1989 *Early Ceramic Population Lifeways and Adaptive Strategies in the Caribbean.* BAR International Series 506. British Archaeological Reports, Oxford.
- 1991 Migration Research in Saladoid Archaeology: A Review. *The Florida Anthropologist* 44:79–91.
- 1995 The Archaeology of Community Organization in the Tropical Lowlands: A Case Study from Puerto Rico. In *Archaeology in the Lowland American Tropics,* edited by Peter W. Stahl, pp. 42–65. Cambridge University Press, Cambridge.

Slama, C. C.
- 1980 *Manual of Photogrammetry.* 4th ed. American Society for Photogrammetry and Remote Sensing, Bethesda, Maryland.

Souterrain Archaeological Services, Ltd.
- 2004 GPS and Archaeology. Electronic document, http://www.souterrain.biz/GPS.htm, accessed August 2006.

Sued Badillo, Jalil
- 1979 La industria lapidaria pretaína en las Antillas. *Revista Interamericana* 8(3):429–462.

Swanson, S.
- 2003 Documenting Prehistoric Communication Networks: A Case Study in the Paquine Polity. *American Antiquity* 68(4):753–767.

Sweeting, M. M.
- 1957 The Karstlands of Jamaica. *Geographical Journal* 124:184–199.

Teenstra, M. D.
- 1836 *De Nederlandsche West-Indische eilanden in derzelver tegenwoordigen toestand.* C. G. Sulpke, Amsterdam.

Terrell, Michelle
- 1998 *What Are You Doing? Examining a Colonial Period Jewish Cemetery in the Caribbean.* Paper presented at the 31st Annual Meeting of the Society for Historical Archaeology, Atlanta. Electronic document, http://www.tc.umn.edu/~terreo11/Resistivity.html, accessed December 29, 2006.

Tilley, Christopher
1994   *A Phenomenology of Landscape: Places, Paths and Monuments.* Berg, Oxford, U.K.
Tite, M. S.
1972   *Methods of Physical Examination in Archaeology.* Seminal Press, London.
Tomlinson, R.
2003   *Thinking about GIS: Geographic Information System Planning for Managers.* ESRI Press, Redlands, California.
Turner, W., R. Langerhorst, G. Hice, H. Eilers, and A. Uijttenbroek
1987   *System Development Methodology.* Pandata, North-Holland.
UNDP/FAO
1972   Groundwater Surveys Report of the Pedro Plains, St. Elizabeth, Jamaica. AGL Documentation Centre: SF/JAM3, Technical Report No. 1, Rome.
U.S. Geological Survey
1918   Map of St. John, 1918.
Veenenbos, J. S.
1955   *A Soil and Land Capability Survey of St. Maarten, St. Eustatius, and Saba, Netherlands Antilles.* Natuurwetenschappelijke studiekring voor Suriname en de Nederlandse Antillen, Publications, No. 11. Utrecht, The Netherlands.
Veloz Maggiolo, M.
1997   The Daily Life of the Taino people. In *Taino: Pre-Columbian Art and Culture from the Caribbean,* edited by F. Bercht, E. Brodsky, J. A. Farmer, and D. Taylor, pp. 34–45. Monacelli Press, New York.
VIFR (Vestindiske forestillings- og resolutionsprotokoller)
1777–1778   July 28 1778; no 733 VIJ 1778. Rigsarkivet (Danish National Archives), Copenhagen.
1781–1782   March 24, 1781, resolution April 18, 1781. Rigsarkivet (Danish National Archives), Copenhagen.
VIJ (Vestindiske journaler)
1779   No 299, VIJ 1779, Oxholm, St. Croix, March 23, 1779. Rigsarkivet (Danish National Archives), Copenhagen.
1780   No 274 VIJ and VIJ(S) 1780, Oxholm, April 5, 1780. Rigsarkivet (Danish National Archives), Copenhagen.
Watters, D. R.
1997   Maritime Trade in Prehistoric Eastern Caribbean. In *Indigenous People of the Caribbean,* edited by S. Wilson, pp. 88–99. University Press of Florida, Gainesville.
Watts, David
1980   *The West Indies: Patterns of Development, Culture and Environmental Change since 1492.* Cambridge Studies in Historical Geography. Cambridge University Press, Cambridge.
Wescott, Konnie L., and James A. Kuiper
2000   Using a GIS to Model Prehistoric Site Distributions in the Upper Chesa-

peake Bay. In *Practical Applications of GIS for Archaeologists*, edited by Konnie Wescott and R. Joe Brandon, pp. 59–71. Taylor & Francis, London.

West Indies Pilot, The

1931 Nautical charts. *The West Indies Pilot*, Vol. II, 8th ed., pp. 52, 54–55. London.

Wheatley, David

1993 Going Over Old Ground: GIS, Archaeological Theory and the Act of Perception. In *Computing the Past: Computer Applications and Qualitative Methods in Archaeology 1992*, edited by J. Andersen, T. Madsen, and T. Scollar, pp. 133–138. Taylor & Francis, London.

Wheatley, David, and Mark Gillings

2002 *Spatial Technology and Archaeology: The Archaeological Applications of GIS*. Taylor & Francis, London.

White, Andrew Marshall

2002 Archaeological Predictive Modeling of Site Location Through Time: An Example from the Tucson Basin, Arizona. Unpublished M.S. thesis, Department of Geography, University of Calgary, Calgary, Alberta, Canada.

White, John

ca. 1585 Map of Grenville's Fort on St. John's Island (Puerto Rico). Department of Prints and Drawings, 1906-5-9-1(4). British Museum, London.

Wilkie, Davis S.

1989 Performance of Backpack GPS in a Tropical Rain Forest. *Photogrammetric Engineering and Remote Sensing* 55:1747–1749.

Williams, J. Mark

1984 A New Resistivity Device. *Journal of Field Archaeology* 11(1):110–114.

Wilson, Samuel

1990 *Hispaniola: Caribbean Chiefdoms in the Age of Columbus*. University of Alabama Press, Tuscaloosa.

Wilson, Samuel M., Harry B. Iceland, and Thomas R. Hester

1998 Preceramic Connections between Yucatán and the Caribbean. *Latin American Antiquity* 9(4):342–352.

Zeidler, James A.

1995 Archaeological Survey and Site Discovery in the Forested Neotropics. In *Archaeology in the Lowland American Tropics*, edited by Peter W. Stahl, pp. 7–41. Cambridge University Press, Cambridge.

Zucchi, Alberta

1984 Nueva evidencia sobre la penetración de grupos cerámicos en las Antillas Mayores. In *Relaciones Prehispánicas de Venezuela*, edited by E. Wagner, pp. 35–50. Fondo Editorial Acta Científica Venezolana, Caracas.

Contributors

Armstrong, Douglas V. (Ph.D.)
Douglas V. Armstrong is the Laura J. and L. Douglas Meredith Professor of Anthropology at Syracuse University, Syracuse, New York. Recipient of the prestigious Maxwell Professor of Teaching Excellence award, his academic interests range from historical archaeology, public policy archaeology, archaeology of the African diaspora, ethnohistory, culture contact, and culture change to the prehistoric archaeology of the Americas. He has written extensively on Caribbean archaeology, with the 1990 publication *The Old Village and the Great House: An Archaeological and Historical Examination of Drax Hall Plantation, St. Ann's Bay, Jamaica* being one of his most seminal works.

Conolley, Ivor (M.A.)
Ivor Courtney Conolley is currently pursuing an M.Phil. degree at the University of the West Indies, Mona, Jamaica. He already holds an M.A. in Heritage Studies (UWI). His particular interest is the indigenous peoples of Jamaica. He is a caver and with his combined knowledge of archaeology and caving has, together with the Jamaican Caves Organization as their archaeology resource person, located a number of hitherto unknown cave sites of indigenous peoples. He is an Executive Member of the Archaeological Society of Jamaica, Jamaican Historical Society, and Jamaican Caves Organization.

Farmer, Kevin (M.A.)
Kevin Farmer is the Curator of History and Archaeology at the Barbados Museum and Historical Society. He holds a Master's degree in Heritage Studies from the University of the West Indies, Cave Hill, Barbados, and is currently pursuing doctoral studies in archaeology at the University of Sussex in the United Kingdom.

Gilmore, R. Grant, III (Ph.D.)

R. Grant Gilmore III is St. Eustatius Island Archaeologist and Director of the St. Eustatius Center for Archaeological Research (SECAR). His excavation experience includes work on a wide variety of colonial period sites located in Virginia (Williamsburg), Netherlands Antilles (St. Eustatius), United Kingdom (Chichester), and Natchitoches, Louisiana. Dr. Gilmore received his Ph.D. from the Institute of Archaeology, University College London at the University of London, with his dissertation entitled *The Archaeology of New World Slave Societies: A Comparative Analysis with Particular Reference to St. Eustatius, Netherlands Antilles.*

Hauser, Mark W. (Ph.D.)

Mark W. Hauser is currently a Visiting Assistant Professor at the University of Notre Dame. He has worked in the Caribbean since the mid-1990s and has had the opportunity to work on archaeological projects in Jamaica, the Virgin Islands, Cuba, Dominica, Guadeloupe, and Martinique. He has published several articles on the development of Caribbean ceramic traditions and their distribution through local economic systems.

Klingelhofer, Eric (Ph.D.)

Eric Klingelhofer is Professor of History at Mercer University, Macon, Georgia. He has published extensively on his primary research interests, which are Medieval archaeology and material culture, English rural settlement and institutions, and early European colonization. Between 1975 and 1979, he was Senior Archaeologist of the Colonial Williamsburg Foundation and between 1972 and 1975 he served as Field Archaeologist in Southampton, Winchester, and Warwick in the United Kingdom.

Knight, David W.

David W. Knight is a freelance cultural resource consultant, historian, and author. He is one of a small group of scholars who in recent years have spearheaded an exploration of the Danish National Archives to bring the rich colonial history of the former Danish West Indies (USVI) into sharper focus. Many of Mr. Knight's published works address the Afro-Caribbean diaspora, but he has numerous studies relating to the broader Danish colonial experience to his credit. He currently serves as President of the St. John Historical Society.

Leech, Roger H. (Ph.D.)

Roger H. Leech teaches historical archaeology in the University of Southampton (U.K.) where he is Visiting Professor. He received his M.A. from the

University of Cambridge and his Ph.D. from the University of Bristol. He was formerly Head of Archaeology for the Royal Commission on the Historical Monuments of England and is a former President of the Society for Post Medieval Archaeology. His principal research interests lie in the historical archaeology and architectural history of the Atlantic world of the fifteenth to twentieth centuries. His many publications include a study of early industrial housing in Frome, Somerset (*Early Industrial Housing: The Trinity Area of Frome, Somerset*), and, most recently, papers focusing on early modern merchant culture.

Lenik, Stephan (M.A.)

Stephan Lenik completed his Master's degree at the University of South Carolina, Columbia, and is presently a doctoral student at Syracuse University, Syracuse, New York. He recently carried out work at Bethlehem Plantation, St. Croix, and has several years of experience working on sites throughout the United States Virgin Islands. He is currently doing background research for his dissertation on early historic settlements on Dominica.

Lyew-Ayee, Parris (D.Phil.)

Parris Lyew-Ayee is currently the Chief Technical Director for Mona Geo-Informatics, Ltd. (formerly Mona Informatix, Ltd.), at the University of the West Indies, Mona, Jamaica. He also lectures in the Department of Geography and Geology at the Mona Campus, where he teaches geographic information systems (GIS) and remote sensing. The title of his doctoral dissertation at Oxford University (United Kingdom) was *Digital Topographic Analysis of Cockpit Karst: A Morpho-Geological Study of the Cockpit Country Region, Jamaica*.

Ramlal, Bheshem (Ph.D.)

Bheshem Ramlal has been a lecturer in GIS, Cartography, and Surveying Engineering at the University of the West Indies since 1992. His research focuses on spatial data issues including metadata standards, National Spatial Data Infrastructure, spatial data sharing and pricing issues, and the application of GIS and visualization tools in archaeology, environmental engineering, and natural resources management. He has served as a consultant to several national agencies in the Caribbean, especially in Trinidad and Tobago.

Reid, Basil A. (Ph.D.)

Basil A. Reid has worked on pre-Columbian sites in Jamaica, Barbados, Haiti, and Trinidad and Tobago. He is currently a Lecturer in Archaeology in the Department of History at the University of the West Indies, St. Augustine, where his major research interests are the pre-Columbian history of the Caribbean, archaeology, and geoinformatics and forensics in the Caribbean. Dr. Reid received his M.A. in archaeology from the Institute of Archaeology, University of London, and his Ph.D. in anthropology from the University of Florida, Gainesville. Not only was Dr. Reid President of the Archaeological Society of Jamaica from 1990 to 1992, but he was also Chairman of the 21st Congress of the International Association for Caribbean Archaeology (IACA) which was held in Trinidad and Tobago in July 2005. He has published in the *Journal of Caribbean History, Caribbean Quarterly,* and *Caribbean Geography.*

Rodríguez Ramos, Reniel (M.A.)

Reniel Rodríguez Ramos is a Ph.D. candidate at the Department of Anthropology, University of Florida, Gainesville. He has a B.A. from the Universidad de Puerto Rico–Rio Piedras and an M.A. from Texas A&M University. His main focus has been the analysis of lithics from precolonial sites of the Antilles. Other research interests include the introduction of pottery and agriculture to the islands, the dynamics of interaction between pre-Arawak peoples and the Huecoid/Saladoid migrants, and the articulation of inter-regional networks between the inhabitants of the insular Caribbean and the Isthmo-Colombian area.

Torres, Joshua M. (M.A.)

Joshua M. Torres is currently working on his Ph.D. in archaeology at the University of Florida, Gainesville. He received his M.A. from the University of Colorado, Boulder, in 2001 and has worked as an archaeologist and geographic information systems (GIS) specialist for the past eight years. Mr. Torres's research interests are GIS applications in archaeology, social landscapes, settlement patterns, the archaeology of communities, and the development of complex prehistoric social systems of the Circum-Caribbean.

Index

aerial imagery, 140, 141. *See also* aerial photography; photogrammetry; satellite imagery
aerial photography, 1, 3, 128, 140–41, 189, 191, 194, 195
African Creole community, 100; land use, 125
Afro-Caribbean ware, 177
AIS. *See* Archaeological Information System (AIS)
Anegada Passage, 22, 25–26
Anguilla: archaeological heritage, 3; microdiversity in, 105
anthropomorphic imagery, 70, 195
Arauquinoid culture, 195
Arawaks. *See* Tainos
archaeological database: Trinidad, 33, 72
archaeological field survey: Nevis, 127–35
Archaeological Information System (AIS), 6, 86, 87–96, 188
Archaeological Museum of Aruba, 3
ArcView GIS (ESRI) software, 6, 42, 81, 86, 87, 91, 92, 142
AutoCAD DXF software, 129

Bahamas, 19, 69; historical archaeology, 193
ball courts, 150
Banwari Trace (Trinidad), 188, 194
Barbados: archaeological resource management, 74–85; coastal sites, 69; cultural resource management, 74–85; heritage management, 75–76, 187–88; land use, 76–77

Barbados Museum and Historical Society (BMHS), 6, 75, 187
Barbados National Grid, 80
Barbados National Trust, 75
Barrancoid culture, 36, 37, 70, 195
batey, 150
Bayesian logic, 196
Blue Mountains (Jamaica), 22, 186, 192
BMHS. *See* Barbados Museum and Historical Society (BMHS)
bohios, 138
Bridgetown (Barbados), 74, 84, 187–88
Brimstone Hill Fortress National Park (St. Kitts), 188
buffers, 2, 19, 84, 187, 196

calabash, 138, 140
caneys, 138
Canoe Bay (Tobago), 4
Caquana (Puerto Rico), 2
Caribbean Basin, 13–17, 28
cartography, 1, 4, 7, 189, 196; Danish West Indies, 105–26; St. John, 105–25
"categorical" data, 43
caves, 75, 138, 140, 150
ceramics, 172, 177, 195, 199. *See also* pottery
Charlotte Amalia (St. Thomas), 103, 110
Cipero watershed (Trinidad), 33–35, 37, 42–44, 46, 49–50, 53–54, 58, 62, 65, 69, 71
Circum-Caribbean region, 19, 25
Citadelle Laferrière (Haiti), 188
Coastal Zone Management Unit (Barbados), 75, 80

Cockpit Country (Trelawny, Jamaica), 138, 146, 148
College of William and Mary (Virginia, USA): research, 170, 174
colonial landscape: Nevis, 127–29, 190
Columbus Bay (Trinidad), 156, 159
conceptual "landfall," 25
conditional independence of evidential themes, 53, 56, 196
contrast values, 43–44, 48
conucos, 138
Coral Bay (St. John), 110, 113, 125
cotton estates, 7, 76–77, 119, 121–24, 138, 172
CRM. *See* cultural resource management (CRM)
Cruz Bay (St. John), 110, 112–13
Cuba, 22, 25, 40, 104, 171, 192
cultural landscapes, 5, 13; St. John, 100, 104, 106, 110, 114, 116, 121, 124–25, 189
cultural resource management (CRM), 3, 5–6, 184, 186, 192, 194, 197; Barbados, 74–85; St. John, 104–25; Trinidad, 33–73, 188
cumulative weights, 54, 197
Curaçao, 182, 188
currents, 25, 29, 185

Danish West Indies: cartography, 105–26; plantation society, 104, 121, 124. *See also* individual islands St. Croix, St. Eustatius, St. John, St. Thomas
Delle, James, 186
DEM. *See* digital elevation models (DEM)
Denmark, 104, 106, 109, 125
descriptive models, 37, 39–41, 58, 69
digital elevation models (DEM), 14, 17, 72, 94–95, 185, 197
digital terrain modeling, 143–44
Dominica, 76, 105
Dominican Republic, 29, 104, 188
dry season: effect on fieldwork, 144, 193

El Dorado, 155
Elizabethan forts: search for, 155–68
English protocolonial expansion, 155, 167–68
English Quarter Sugar Plantation (St. Eustatius), 8, 170, 174–78, 181–83, 192

estate consolidation, 189; Nevis, 6, 127–36, 190
evidential themes, 5, 33, 37, 39, 40, 42–44, 46–53
excavations, 4, 103, 150, 170, 175, 181, 193, 194; "targeted" excavations, 4, 193
exploration (evidence) themes, 37, 39–40, 42

Falmouth (Trelawny, Jamaica), 138, 187
fluxgate gradiometer, 170, 175–77, 183, 198
France, 171, 172
free colored group. *See* free persons of color
"free" data, 43
free persons of color, 99, 121, 189; St. John, 7

Gandhi Village (Trinidad), 185–86
geographical information systems (GIS) 1, 4–7, 72, 198; and heritage management, 79–85; software, 129; utilization in archaeology, 86–96, 120–26, 137–51, 185–90; utilization in Barbados, 74–85; utilization in Trinidad and Tobago, 88–96
geoinformatics, 1, 3–4, 198; training programs, 187; use in Caribbean archeology, 184–94
geophysical surveys, 1, 2, 4, 8–9, 175–77, 181, 183, 192–94
geophysics: in archaeological research, 8, 155–68; in Caribbean archaeology, 192–94; in St. Eustatius archaeology, 170–83, 192; in Trinidad archaeology, 155–68; in volcanic Caribbean islands, 170–83
Geoplot program, 176
geothermography, 162–65, 192
ginger, 77
GIS. *See* geographical information systems (GIS)
GIS environment, 7, 79, 137, 189–90
global positioning systems (GPS), 1, 4, 7–8, 71, 79, 80, 81, 100, 103, 126–35, 137, 140–42, 189, 190–91, 198; handheld GPS, 7, 129; mapping grade GPS, 129, 135; navigation grade GPS, 129, 190; survey grade GPS, 129; surveys, 103, 126, 132, 141–42, 190
GPS. *See* global positioning systems (GPS)
gradiometry, 170–83
Grand Bay (Carriacou), 2–3

Great Britain, 128, 171
Greater Antilles, 3, 25–26, 138
Grenville, Sir Richard, 156, 166, 168
grid cell size, 43
ground resolution, 194, 199
ground visibility, 36, 71
Guadeloupe, 103–4, 171, 193; historical archaeology, 193
Guayabitoid culture, 36, 37, 39, 41, 69, 70
Guayanilla River (Puerto Rico), 166–68

HABS/HAER. *See* Historic American Buildings Survey/Historic American Engineering Record (HABS/HAER)
hand-drawn maps, 72
handheld GPS, 7, 127, 136, 141. *See also* global positioning systems (GPS)
heritage management, 3, 75–76, 79, 187–88; archaeological, 71–72
Higman, Barry, 104, 124; *Jamaica Surveyed*, 189–90
hilltop settlements, 69, 138, 185–86
Hilton, Mr.: map, 128, 130
Historic American Buildings Survey/Historic American Engineering Record (HABS/HAER), 118
historical GIS, 7; St. John, 116, 124–25, 189
Historic Sites and Monuments Record (HSMR), 79–82, 85
HSMR. *See* Historic Sites and Monuments Record (HSMR)

IACA. *See* International Association for Caribbean Archaeology (IACA)
Ichirouganiam, 76
Iles's map, 128
Institute of Jamaica, 3
insularity: in the Caribbean, 5, 13, 15
interaction spheres, 13, 15, 22
interconnectivity: Caribbean region, 16, 22, 26, 28
International Association for Caribbean Archaeology (IACA), 2
intersecting visibility, 16, 22, 26
isolationism in the Caribbean, 5, 13

Jamaica: geographical information systems (GIS), 137, 142–44; global positioning systems (GPS), 137, 140–42; heritage management, 187; pre-Columbian communities, 40, 69, 191; Taino sites, 137–52, 185, 186, 192
Jamaica National Heritage Trust, 3
Jewish Cemetery (Nevis), 2

karst landscape, 138, 144
Keegan, William, 2, 61

land capability, 33, 39–42, 46, 48, 50–54, 56, 58, 61, 68–69, 70
land cover, 140, 144, 146, 191; characteristics, 141, 146; classification, 144, 147
landforms, 33, 39–42, 46, 48–52, 54, 56, 58, 61, 69, 143–44, 191
land relief, 33; Danish West Indies, 106, 125; Jamaica, 143–46; Trinidad, 39, 40–41, 46, 48–58, 69
Landsat imagery, 142, 186–87, 194
landscape conceptualization, 1, 13, 28
land tenure, 189, 194; Danish system, 99, 189
land-use management, 33, 72; Barbados, 80–85
land-use patterns, 72–73
Little River site (St. Ann, Jamaica), 22, 69
local geology, 193–94
Long Pond Sugar Factory (Trelawny, Jamaica), 140
Los Gallos Point (Trinidad), 155–61, 166, 168, 192, 193

magnetometer, 155, 156, 158–59, 161–64, 199
magnetometry, 156–61, 192
mapping. *See* cartography
mapping-grade GPS, 129, 135, 199. *See also* global positioning systems (GPS)
Martha Brae River (Trelawny, Jamaica), 138, 148, 150; hydrologic system, 140
Martinique, 126, 171
Mayoid culture, 36, 199
Mercer University Team, 8, 155, 166, 168
missing data, 53; integers, 200
Mona Passage, 26, 29
monocultural landscapes, 13
Montserrat, 130
"Mosquito Bay" (Puerto Rico), 166
Mr. Hilton's map. *See* Hilton, Mr.

multiscalar analyses, 104, 116, 194
multispectral IKONOS imagery, 142, 187

National Archaelogical Committee (Trinidad and Tobago), 155
National Conservation Commission (Barbados), 75
National Geodetic Survey (U.S.), 167
National Museum (Trinidad and Tobago), 87
National Park Service of the United States, 103, 104, 118, 125, 126
National Trust of Trinidad and Tobago, 72, 188
Native American sites, 36
negative space, 22, 25–26
negative weight, 44, 200. See also weights-of-evidence analysis
Nevis, 1, 2, 7, 105, 126–35, 171–72, 190
Nevis Heritage Project, 127–35
New World, 155, 156, 166, 171, 174, 183
nongovernmental organizations (NGOs), 75, 82

ocean currents. See currents
Orinoco River (South America), 13, 155
Oropouche, South, watershed (Trinidad), 33–35, 37, 41, 42–44, 48, 50–51, 53–54, 58, 63, 66, 69, 71
Ortoiroid (Archaic) culture, 36–37, 41, 73
Ostionoid culture, 16, 200
Oxholm, Peter. See Oxholm's maps
Oxholm's maps, 7, 100–104, 106, 109–16, 119, 124–26, 189

parallax. See X- and Y-parallax
Parris's Garden (Nevis), 130, 134
"passage area" concept, 26
PDA-type pocket computers, 135
Pernambuco model, 78
petroglyphs, 2, 138, 140, 144, 150
phenomenology, 13, 184
photogrammetry, 1, 4, 8, 140–41, 189, 191–92, 194, 201
Pitons (St. Lucia), 191
Pleasures Estate (St. Eustatius), 8, 170, 174–83, 192
Polynesians, 25

positive relief features, 143, 144, 146
positive weight, 44, 201. See also weights-of-evidence analysis
pottery, 37, 71, 138, 140, 144, 150, 151, 195, 199, 200, 202. See also ceramics
pre-Columbian migrations, 13, 184, 194
predictive models and modeling, 5–7, 61, 186, 201; Barbados, 82–84; Jamaica, 137, 151, 191; Trinidad, 5, 33, 36, 41, 44–46, 48, 50, 53–54, 71–72
protocolonial expansion. See English protocolonial expansion
Puerto Rico, 16, 22, 26, 40, 70, 104, 165–68, 192

Quill volcano (St. Eustatius), 170, 171

rainy season. See wet season
Raleigh, Sir Walter: outpost on Trinidad, 8, 155–68, 192
Raleigh's fort. See Raleigh, Sir Walter
relief. See land relief
remotely sensed data, 8, 191
resistivity, 161–65, 170–83, 192–93
resistivity meters, 8, 155, 161–62, 168, 170, 175–78, 183, 193, 201
response themes, 37, 50, 53, 201
Rest North watershed (Trinidad), 33–35, 37, 42–44, 48, 52–54, 56, 58, 64, 67, 70–71
Roanoke Island (North Carolina, USA), 156, 166, 168
Royal Commission on Historical Monuments, 128

St. Catherine (Jamaica), 4
St. Croix, 99, 104; cartography, 105–10, 114–15, 125
St. Eustatius: archaeological research, 170–83; geophysical surveys, 175–83; historical archaeology, 174–75
St. John: archaeological research, 99–125; cartography of, 105–116
St. Kitts, 2, 171–72; cartography, 128, 190; heritage management, 188
St. Lucia, 76, 191; heritage management, 188, 190
St. Quentin Estate (Trinidad), 156

St. Thomas, 99, 103, 104; cartography, 106, 109, 110
St. Vincent, 76
Saladoid culture, 16, 36–37, 39, 41, 69–70, 185, 192, 202
San Juan National Historic Site (Puerto Rico), 188
Sans-Souci Palace (Haiti), 188
satellite imagery, 1, 4, 6–8, 202; use in cartography, 79, 81, 124, 129, 190–91; use in locating sites, 137, 140–41, 189, 194
sea currents. *See* currents
settlement patterns, 2, 39, 185, 191
sharecropping, 78
Sierra Maestra (Cuba), 22
silk cotton trees, 140
Sites and Monuments Inventory System (Barbados), 6, 74, 80, 187, 188
slash and burn, 76
slave quarters, 8, 170, 177, 181–82
slave residences. *See* slave quarters
slave-to-quarter ratios, 182
soil sampling, 155, 159, 192
soil texture: Trinidad, 39, 41, 42, 44, 48–49, 52–53, 56, 58, 70
soil thermography, 155
spatial autocorrelation, 186, 194
SPOT imagery, 152, 187
SQL. *See* structured query language (SQL)
Statia. *See* St. Eustatius
Steward's Circum-Caribbean Theory, 22, 202
stratigraphy, 155, 159, 161
structured query language (SQL), 92, 202
study area theme, 202
sugar production: Barbados, 76–79; Nevis, 127–30; St. Croix, 114; St. Eustasius, 8, 170–72, 179–82, 186; St. John, 7, 105, 116, 119–24; Trinidad, 71
survey-grade GPS, 129, 202
system development, 87, 92

Tainos, 70, 137–52; artifacts, 138, 144, 146; cosmology, 140
Taino sites, 7–8; Jamaica, 137–51, 185
tax records *(matricals)* (St. John), 7, 99, 100, 103, 110, 115, 119, 121, 124, 125, 189

test pits, 159
three-dimensional surfaces from imagery, generation of, 142–44
tobacco: Barbados, 76–77; St. Eustatius, 171
Tobago Trust, 3
Tobler's Law of Geography, 186
topographic index, 143
Town and Country Planning Authority (Jamaica), 3
Town and Country Planning Department (Barbados), 75
Town and Country Planning Division (Trinidad and Tobago), 3
training sets for weight-of-evidence modeling, 37, 41–44
Treaty of Paris, 171
Trelawny (Jamaica): Taino sites, 7–8, 137–51, 191
Trimble ProXR differential GPS unit, 141
Trinidad and Tobago: Archaeological Information System (AIS), development of, 86–96, 185–86, 188; pre-Columbian sites, 33–73

UNESCO, 80, 81, 187; Convention, 75, 84, 188; grants, 6, 74. *See also* Sites and Monuments Inventory System (Barbados); World Heritage Center; World Heritage sites
United States Virgin Islands. *See* Danish West Indies
Universal Transverse Mercator (UTM), 40, 81, 203
University of the West Indies, 40, 72, 187; Archaeological Centre, 6, 86–87
Upper Rawlins plantation (Nevis), 130
"Upper Woodland" plantation (Nevis), 130, 133. *See also* Woodland (Nevis)
user needs assessments, 87–89
UTM. *See* Universal Transverse Mercator (UTM)

vector data sets, 39–40, 79, 203
Vieques Sound, 26
Virgin Gorda, 22, 105
Virgin Islands Department of Planning and Natural Resources, 104

Virgin Islands National Park, 103, 116, 125
visibility models, 5, 185–86, 189
visibility ranges, 17, 19, 22

WAAS. *See* Wide Area Augmentation System (WAAS)
watersheds. *See* Cipero watershed (Trinidad); Oropouche; Rest North watershed (Trinidad)
"wattled and plastered" slave houses, 193. *See also* slave quarters
weights-of-evidence analysis, 5–6, 33, 36–73, 185. *See also* negative weight; positive weight
wet season: effect on fieldwork, 193
WGS. *See* World Geodectic System (WGS)

Wide Area Augmentation System (WAAS), 129, 141, 190
Woodland (Nevis), 130. *See also* "Upper Woodland" plantation (Nevis)
World Geodectic System (WGS), 79, 80, 81
World Heritage Center, 75. *See also* UNESCO; World Heritage sites
World Heritage List, 75. *See also* UNESCO; World Heritage sites
World Heritage sites, 84, 188, 191

X- and Y-parallax, 142–43

Yucatan Peninsula, 3, 13

zoomorphic, 203